Baedek

Budapest

www.baedeker.com

Verlag Karl Baedeker

SIGHTSEEING HIGHLIGHTS ★★

The Castle District, Chain Bridge and Parliament – the most famous sights can hardly be missed. For the rest of your sightseeing programme we have summarized the highlights here, to ensure nothing has been overlooked by the end of your Budapest visit.

Gellért Bath
Ornamental dream: spa inspired by Turkish baths

Arts and Crafts Museum
In the style of Indian palaces

Lion Gate
Roaring sentinel at a gateway in the Royal Palace

BAEDEKER'S BEST TIPS

Of all the Baedeker Tips in this book we have gathered together the most interesting for you here! Experience and enjoy Budapest from its best side.

Men …
… have this part of the Gellért Bath to themselves

Opera House ...
... from the glittering era of the genre

Fancy an old Baedeker?
Hunt around, browse, discover ...
▶ page 211

Domes and constructions
Budapest from above after ascending to the dome of St Stephen's Basilica
▶ page 237

Ice skating in the woods
Like a scene from Brueghel's paintings: ice skating for all ▶ page 250

Skating
Winter pleasures in Városliget woods

Café New York
The world-famous coffee house re-opened after extensive renovation in 2006 ▶ page 209

Beware of the sharks!
Underwater wonders close enough to touch without getting your feet wet
▶ page 210

Outdoor fountain of youth: the Széchenyi Bath
► page 252

BACKGROUND

The Socialist monuments are obsolete.
► page 237

PRACTICALITIES

Two landmarks at once: Chain Bridge and Royal Palace
► **page 163**

TOURS

In the Ethnographic Museum
► **page 169**

The most important church in Budapest: Matthias Church

► **page 201**

SIGHTS FROM A to Z

Vajdahunyad Castle in the Municipal Forest

► **page 251**

Paprika – a national feast for the eyes and the palate.
▸ **page 129**

Background

ABOUT THE CITY ON THE DANUBE, THE COUNTRY AND ITS PEOPLE, ECONOMY AND POLITICS, SOCIETY AND DAILY LIFE ...

TWO SISTERS ON THE RIVER

»Budapest and the Danube form one of the most beautiful city and river landscapes in existence, equal to London and the Thames or Paris and the Seine ...« wrote the French writer Jules Romains, enraptured, in the mid-20th century.

Much water has flowed down the Danube since then. The era of pomp and magnificence, the famous Dual Monarchy of Austria-Hungary, was followed by the First World War. Then came the bourgeois democratic Hungarian Republic, which had an unhealthily close relationship with Hitler's Germany before the Second World War. Liberation by Soviet troops almost inevitably led to the foundation of the Socialist People's Republic which, however, was later allowed to follow the somewhat freer path of so-called Goulash Communism. The great changes in the early 1990s, which ended with membership of the European Union, are the latest chapters in a diverse history. And still the Danube takes its quiet and majestic course through the city, past imposing monuments that impressed travellers and visitors to the city long time Jules Romains' time, separating the two unequal sisters of Buda and Pest, to the right and left of its banks. Lit up by the glow of many lights at night, the river exudes the mystery of waters that have seen much along their shores and the long journey east.

Tradition *The top-class Gundel restaurant has welcomed prominent guests for over 120 years.*

The Long Road to the Present

Actually three sisters were united to form the Hungarian capital as recently as 1873: medieval, small and hilly Buda; flat Pest, crossed by broad boulevards; and Óbuda, which until then was a sleepy small town built on the ruins of an old Roman settlement. Today Budapest makes a bustling impression on the road to a modernity that was unthinkable for so long: there is a tremendously enthusiastic atmosphere of growth and development. Since membership of the European Union the city really has arrived in the modern world. The economy is flourishing, the mood is optimistic. During the past ten years Budapest has evolved into the continent's number one destination for

Moments of glory
Recent events beneath the dome of Parliament have mostly been positive: for example, Hungary's admission to the European Union.

Feel like sunshine?
Budapest is spoilt for sunshine. On average, it will light up your face for eight hours a day from April to September.

Step inside!
Budapest's wonderful art nouveau baths are a heritage unmatched elsewhere in the world, and there is no need to choose between sightseeing and relaxation.

Meeting places
Famous and always lively, Budapest's coffee houses recall the atmosphere of the late 19th century.

The ravages of time ...
... gnaw at many once magnificent buildings. Yet the will to restore is great, and the Andrássy út boulevard has even become a UNESCO World Heritage site.

Ascend gracefully
The organic forms of the Secessionist style are very common in the city

studies. Students come to this rejuvenating city from all over Europe. They appreciate the high quality of teaching and the pulsating vitality.

Paprika, Pepsi and Pop Culture

In addition to its very new »citizen of the world« attitude, Budapest also boasts many traditional superlatives: 130 thermal and healing baths, Europe's largest parliament building and, after London, the continent's oldest underground railway system; but also 237 artistic monuments, 223 museums and galleries, and 40 theatres. Music, especially, has been honoured with 'temples' such as the opera and the music academy, evidence of a highly valued cultural tradition that was never just for show, but rather a need, and even a support. In fact, all facets of musical expression flourish alongside each other: the lively youthful Pepsi-Sziget-Festival and the pure classical music of the State Opera; operetta and virtuoso folk music; musicals, czardas and – an essential part of the city atmosphere – the soulful melodies of the romantic violinists in the bars in Buda's Castle District. Many other things also thrive happily side by side here: the styles of the Dual Monarchy and art nouveau, paprika and salami, high fashion and folk art, coffee-house culture and fast food empires, traditional bathing and modern spa treatments. Budapest wants to please its international visitors, and a great deal of old glamour has been given a new shine. For example, the East and the West Railway Stations, the central market and the metro stations of the original number one line which, incidentally, is counted as part of the UNESCO world cultural heritage along with Andrássy út, the Castle District, and the banks of the Danube. The latest treat is the complete restoration of the opulent art nouveau Gresham Palace. This former insurance building is now home to an international luxury hotel aimed at illustrious and prominent customers. But new superlatives are also getting noticed: thus the largest oceanic aquarium in central Europe opened in Budapest a few years ago. By the way, fish are swimming in the Danube once again, and a good way to enjoy them is in halaszle, the famous spicy fish soup.

Modernity
A whole island rocks at a week-long mega-event for the young: the Sziget Festival.

Facts

Budapest is aglow, emanating a new self-confidence and optimism. It knows how to live too. Rarely does it rest, for a generation of dedicated young Europeans work the world markets during the day, so they can meet in the bars until late into the night. Never forget: the motto here is »live now!«.

Population · Politics · Economy

Population

Population expansion

The independent towns of Óbuda, Buda and Pest had a combined population of 12,200 in 1720. By the time they were amalgamated into Budapest in 1873, the total number of inhabitants had already passed the 300,000 mark. When Budapest became the capital of Hungary in 1867, the city experienced a boom without precedent, which also took the form of a dramatic increase in population. By the beginning of the 20th century, a million people lived in Budapest. Incorporation of surrounding districts during the 1970s resulted in the two million mark being passed, but in the 1990s many Budapest residents turned their backs on an increasingly expensive city. Today Budapest has around 1.6 million inhabitants at a density of approx. 3600 per sq km/9300 per sq mi.

Immigrants usually came from the east

The development of the Hungarian capital was influenced by immigrants from former German and Austrian territories, as well as by Czechs, Slovaks, Serbs, Croats and Bulgarians, particularly during the 18th and 19th centuries. After the Second World War many Greeks came to the city. In recent times, numerous immigrants, officially »tourists«, from the Ukraine, Russia and countries from the Near, Middle and Far East have settled in greater Budapest.
Hungarian Jews, whose deportation in 1944 comprised the last major action of the Holocaust, have survived mainly in Budapest (►Baedeker Special p. 184). Before World War II over 200,000 Jews lived in Budapest. Their present 80,000-strong community is the largest in all of eastern Europe. They have settled mostly in the VII quarter (Elizabeth Town), where the main synagogues of the Orthodox and other communities are to be found.
The largest ethnic minority in terms of numbers is made up by the Sinti and Roma. Instability in Hungary's neighbouring countries since the 1990s has caused an additional influx from these groups to the wider Budapest area.
The second-largest minority in the country consists of the 87,000 Hungarian citizens who described themselves as culturally German Hungarian in the 2001 population census.

Religion

The majority of Budapest residents who acknowledge a religious affiliation, presently 65%, are traditionally Roman Catholics. A quarter are Protestants, the overwhelming majority followers of the Reformed (Calvinist) Church. The rest consists of other religious groups, in particular Orthodox Christians, Baptists and Jews.

← Two sides of the coin: the city is resplendent, but life is hard for those who have not found a place in this new world.

Budapest districts

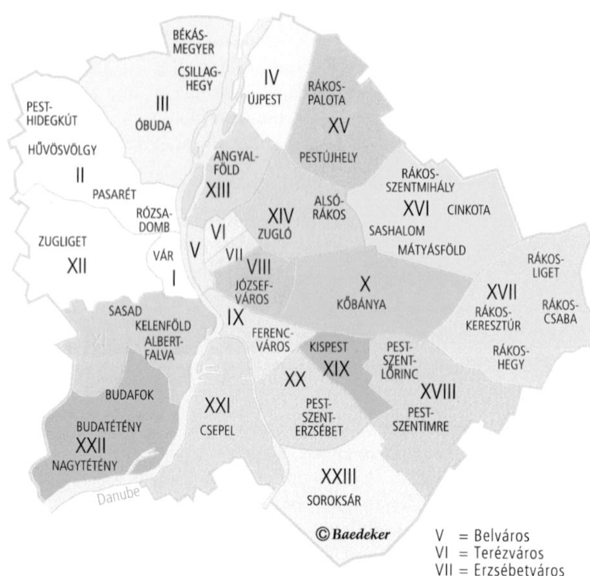

City Structure and Politics

Municipal districts The city of Budapest is divided into 23 municipal districts or boroughs. The central shopping district of the Hungarian capital is almost identical in extent with the V district (on the Pest side of the Danube): not only numerous department stores, shops, boutiques and top-class hotels can be found on little more than 2.5 sq km/1 sq mi, but also government departments, finance and trading institutions, and significant cultural and scientific establishments. Far in excess of 100,000 workers commute daily to the V district.

City administration The city is ruled by the Senate (Közgülés). The city's leader, the mayor, is nominated by the party or coalition which has a majority in the Senate. The municipal districts are each managed by a magistrate controlled by the Senate.

Twin cities The Hungarian capital is twinned with the German financial metropolis of Frankfurt am Main, the Finnish capital Helsinki, the Lithuanian capital Vilnius and the Texan city of Fort Worth in the United States. Others include Berlin, Germany; Lisbon, Portugal; Zagreb, Croatia; the most recent addition is Dublin, Ireland in 2006.

Facts and Figures Budapest

Location

- 47° 29' north latitude
- 19° 08' east longitude

Area

- 525 km^2/202 mi^2,
  of these
- 173 km^2/68 mi^2 east of the Danube and
- 353 km^2/136mi^2 west of the Danube.
- About half of the city's area is developed; the rest is green space.

Highest elevation

- John Hill (János-hegy):
  529m/1,736ft

Population

- 1.6 million (2007)
  Compared to: Berlin 3.4 million
  Paris 2.1 million
  New York 8.1 million
- Population density:
  3,230 per km^2/1,247 per mi^2

Religion

- 65 % roman catholic, 25 % protestant, 4 % hungarian greek catholic, 6 % other

Administration

- 23 city districts
- Administrative head: High mayor

Economy

- Financial and economic capital of Hungary
- 74 % of the employed work in the service sector
- average monthly income:
  gross 170,000 HUF
  (ca. 595 Euro, 444 GBP)
- Unemployment rate: 3 %
  (Hungary 7.5 %)
- 360,000 registered businesses (of these 267,000 are actually doing business)

Traffic

- Airport: Ferihegy, with 6.3 million passengers annually the largest airport in Hungary (2006)

Public transport

- More than 200 bus lines, almost 40 streetcar lines, three metro and four suburban commuter lines transport local people and tourists.

Adresses

- The Roman numerals in the addresses refer to the city district.

Education

- 100,000 students are registered in the universities and schools of higher education in Budapest, twice as many as ten years ago.

Heart of the Hungarian Economy

Economic centre Budapest is one of the leading economic centres of eastern central Europe. At present almost a quarter of Hungary's gainfully employed work in the economic area of Budapest. The vast majority work in the service sector, administration and trade. Furthermore, the city is characterized by a high number of export-orientated industrial sectors. To these belong in particular the car and machine production industries, the chemical and pharmaceutical industries, as well as the electrical and electronic industries.

Industrial development The particularly good transport links and coal deposits in the near vicinity were and remain the ideal basis for Budapest's economic development. The city, made capital of Hungary in 1867, soon became the main seat of significant industrial companies. After the Second

Budapest too has its bright new supermarkets and shopping malls, but the buying power of the average family is not yet enough for splashing out.

World War, raw material imports from the Soviet Union enabled the establishment of new oil-processing and chemical industries. The Ikarus plant not only delivered buses to countries in COMECON (Council for Mutual Economic Assistance, the eastern European counterpart to the European Union), but also to clients in the West. After the collapse of Communism at the end of the 1980s, the free market was quickly re-established and businesses were privatized. The fundamental political changes in eastern Europe attracted a huge stream of investment capital, especially from Germany, to Budapest, where companies – now not only multinationals – have created platforms by buying existing companies or establishing new ones.

Trade

Budapest has a long tradition as a centre of trade due to its good geographic and transport location. This applies in particular to the district of Pest, where all strands of Hungarian business management come together today. The large shopping centres and commercial markets that have now arisen in the outer districts or on the periphery of the city can match those of any other European metropolis. Even after membership of the European Union, Germany remains the most important trading partner. Budapest's Ferihegy Airport has succeeded in becoming one of the most significant air-freight handling centres within the space of a few years, while the free port of Csepel has become the most important transhipment centre on the Danube.

Banking and insurance

Thanks to its economic strength, Budapest is now one of the principal financial centres of eastern central Europe. Numerous foreign banks have branches in Budapest and, as becomes a European capital, there is also a stock exchange in the city. Hungary's largest insurance companies are at home in Budapest.

Trade fairs

As one of the leading trade fair centres of eastern central Europe, Budapest fully participates in the national and international calendar of exhibitions and congress activities. The internationally most important trade fairs that take place regularly include the Utazás Tourism Fair; the agricultural machine fair Agro-Masch in March; the Budapesti Nemzetközi Vásár (BNV), with its concentration on technical and consumer goods, in September; the Budapest car fair Autosalon in October; and Snowshow, the fair for winter sports in November.

Tourism

Budapest has been among the top destinations for European city breaks for years. The majority of the around 25 million annual visitors to Hungary visit Budapest. Austria, Germany, Italy, the Netherlands, Switzerland and Israel, as well as the USA and Canada, are the main contributors to tourist earnings.

City History

First came the Romans, then the Magyars; for a long time the Turks ruled. Only after that does the history of this city, which never really existed before, begin. It became the eastern seat of the Austro-Hungarian Dual Monarchy, experienced a golden age after 1867, was then a pawn in grim world events, and now follows a European democratic path in the new millennium.

Romans, Huns and Árpáds

895–896	Invasion of the seven Magyar tribes
1000	Stephen (Istvan) I becomes King of Hungary
1241–42	The Mongols destroy Buda and Pest
1308–1386	Rule of the House of Anjou
1458	Matthias Corvinus becomes king

Pre-history

So far the earliest known traces of settlement are on the Buda side of the Danube and go back to the early Stone Age, around 14,000 BC to 12,000 BC. By about the second millennium BC both banks of the Danube had been settled. Several fields of urns have been discovered over the entire area of the present-day Hungarian capital dating from the Bronze Age. Nomadic Scythians from the Black Sea region settled in the Budapest area in the 6th century BC, and in the 4th and 3rd centuries BC Celtic tribes appeared.

Roman rule

The Romans conquered the region west of the Danube around 10 BC. The **Roman fortification of Aquincum** in the present-day quarter of Óbuda became the capital of the province of Pannonia Inferior. The residential and garrison town of Aquincum experienced its heyday at the end of the 2nd century AD.

Invasion of the Huns

The power vacuum caused by the fall of the Roman Empire allowed the Huns to penetrate into Europe. In the year 409 Aquincum fell to the nomadic people from the east by agreement – a rarity in the history of the Huns. Bloody campaigns of conquest were the foundation for the Hun empire under **King Attila**. With the death of Attila the Hun in 453, the empire, already weakened by its defeat in Gaul in 451, collapsed. Ostrogoths, Lombards and Avars from the steppes settled along the Danube in the aftermath.

Invasion and rule of the Árpáds

Seven Hungarian tribes belonging to the Finno-Ugrian linguistic group moved into the Carpathian basin and continued their migration up the Danube, settling in present-day Óbuda around 895–896. These tribes, the Nyék, Megyer, Kürtgyarmat, Tarján, Jenö, Kér and Keszi, were led by the chieftains Árpád, Elöd, Ond, Kond, Tass, Huba and Töhötöm, who are all portrayed as a bronze equestrian group on ►Hösök tere (Heroes' Square). This phase, from 895 to 972, characterized by the Magyar invasion of the Carpathian basin as well as their raids into western and southern Europe, is known as the Age of Migrations. Árpád ruled the unified Magyar tribes as

← *Famous date in Hungarian history: the anti-totalitarian uprising on 23 October 1956*

chieftain after the blood-brother union of Szeged, and his descendants ruled until 1301.

Feudal state and Christianity Stephen I (István I) became King of Hungary in the year 1000. He organized a feudal state on the central European model and introduced Christianity. His residences were in Esztergom and Székesfehérvár. With the settlement of merchants from central and western Europe in Buda and Pest in the 12th century, these towns on the trade route to eastern Europe increasingly gained economic significance.

Invasion of the Mongols In the middle of a period of economic boom, the up-and-coming Danube towns of Buda and Pest were stormed and destroyed in the years 1241–1242 by Mongols. After the terrible experiences of the Mongol invasions, King Béla IV had a castle built on Buda hill and the Castle District was built to his plans. The new city was soon given the right to hold markets.

From the House of Anjou to the Turks With the death of Andrew III in 1301, the male line of the Árpád dynasty died out. The house of Anjou took over the Hungarian throne. The rule of Charles Robert (1301–1342) and Louis I (1342–1382) gave Hungary an era of domestic political stability and economic development. Under the rule of Louis, Hungarian power stretched all the way to Bosnia, Serbia, and Bulgaria, and on to Walachia and Dalmatia – with access to the sea. From 1387 to 1437 **Sigismund**, later Holy Roman Emperor, ruled Hungary and had a palace built on Castle Hill.

Symbol of the Hungarian monarchy: the coronation insignia

Matthias Corvinus (Mátyás Hunyadi), son of the conqueror of Turks János Hunyadi, was crowned King of Hungary by the nobility in 1458. Buda developed into a **centre of Renaissance culture** during his rule, which lasted until 1490. The Buda royal palace was extended and the Corvina Library became one of the largest libraries in Europe.

Peasant revolt In 1514, Captain György Dózsa gathered an army before Pest by order of the Church, intended to fight the advancing Turks. However, this army, predominantly made up of farmers and serfs, turned against the despotism of the Hungarian nobility. The peasant revolt was brutally crushed by the feudal lords.

The Coming of the Turks

1541–1686	Turkish rule
1686	Charles V, Duke of Lorraine, expels the Turks

Time of the Turks

After their victory over Hungarian troops at Mohács, when the Hungarian King Louis II was killed, the Turks temporarily occupied Buda Castle.

Division of Hungary

The dispute over succession after Louis II's death led to the division of Hungary: to protect the crown from Habsburg aspirations one faction of the Hungarian nobility elected King John I (János Szapolyai), while another elected the Habsburg Archduke Ferdinand I of Austria, who was forced to restrict his rule to the western regions of Hungary. Through Ferdinand's rule over parts of the Hungarian territory, the country became the setting for warfare between the Habsburgs and the Ottoman Turks.

Historic view of Buda and Pest dating from 1617

Second era of Turkish occupation Buda and Pest were occupied by the Turks under Sultan Suleiman I from 1541 onwards. Many churches were turned into mosques during this time, fortifications were renewed, and magnificent bathhouses were built. Buda became the seat of a vizier. The Ottoman Empire's rule over central Hungary meant the country was divided into three. Óbuda, Buda and Pest were retaken for the Habsburgs by Charles V, Duke of Lorraine, only in the year 1686.

The Danube Monarchy

1740–1780	Rule of Empress Maria Theresa
After 1789	Early attempts at civil reform
1848	Bourgeois revolution
1867	Hungary gains an independent government

Rule of the Habsburgs During the Hungarian Diet called in 1687, the Habsburgs were granted the right of accession to the Hungarian throne in return for freeing Hungary from the Turks, and Hungary was incorporated into the Habsburg Empire at the Peace of Karlowitz in 1699. However, opposition to rule by the Habsburg emperors, with their court in Vienna, developed as early as 1697. **Ferenc Rákóczi II** (1676–1735), Prince of Transylvania, who initially refused to lead the fight against the Habsburgs, took over as leader of the freedom movement from 1701, allying himself with the French king, Louis XIV. But, apart from feudal privileges guaranteed to the Hungarian nobility by the Peace of Szatmár in 1711, his military campaigns were mostly unsuccessful.

Recalling the coronation: mosaic in the Matthias Church

Maria Theresa's rule of **enlightened absolutism** as Habsburg empress (1740–1780) was characterized by a modernization of the Habsburg Empire and a simultaneous strengthening of the absolutist feudal system. Technical, social and economic reforms did strengthen civil society, however, and led to tentative economic growth. Numerous immigrants from German-speaking regions, especially from Upper Austria and southern Germany, settled in Buda and Pest during this phase. The university founded in Nagyszombat by Peter Pázmány in 1635 was initially moved to Buda in 1777, and then to Pest.

Spread of revolutionary ideas

The Hungarian nobility restricted the reform policies of enlightened absolutism. By clinging to its political and social privileges, however, it made the population receptive to the message of the French Revolution. The emerging liberation movement was destroyed by terror: numerous Hungarian supporters of republican ideas were executed on the Bloody Field (Vérmezö) below Castle Hill in 1825.

Renewed attempts at reform

In 1825 the failed reform ideas of the late 18th century once more became the object of political discussion, during the course of which – among other things – the nobility's tax privileges were reduced. One of the key figures of the reform era was **Count István Széchenyi** (1791–1860), who aimed to counteract Hungary's economic, technical and social backwardness by the foundation of the Hungarian Academy of Sciences. He brought this project to fruition with a generous donation. The urban development of the two neighbouring cities of Buda and Pest during the first half of the 19th century followed the example of western and central European cities. Bourgeois society set the tone. Many areas of life received further reforms, and trade blossomed. The Hungarian language was also renewed: Latin was dropped in favour of Hungarian, and national feeling awakened.

Bourgeois revolution

Revolution broke out in the year 1848, led by liberal nobles fighting the Austrian hegemony in Hungary. Count Lajos Batthyány (1806–1849) formed a government responsible to the Hungarian parliament and Lajos Kossuth (1802–1894; ►Famous People) rose to become a significant political leader; the poet Sándor Petöfi (1823–1849; ►Famous People) died in battle. The Habsburg monarchy crushed the freedom movement with the help of tsarist troops from Russia. Kossuth fled into exile, while Batthyány was executed.

The Hungarian Compromise with the Austrian rulers was not achieved until 1867, with the help of **Ferenc Deák** (1803–1876). Hungary was granted a considerable amount of independence and its own government, although the Austrian emperor continued to be King of Hungary, which is why the **Austro-Hungarian Dual Monarchy** was sometimes derided. Emperor Franz Joseph I and Empress Elizabeth (Sisi) were crowned in the Matthias Church in 1867, the final act in the establishment of the Austro-Hungarian Monarchy. In 1873, Óbuda, Buda and Pest were united to form the Hungarian capital.
On the occasion of the **1000th anniversary** of the arrival of the Magyars in the Carpathian basin, an impressive jubilee exhibition was

? DID YOU KNOW ...?

- The revolution of 1848 broke out when Sándor Petöfi recited his »National Song« in front of the Hungarian National Museum.
  Useless villain of a man
  Who now, if need be, doesn't dare to die
  Who values his pathetic life greater
  Than the honour of his homeland
  By the God of the Hungarians
  We vow that we will be slaves
  No longer!

mounted. During the course of the millennium celebrations in 1896, the decision was made to honour the heroes of Hungarian history with a major memorial: ► Heroes' Square). The first underground railway on the European continent was initiated. The Parliament building was completed in 1902.

Hungary up to 1945

1918	End of Habsburg rule and establishment of a republic
1919	Republic of Councils under Béla Kun
1920–1944	Miklós Horthy, Regent of Hungary
1941	War on the German side
1944	Invasion of German troops, murder of approx. 500,000 Jews
1945	Soviet troops liberate Budapest

First World War and inter-war years

Budapest suffered severe setbacks in its economic development during the First World War. With the defeat of Austria-Hungary, which fought on the side of the Germans, Habsburg rule was at an end in Hungary too. On 16 November 1918, a civil democratic republic was announced. Its first president was **Count Mihály Károlyi** (1875–1955). The Republic of Councils installed by Social Democrats and Communists in March 1919 only held for a few months. In November **Miklós Horthy** (1868–1957) took power and re-established the monarchy in Hungary. As a return of the Habsburgs was unthinkable, he ruled as their regent. Thousands of supporters of the Republic of Councils fell victim to his White Terror.

Peace Treaty of Trianon

The Treaty of Trianon resulted in Hungary losing two thirds of its territory and 60% of its population to neighbouring states. This decision by the victorious Allies shocked the Hungarian population, and it is not surprising that Hungarian foreign policy during the inter-war years made a revision of the Treaty of Trianon its goal. All means were acceptable to achieve the end of a revision of the treaty and any strong partner was a welcome ally. As an irony of fate it was an Austrian who appeared to hold the solution to Hungary's problems. The closer association of Hungary with Hitler's Germany after 1933 should be seen in the context of Hungarian efforts for revision: Germany became the ideal alliance partner, an aggressive and effective support in the question of a reversal of the Treaty of Trianon. By 1940, the lost territories had successively been handed back to Hungary through the two Arbitrations of Vienna in 1938 and 1940, as well as through the occupation of the Carpathian Ukraine by Hungarian troops in 1939. With Germany as its ally, however, Hungary had to pay a high price for its persistent policy of revision: joining the Second World War on the side of the German Reich in 1941.

Second World War

Hungarian troops were not spared their Stalingrad: in January 1943, the 2. Hungarian Army was destroyed at Voronezh; almost 300,000 soldiers died. When the defeat of Nazi Germany became obvious the Hungarian leadership began to think about a timely exit from the war. Hitler's reaction was swift: German troops occupied Hungary on 19 March 1944. There were arrests in Budapest, which also affected renegade representatives of the Horthy regime who had wanted to cancel the pact with Hitler. The bombing of the city began in the summer. After Rumania's exit from the war coalition, Soviet troops easily moved in the direction of Hungary. Nevertheless the **deportation of the Jews** was initiated outside Budapest. The persecuted were gathered in so-called Jews' houses in the Hungarian capital. Later a ghetto was established. The Swede **Raoul Wallenberg** (►Famous People), the papal nunciate, as well as other significant personalities and institutions tried to help the Jews (►Baedeker Special p.184). Miklós Horthy left the alliance with Adolf Hitler on 15 October 1944. The German occupation removed the regent and handed power to the **Arrow Cross Party** led by Ferenc Szálasi. Shortly afterwards Soviet troops surrounded the Hungarian capital and there was heavy street fighting. Wehrmacht and Waffen-SS troops barricaded themselves in Buda Castle. Arrow Cross party members murdered many thousands of Jews in the ghetto and on the banks of the Danube. In January 1945, Soviet troops advanced towards the Danube from the Pest side. Hitler's troops destroyed all Danube bridges. The German soldiers barricaded in the castle failed to escape and the battles ended on 13 February 1945, when Budapest was liberated.

The Communist Era

1946	The Hungarian Republic is declared
1949	Hungary becomes a People's Republic
1956	Popular revolt

Hungarian Republic

The first post-war elections during the national assembly of November 1945 lead to a defeat for the Communist Party, which had to make do with 17% of the votes. The winner, with 57% of the votes, was the Party of Small Farmers, and the first government leader of the post-war era was **Zoltán Tildy**. The **Hungarian Republic** was declared in Budapest on 1 February 1946. During the period that followed, the Communist Party tried to regain a share of power with its so-called salami tactic: trying to remove the power of the democratic government slice for slice. The goal was a socialist society on the Soviet model. There were ever fiercer disagreements within the coalition government.

Dictatorship of the proletariat Arbitrary methods were used in an attempt to establish a dictatorship of the proletariat. There were show trials and other repressive measures, and even the smallest businesses were nationalized. Finally, the new constitution of the **People's Republic** came into force on 20 August 1949.

Development of infrastructure The city of Budapest was substantially enlarged by incorporating surrounding districts in 1950. The new Ferihegy Airport was opened the same year, and good progress was made with rebuilding the destroyed neighbourhoods and the Danube bridges. The expansion of heavy industry around Budapest was promoted with great enthusiasm in the early 1950s. By comparison, housing development was seriously neglected.

Relaxation of the political climate Changes within the Soviet leadership caused by the death of Stalin made for an improved political atmosphere, in Hungary as elsewhere, from 1953 onwards. **Imre Nagy** (1896–1958; ▸ Famous People), Rákosi's challenger, who was considered a liberal Communist, became Hungarian prime minister in July 1953. Tentative changes were made under pressure from reformers within and without the Hungarian Communist Party. Nevertheless, Prime Minister Nagy was beaten by arch-conservative post-Stalin Rákosi supporters and pushed from office in 1955. Battles over the political direction brought economic development to a standstill. The general disaffection of the population increased.

The 1956 uprising After the 20th Congress of the Communist Party of the Soviet Union, groups pressing for a democratization and modernization of socialism formed. Rákosi gave his last speech in the Budapest Sports Palace, but his successor Ernö Gerö had not the slightest interest in political reforms. On the occasion of a student demonstration on 23 October 1956, his resignation was demanded, along with a call for political renewal.

A **popular uprising**, and finally an armed battle ensued. The greatly weakened Hungarian regime called on the help of the Soviet army, and bloody confrontations were the result. Soviet troops moved into Budapest on 4 November and, led by **János Kádár** (1912–1989; ▸ Famous People), the resistance inspired by national and social ideas was crushed. Kádár was the first secretary of the newly founded Hungarian Socialist Workers Party, and he entered the political stage as prime minister of the Government of Revolutionary Hungarian

Street cleaners in the socialist workers' state →

Workers and Farmers. Budapest's city centre was devastated. 25,000 Hungarians were killed; over 200,000 left their homeland.

Socialism Hungarian-style The years 1957–58 were characterized by a settling of scores with the fighters of 1957 and consolidation by political means. The focus moved to raising the standard of living and building of housing. A democratization of the system was also risked, but the execution of Imre Nagy and four of his closest associates for high treason in 1958 caused profound shock. Socialism Hungarian-style had its heyday in the years between 1958 and 1968. Kádár permitted a cautious, but nevertheless dynamic, development of the Hungarian economy and society. The education and healthcare systems were reformed and the development of science and technology was especially promoted. From 1960 onwards, large urban building programmes and the expansion of the transport system were realized.

Goulash-Communism A new economic system – so-called Goulash Communism – was introduced at the end of the 1960s. It contained elements of a market economy, allowed personal freedoms and participation in decision-making by the collectives. The realization of this plan was continued even after the invasion of Czechoslovakia by Warsaw Pact troops.

The bloody end of the Hungarian vision of a modernized socialism: Soviet troops invaded Budapest in 1956.

With the exemplary restoration of the historic quarters of Buda, especially the castle and the Castle District and, after 1975, of Pest, tourism blossomed and several large hotels were opened. Hungarian foreign and economic policy sought contact with Western countries and, after the Conference on Security and Co-operation in Europe held in Helsinki, the leaders of various Western states visited Budapest.

Contact with the West

Democracy and Integration with the West

1987	The peaceful change of system begins
1989	The third Hungarian Republic is declared
1991	The Soviet Army leaves the country
1999	Hungary becomes a member of NATO
2004	Hungary joins the European Union

Turning away from socialism

Small business were already permitted at the beginning of the 1980s. In 1985, several candidates stood in one local election, which was a novelty in the history of the Communist bloc. The General Secretary of the Hungarian Socialist Workers Party, János Kádár, was deposed in 1988. His post was taken by **Károly Grósz**, who had, in the meantime, been elected prime minister. That same year workers' organizations and political groups independent of the Party constituted themselves in a first step towards a multi-party system. In 1989, the Hungarian Socialist Workers Party dissolved itself. Leadership of the Council of Ministers was taken over by **Miklós Németh**, who remained in office until the elections of 1990. A re-evaluation of the events of 1956 took place. On 16 June 1989, hundreds of thousands paid their respects once more to the former prime minister Imre Nagy, who was the most prominent victim of the 1956 uprising. An increasing number of features of a free market economy began to emerge in the system of the previously socialist planned economy. The Iron Curtain along the Austro-Hungarian border was dismantled. The liberal attitude of the Hungarian authorities enabled tens of thousands of East German citizens to leave for Austria and the Federal Republic of Germany.

Free elections

By the early 1990s Hungary had finally said good-bye to socialism and become a republic on the Western model. The Democratic Forum and the Association of Free Democrats emerged as the strongest groupings after the first free elections in 45 years. The parties of the Left suffered defeat. **Árpád Göncz** became state president. The constitution was changed in several points: instead of a Hungarian People's Republic, there was now a **Hungarian Republic**; the old state coat of arms with the Crown of St Stephen was reintroduced; the Hungarian Constitutional Court began work and the entire state apparatus was remodelled. The administration, military and police were given new structures. Hungarian economic and foreign policy turned to the West even more than before. Important heads of state from Western countries, among others US President George Bush senior and France's President François Mitterrand, supported the efforts of the new Hungarian government. The most extraordinary event was the visit by the Pope in August 1991.

Integration with the West and free market economy

The economic restructuring of post-Communist Hungary caused severe disturbances in 1992. Increasing unemployment and inflation were the result.

In April 1994, the Hungarian government applied for membership of the European Union. An association agreement that envisaged the step-by-step reduction of customs duties within nine years had already come into force in February 1994.

In the parliamentary elections of May 1994, the opposition Hungarian Socialist Party (MSZP) achieved an absolute majority with 209 out of 386 seats. **Gyula Horn**, who had signed up to a continuation of the path towards a free market economy, became the new prime minister.

Recession

The opening up of the Hungarian market encouraged recession: the rate of inflation stood at almost 19%, unemployment at 10%, and there were few wage increases. The Hungarian capital was forced to cancel its planned Expo 1996 due to lack of funds. The government took measures to reduce domestic debt by, among others things, reducing the value of the forint and limiting state expenditures by, for example, reducing wages in the public sector and shortening the period of income support after illness.

Kosovo crisis and membership of NATO

The Kosovo crisis of 1999 affected life in the Hungarian metropolis. Hungary, which had been a NATO member since March 1999, and especially Budapest, not only became the destination for many refugees from the areas of former Yugoslavia hit by NATO bombs, but also became a logistical base for NATO troops operating in and around Kosovo. Shipping on Europe's second-longest river suffered lasting damage because of the destruction of the Danube bridges in Serbia. The transhipment of goods at Budapest's Csepel port was also greatly reduced.

Coronation jubilee of Stephen I

The year 2000 began with the thousandth anniversary of the coronation of Stephen I. During the course of celebrations, the Crown of St Stephen was carried from the National Museum to Parliament on the first day of the new millennium.

EU membership

The most recent highlight of the country's journey towards joining the community of democratic market economies was Hungary's membership of the European Union on 1 May 2004. It is not expected that Hungary will meet its goal of introducing the Euro as its currency by 2010, but it is quite possible that it will do so by 2012-2013.

Disturbances in 2006

In September 2006, Hungary was gripped by protest. During a party meeting Prime Minister Ferenc Gyurcsány – only re-elected in April 2006 – discussed false promises made by his government in the recent elections. When a recording of his comments was played to the media, Budapest experienced its worst disturbances since the beginning of the post-Communist era. The »speech of lies« provided the opposition (FIDESz) with a massive victory at the communal and regional elections of October 2006, the mark of a massive loss of faith in the government. The increased cost of living since joining the European Union contributed towards a latent dissatisfaction in the population, and there were yet more demonstrations against the government and its policies in 2007.

Art and Culture

Where can traces of the Romans be found? When was Budapest's Belle Époque? What did the city grant itself for its 1000th anniversary? Which cultural circle inspired Ödön Lechner, the art nouveau architect? And what connects Budapest's Western Railway Station with the Eiffel Tower?

Architecture

Architectural Epochs in the City

Medieval remains in Buda

Far into the 19th century, the Buda side still had a mostly Baroque appearance. However, many houses of the Castle District that were rebuilt in the 18th century in the Baroque style after the reconquest of Buda from the Turks have medieval foundations from earlier buildings. Traces of this can often be found, most obviously in the seating niches with pointed arches or blind tracery in some entrance gates, for example at Országház utca 2. The appearance of Buda showpieces today, such as the royal palace and the Matthias Church, is characterized mainly by the designs given to them during the millennium years after a turbulent history.

Historicism

During the time of the Austro-Hungarian Dual Monarchy (1867–1918), **historicism**, with its multi-faceted use of the great historical architectural styles, was the characteristic building style in Budapest. It was during this time that all the public and commercial buildings, churches, private mansions and industrial headquarters with neo-Romanesque, neo-Gothic or neo-Baroque façades were created. The 1870s and 1880s are considered the true foundation years of the city. Many significant public building works were only undertaken after 1873, when the formerly independent towns of Buda, Pest and Óbuda were officially united. The buildings from this period include the **Nyugati (West) Railway Station** (1877); the **Keleti (East) Railway Station** (1884); the **Margaret Bridge** (1884); **Andrássy út** (completed in 1885), part of the **Great Ring Road**; the **Basilica of St Stephen in Lipótváros**; the **Opera House** (opened in 1884); most of the **university buildings**; the **Customs House** on the Pest bank of the Danube, as well as the massive **Parliament Building** (1885–1904). This rapid pace of development occurred on the busy Pest side, in particular, where an official commission for beautifying the city had been responsible for systematic urban planning since 1808. The grid of streets was planned and the first apartment blocks were built. Several surviving houses in Lipótváros (Leopold Town), for example on József Nádor tér, or in Terézváros (Theresa Town), especially on Király utca, give an impression of the architecture of the first half of the 19th century. The cultural and political perspectives of the independence movement of the mid-19th century are evidenced by pioneering works such as the building of the **Chain Bridge** (1839–1849), the first Danube bridge, which was built from plans by the English engineer W. T. Clark; construction was supervised by Adam Clark. Other buildings that date from this era are the

← *Collector and patron: Count Ferenc Szechenyi donated his art collection to found the National Library and National Museum.*

National Museum (1836–1846), the **synagogue** on Dohány utca (1854–1859), the concert hall known as **Vigadó** (1859–1864), and the **Hungarian Academy of Sciences**, whose main buildings on Roosevelt tér were built between 1862 and 1864.

Hauszmann's Baroque dome rose above the Royal Palace until 1945.

At the turn of the 20th century, architects with a historicist perspective continued to win the most prestigious building contracts. For example, Alajos Hauszmann, who was responsible for the extension of the Buda **palace buildings** from 1891 to 1905, also supplied the plans for the former Palace of Justice, today's **Ethnographic Museum** on Kossuth Lajos tér. He adorned this building with architectural decorations and gilded adornments as sumptuous as those of the former headquarters of the **New York Insurance Company**, with its well-known café on the ground floor. Between the magnificent outer façades and the interior, however, the building was partly supported by reinforced concrete. The same generation also produced architects whose Hungarian variations on art nouveau still attract attention today. Ödön Lechner, the main representative of the Hungarian Secession style, sought his inspiration for an original and independent architecture not in the academic European styles, but in the East. However, he later wrote of the ornamental decoration of his **Arts and Crafts Museum** (1891–1896) that it had »turned out a little too Indian« after all. Apart from considerations of style, in his extensive use of washable ceramic elements he also already took account of problems caused by pollution in the city.' From the beginning, Hungarian Secession had a second focus that worked to a different agenda: for architects such as Károly Kós (1883–1977) the roots of an architecture appropriate to a Hungarian style lay in folk art and medieval art. Kós was given commissions that gave him an ideal opportunity for experimentation in the use of traditional building methods from different Hungarian regions, even in the city, with buildings such as the **Budapest Zoo** (1910) and the **Wekerle telep** (from 1912) housing project in Kispest.

New building

A transitional position is held by Lajos Kozma (1884–1948), who took art nouveau as his starting point and attached himself to the avant-garde tendencies of Modernism. In contrast to many of his colleagues, who had planned in Modernist style elsewhere as emigrants from the 1920s, he was able to complete typical examples of Modernist architecture in Budapest. These include, among others, the **Atrium House** (1936) and the **cinema** at Margit körút 55, with its generous and elegant interior. A **showcase housing development** (1931), in which most of the modern architects working in Budapest at the time participated, lies in the II district, on Napraforgó utca.

History reflected in modern architecture: glass façade of the Hilton Hotel.

However, the ideas of classic Modernism could only be revisited and developed into functional solutions, especially for industrial, transport, leisure and housing buildings, after the Second World War and after the »iron« Fifties. Buildings, such as the **Hotel Budapest** (Szilágyi Erzsébet fasor 47), built by György Szrogh in 1969, emerged, as well as **terraced houses and apartment blocks** such as the complex on Körösi utca, built by György Vadász between 1967 and 1969. The **Elizabeth Bridge** was built between 1961 and 1964, and the **Metro 2** line was opened in 1973.

In the 1970s and 1980s, elements of Secession architecture came back in fashion. During Expo 1992 in Seville, Hungary presented itself with a pavilion by Imre Makovecz, who said of his return to pre-industrial building designs: »I call my work, which is influenced by the turn of the 20th century, **organic architecture** ... «. In Budapest, it is possible to get an idea of this organic architecture in the wealthy neighbourhoods of the II district, from several private villas such as House Pete at Kondorkert utca 9, or House Gubcsi at Törökvész lejtö 25. Today, in contrast to these buildings, there are architectural concepts that work with ideas of urbanity and try to underline what is typical in the city. An example of this trend that comes under the heading of Deconstructionist is the interior of the **Nane Gallery** (IX district, Lónyay utca 41), by Gábor Bachman.

Left: organic forms, opulent materials and playful details – art nouveau Hungarian-style had a political dimension as well as an aesthetic one.

Right: gable mosaic on the Török Bank on Szervita tér

A NATIONAL STYLE

The search for a national heritage and identity and the quest for a unique tradition were the issues of the day for Hungarian intellectuals at the end of the 19th century. The establishment of a typically Hungarian style was intended to create a counterweight to Austrian hegemony in Hungary. Architecture and art became the means to achieve national emancipation.

In 1886, the Budapest Arts and Crafts Museum made a purchase in Antwerp that was of special significance for the Hungarian national self-image. It was the complete interior of an Arabian room, and the objects of interest were the rich and exotic ornamentation on the room's component parts. Their mystery provided the impetus for speculation on the origin and identity of Hungary itself.

Art and Identity

Often art has been used as evidence for daring theses on the origin of a national heritage and for the construction of a mythical origin. The reason why an Arabian interior should have been of interest to Hungarians lay in the contemporary method of proving cultural associations with even distant regions by identifying similarities in the decorative style of common objects. The Orient proved to be an endlessly rich source of counterparts to the Hungarian love of decoration and the tulip motif known from folk art, a central motif of Ottoman architectural art. Looking to the East signified a distancing from the cultural traditions of Europe, which had led to an eclectic mixture of artistic styles. In this »golden age of the surrogate«, as critics at the end of the 19th century dubbed it, there was increasing dissatisfaction with beautiful imitations. There was a yearning for something indigenous and original with which to confront Austrian hegemony.

Folk Art as a Model

The desire for an original tradition and a »national style« became pressing. A host of political and artistic directions developed that investigated the matter from all manner of perspectives. For example, Jósef Huszka, who worked as an art teacher in the eastern region of Transylvania, produced extensive books of patterns taken from Hungarian folk art. His collections of motifs, intended as examples for artists and architects, were successively published over a quarter of a century and had a great impact. In fact, his dedicated collecting was inspired by a very similar idea to that which had led to the purchase of the above-mentioned Arabian interior: namely to prove and rediscover ancient connections with the great eastern cultures.

Lechner's Architecture

This legendary relationship was taken up with great enthusiasm in several artistic circles. Among architects, it was Ödön Lechner in particular who found himself inspired by the mythical East and the sheer inexhaustibility of its wealth in forms. He pursued the contemporary desire to find a national style by a method in which he wove all kinds of inspirations together. His motto, »a Hungarian language of forms is not the past but the future«, not only allowed him to mix ancient Hungarian motifs with exotic ornamentation, elements from English colonial architecture and the impressions he gained from plaster casts of Indian architectural details from the Trocadero in Paris, but also allowed him to pursue his preference for the contemporary relevance of ceramic techniques. For Lechner, ceramics combined all the elements of his artistic claim: the possibilities inherent in rich colour schemes and ornamental design, its folk traditions, the durability of the material in an

Glazed tiles and playful forms – a masterpiece by the doyen of Hungarian art nouveau, Ödön Lechner: Post Savings Bank building of 1901

urban environment, and the long-established tradition of the craft itself. He argued that »the largest and most Hungarian part of the country is the Great Plain, where people only know from hearsay of stones, for which transport is extremely expensive, but where tile making is one of the most ancient traditions«. Lechner had first-hand experience of the techniques involved in working with clay – he came from a family of tile producers – and was also a friend of the famous terracotta and porcelain producer from Pécs, Vilmos Zsolnay. However, in his search for the roots of motifs he was often dependent on chance and speculation. For example, he admitted that his design for the Arts and Crafts Museum was largely inspired by the impact of photographs and publications on Persian and Indian art. To this day, the Arts and Crafts Museum, built with Gyula Pártos, as well as Lechner's buildings for the Geological Institute and for the Post Savings Bank, built at the beginning of the 20th century, count as key examples of Hungarian architecture.

Liberation from Established Styles

Lechner's direction, however, was not uncontested by his contemporaries. Confirmed opponents, such as the historicist and long-term professor at the technical college, Alajos Hauszmann, demanded a clear differentiation between folk art and national art. Lechner's like-minded fellows from the Secessionist camp, too, were certainly capable of taking their cues from different models and artistic movements. The common goal was simply to emancipate themselves from the cultural background of the established academic styles.

International Focus

Some representatives of the movement even had an international orientation. These included, for example, Henrik Böhm and Armin Hegedüs, who opened a practice together in 1896. Ten years later they had a notable success: the Turkish bank built to their plans on Servita tér was unveiled to the public. With its intricate exterior glass façade and its more or less open-plan interior, the bank became a symbol for modern building. The showpiece of the bank was the monumental gable mosaic whose theme, in turn, of »Honour to Hungaria« was thoroughly in tune with the contemporary zeitgeist. Later too, Hegedüs participated in image-laden building projects for the prestige of Budapest's business world, such as the new luxury Gellért Hotel with its attached bath house.

Much has changed in the Budapest cityscape since the end of the 1980s. Street names were changed, sculptures and memorials were removed, and the red stars disappeared from public buildings and squares. Post-modern department stores appeared with impressive rapidity, their glass façades contributing to the appearance of the inner city today.

Change

Buildings for the 1896 Millennium Celebration

1896 – 1000 years of Hungary

The urban architectural development which blossomed at the time of the millennium celebrations gave Budapest the characteristics that mark it out as a 19th-century metropolis to this day. The architectural heritage of this epoch, which was decisive for the city, can be encountered by visitors at every step, especially in the city-centre districts on the Pest side. The 1896 millennium festivities were staged to recall the arrival of the Hungarian tribes in the Carpathian basin and to record the »glorious thousand-year past« as national history.

Andrássy út, Hösök tere (Heroes' Square)

The buildings that were constructed on the occasion of the millennium stand predominantly along the north-eastern end of Andrássy út. Even then, the massive Heroes' Square (Hösök tere), which is totally dominated by the millennium memorial, could be reached directly via the freshly inaugurated »Little Metro«, the first underground railway in continental Europe, which runs underneath the showpiece street. Work on the bronze equestrian statue of the seven Hungarian tribal chieftains by György Zala (1858–1937) was not completed until the late 1920s. The design for the columned architecture of the memorial was provided by Albert Schickedanz (1846–1915), who also designed the two museum buildings that flank the square: the Museum of Fine Arts and the Palace of Art.

Temporary exhibition buildings

Few traces remain of the temporary millennium buildings that spread over the area stretching from present-day Heroes' Square to the distant wooded area of Városliget, far beyond. The memorial was initially the site of the main entrance to the exhibition area, a colossal gate in French Renaissance style, about which the contemporary press wrote that this fake had »succeeded wonderfully in imitating a stone building, and was uncannily real«. The exhibition architecture consisted of 230 similar stage set buildings. Of all those, the only survivors are the »group of historic main buildings«, whose design was intended to display the entire architectural history of Hungary and which exhibit motifs from many important buildings from all parts of the country in creative combinations. Over time this group of buildings became known under the collective name of Castle Vajdahunyad (Vajdahunyad vára), after the Knights' Hall which inspired it, the original of which is in Transylvanian Vajdahunyad (today Hunedoara in Rumania). Castle Vajdahunyad is located in what is now the Municipal Forest.

Fine Arts

19th century
Artists' meeting places ►

Guests entering one of the coffee houses in the district of the capital's art and exhibition centres during the time of the Dual Monarchy (1867–1918) would, in all probability, have met a social gathering in lively debate about the cultural and political questions of the day. For the artists of that time, the circle of regulars at the local café was the most important forum for discussing their concerns. The composition of the individual circles more or less mirrored the main artistic trends and their adherents at the time.

The older generation

The older generation, representatives of the academic style, met in a side room at Virágbokors (bunch of flowers). To these belonged **Bertalan Székely** (1835–1910), a friend of the Munich historical painting movement, who liked commissions for monumental wall paintings best; **Károly Lotz** (1833–1904), the most successful fresco artist of his day, who from the 1870s onwards worked on the majority of new buildings for official representation, such as the great hall in the Palace of Justice, the staircase of Parliament, the ceiling in the auditorium of the opera house, and the main hall in the Academy of Sciences; **Gyula Benczúr** (1844–1920) dazzled visitors to the millennium exhibition with his 3.5m x 7 m (11ft x 23ft) oil painting on the *Reconquest of Buda Castle*, which today hangs in the country's National Gallery. The different circles of the popular Salon and genre painters gathered in the Abbázia Cafè or the Royal Café. Several groups of youthful Secessionists met at the Mücsarnok kávéház, the café in the Palace of Art.

The younger generation

At the end of the 19th century and the beginning of the 20th century, the Japán kávéház was the most important artists' meeting place. It was the favourite café of innovators, such as **Pál Szinyei Merse** (1845–1920) who, independent of Parisian influences, had already experimented with painting outdoors around 1870. His main work, *Breakfast Outdoors«, of 1873, is in the Hungarian National Gallery.* **Károly Ferenczy** (1862–1917) also dropped in here when he had business in the city, and was not at the artists' colony of Nagybánya. He was one of the most influential exponents of non-academic methods and directions, from Pleinair to Impressionism, and from art nouveau to Symbolism, that were represented and developed by the »Nagybánya School« from 1896 onwards. Examples of his work can also be admired in the National Gallery, such as *The Painter* (1903) or *Sunny Morning* (1905). The »greats« that patronized the Japanese café also included **József Rippl-Rónai** (1861–1927) who, after his intensive and frequent visits to France, reported on the latest artistic events there, and also reacted to them in his own work. A not very sociable and, in his day, not seriously respected member of the circle was **Tivadar Csontváry Kosztka** (1853–1919), who was convinced that his pictures would one day »shine as lone stars in the sky«. This attitude, which he expressed in monumental landscape paintings in expressive colours with motifs from the Near East or southern Italy – such as, for example, *The Ruins of the Greek Theatre at Taormina* from 1904/1905, in the National Gallery – still causes debate among art historians today about Csontváry's merits.

The inter-war years

Most of the artistic avant-garde that began to develop in the revolutionary climate of the 1910s had to continue its activities abroad after the collapse of the People's Republic in 1919. Vienna and Berlin, where the relationship with German Expressionists and Dadaists, Italian Futurists or Russian and Dutch Constructivists could be developed especially well, became the centres of Hungarian emigration. Today the career of Lajos Kassáks (1887–1967), the main organizer of the Hungarian Activist circle, and his activities as an artist, writer and publisher of a number of avant-garde publications, can be can be viewed in the Budapest Kassák Museum in Zichy Palace in Óbuda, as the artist returned to his homeland after years of exile. Quite a few artists connected with Hungarian Activism went to the Bauhaus, where they were able to lay the foundation for their international recognition. The most famous among them are **László Moholy-Nagy** (1895–1946), **Marcel Breuer** (1902–1981), **Farkas Molnár** (1898–1944) and **Sándor Bortnyik** (1893–1976).

»Poultry Market« by Lajos Déak-Ebner

Art after 1945

Lajos Kassák remained a defender and supporter of the avant-garde right up to his death, even of the newest trends of New Abstraction, happenings, Flux and Pop Art. In the 1960s and 1970s, however, several exhibitions oriented towards the international scene were closed down early, despite support from famous personalities. Newspaper projects were foiled, and several theatre productions banned. Protagonists of that Underground era were, for example, **Sándor Altorjai** (1941–1979), **Ilona Keserü** (born 1933), **Béla Kondor** (1931–1972) and **Dóra Maurer** (born 1937). The heroic sculptures that were created for Budapest's streets and squares on official commissions from the 1950s to 1980s will probably not leave their present location any time soon: they are all gathered in silent pathos in the ►sculpture park on the city's edge, designed as if it were a final resting place (Szobor Park, Szabadkai út).

Contemporary art scene A unique aspect of the Hungarian art scene is that it is less characterized by private galleries and the art trade, and more by the associations, free groups and independent initiatives of the artists themselves. This is still the case today, as the Hungarian avant-garde's desire for independence from official tastes in art has a strong tradition. The search for alternatives to the mainstream, to the lucrative safe posts, with all their excess of virtuosity and socio-political dependence, inspired the creation of a number of more or less autonomous artists' colonies as early as the beginning of the 20th century. After the First World War, whole groups of artists joined the political fray on their own behalf, for example the **Group of »Eight«** and the **»Activists«**; in the 1930s and 1940s too independent artistic groups emerged, such as the **Szentendre circle of artists**. During the years of the Hungarian People's Republic, the art scene laid claim to several unconventional places in which to offer its newest work for public discussion. For example, such exhibitions and art events took place in the Budapest zoo, in the Research Institute for Physics, at the airport and, very often, in private apartments or studios. Beyond the traditional art institutions, many forms of expression which challenged social conventions were tried out. The myth of several confrontational and scandalous performances and actions in the 1970s and 1980s by **Miklós Erdély** and **Tibor Hajas**, still resonate today. Today, too, the liveliest sector of the art scene is sustained by initiatives of the artists themselves, which occur at changing venues without fanfares or publicity. These events are almost always exclusively advertised by word of mouth. One of the most active venues is the **Liget Gallery**, a non-commercial artists' gallery by a small municipal wood in the XIV district (Ajtósi Dürer sor 5), where a new exhibition opens almost every two weeks.

Budapest: City of Culture

Cultural centre Budapest is Hungary's most important cultural centre. It is not only the home of the Hungarian Academy of Sciences, thanks to a generous donation by Count Széchenyi, but also the city in which most of the country's universities and colleges are concentrated. The Music School, the Opera, as well as the Operetta, which successfully competes with Vienna and Paris, make the city on the Danube a centre of musical art. Furthermore, over two dozen theatres, superbly equipped museums and galleries underscore Budapest's reputation as a city of culture. Several poets and writers have succeeded in helping a rich Hungarian literature to achieve international fame, despite its linguistic isolation.

City of Music

»In relation to songs and other forms of entertainment, Pest is ahead of Vienna«, thus wrote the Vasárnapi Ujság (Sunday News) in 1873. In fact, Budapest was so successful that connoisseurs such as Johannes Brahms travelled there especially to hear a good performance of *Don Giovanni*. That was around 1890, when Gustav Mahler was the director of the Royal Hungarian Opera. External influences were many and various during the development of the city's culture. Conversely, however, Hungarian traditions were also received in the cultural centres of Europe took place, a phenomenon particularly evident in music. Musicians such as Brahms or Schubert liked to use themes that originated in the Verbunkos instrumental dance music of the 18th century. Originally, Verbunkos melodies and dances were used in recruiting of soldiers.

Music performances

First-class music can be experienced at the Budapest Opera, which has been under the artistic direction of such eminent persons as Gustav Mahler, Sergio Failoni, Aladár Tóth, Kálmán Nádasdy, János Ferencsik and András Mihály. Furthermore, there are concerts at the Academy of Music, the Pest Redoute, in the new Congress Centre and, on various occasions, in the Matthew Church and the Dohány Street Synagogue.

During the summer months, there is a programme of operatic and ballet performances on the open-air stage on Margaret Island. Significant musical occasions can also be experienced during the course of the major annual cultural events: the »Budapest Spring Festival« and the »Budapest Autumn Festival«.

Renowned orchestras

The Hungarian National Philharmonic, the Budapest Philharmonic, the Orchestra of the Hungarian Radio and Television, the Festival Orchestra, the Budapest Madrigal Ensemble, the Franz Liszt Chamber Orchestra, the Budapest Chamber Ensemble and the Schola Hungarica are famous far beyond Hungary.

Theatre

Venues and ensembles

Theatrical venues in the Hungarian capital reflect cultural changes and influences. In the second half of the 19th century, the Viennese architectural practice of **Ferdinand Fellner and Hermann Helmer** built countless theatres. In Budapest, their first commission was a theatre that no longer exists; their last was the Vígszínház Theatre on Szent István körút, which was built in 1895–96. Their most interesting project was the Somossy Orfeum, today the home of the Operetta (Fövárosi Operett Színház), which they had to fit into a narrow plot at Nagymezö utca 17, in 1893–94. The stages and auditoriums of the two Viennese architects always followed Baroque models. In contrast, the Erkel Theatre in VIII district, Köztársaság tér, was built in art nouveau style in 1911 by pupils of Lechner, Marcel Komor, Dezsö Jakab and Géza Márkus, though it has had to endure many rebuildings. Today around fifty ensembles covering a wide spectrum perform theatre in Budapest. Popular opera, Hungarianized musicals, well-known operettas and light music dominate the programme of the major Budapest stages. However, the Opera House (Magyar Állami Operáház, VI district, Andrássy út 22) increasingly offers out-of-the-ordinary productions. Built to designs by Miklós Ybl between 1875 and 1884, the Opera House remains the city's most significant venue, even if, in recent years, artistic innovations and experiments in content and organization have generally been developed for small stages, such as the József Katona Theatre on Petöfi Sándor utca 6. With the inauguration of the Hungarian National Theatre in March 2002, Budapest gained a further important venue. The controversial building, designed by Mária Siklós, eventually found a home in the IX district, at Soroksári út on the banks of the Danube, after long arguments at the highest political level over its siting.

A renowned institution: the Franz Liszt School of Music

The Mikroskop Theatre and the Comedy Theatre predominantly host cabaret. The capital's circus is a venue for rock operas, musicals and mime, and the Arany-János Theatre, or Budapest Puppet Theatre also deserve a visit.

Universities

The first Hungarian university was founded in Nagyszombat (present-day Trnava in Slovakia) in 1635 and initially moved to Buda in 1777, and finally to Pest in 1784. From this emerged today's Eötvös Loránd Tudományegyetem, the city's and the entire country's foremost university. It is named after the physicist and researcher of gravity Loránd Eötvös (1848–1919), who invented the torsion balance that carries his name. The various faculties of the university are housed in different buildings, occasionally far away from each other.

The majority of humanities subjects are taught in the buildings encompassed by Váci utca und Pesti Barnabás utca, which is also where the university theatre (Egyetemi Színpád) is housed. The former school of the Piarist Order, which was built between 1913 and 1915, was nationalized after the Second World War and given to the university. In recent times it has been the subject of heated discussions on restitution claims by the church.

Of the almost 60 institutes of higher learning in the country, a quarter are found in Budapest alone. Many subjects can be studied only there. The most important seats of learning and research, which also played a significant role in the development of the city, are the Technical University (Budapest Müszaki Egyetem), the School of Veterinary Medicine (Allatorvostudományi Egyetem), the Music School (Liszt Ferenc Zenemüvészeti Föiskola), and the Art School (Magyar Képzömüvészeti Föiskola).

Andrássy University

The German-language Andrássy Gyula University was founded in 2002 and housed in the palace of the Festetics noble family, behind the National Museum. The name is taken from Count Gyula Andrássy, the most significant Hungarian reform politician of the 19th century. The university has a European focus and offers subjects such as, International Relations, Comparative Schools of State and Law, and Central European Studies.

Famous People

Who went down in history as the »saviour of mothers«? By which name does the film world know Mihály Kertész? Whose career went from locksmith to prime minister and ended in a tragic traitor's death? Short testimonials to people who are associated with Budapest.

Árpád (probably 850 to 907)

First king of the Hungarians

Árpád was the founder of the first Hungarian royal dynasty, the Árpáds, who ruled the country from the 9th century until the year 1301. The nomadic Hungarian tribes of the ninth century had two types of leaders, the kende (religious leader) and the gyula (chieftain and judge). Árpád was a chieftain when he penetrated the Carpathian basin via the Verecke Pass in present-day Ukraine, and conquered the regions east of the Danube during the first phase of the Great Migrations. After the death of the kende in 904, Árpád took over this role too and became sole leader as chieftain.

Béla Bartók (1881–1945)

Composer

Béla Bartók became famous as a composer far beyond the borders of Hungary. He studied at the Budapest Music School and took on a professorship for piano there in 1907. His interest in folk music, which he researched himself in Hungary and in formerly Hungarian regions, was inspired by his friendship with Zoltán Kodály. As a composer, Bartók succeeded in joining the European avant-garde; his works combine modern musical language with Hungarian folk music. With his *Mikrokosmos*, comprising 153 piano pieces, Bartók created a progressive textbook between 1926 and 1937. On the occasion of the 50th anniversary of the unification of Buda and Pest in 1923, he composed the *Dance Suite*, which had its premiere together with Kodály's *Psalmus Hungaricus*. Developments in Hungary caused him to emigrate to the USA in the autumn of 1940, where he died in impoverished circumstances in 1945. His remains were transferred to Budapest in 1988.

Dénes (Dennis) Gábor (1900–1979)

Physicist

The Budapest-born physicist Dénes Gábor went down in the history of science in 1947, when he invented holography. After his studies in Budapest and Berlin he emigrated to England in 1934, where he became a lecturer at London's Imperial College from 1949, and Professor of Electrophysics from 1958 to 1967. After the invention of laser light in 1960, his technology gained great practical significance. Dénes Gábor was honoured with the Nobel Prize in Physics in 1971.

Theodor Herzl (1860–1904)

Zionist

Budapest is the birthplace of Theodor Herzl, the founder of political Zionism. Herzl studied law in Vienna and after the completion of his

← *Lajos Kossuth, the Hungarian national hero of the 1848 revolution, fought for independence from Austria.*

final examinations in 1884 worked as a foreign correspondent for an Austrian newspaper in Paris. He came to Zionism there, where large sections of society were increasingly anti-semitic. In *The Jewish State*, published in 1896, he demanded the foundation of a sovereign Jewish state with the argument that Jews were not only a religious group, but also a nation. He called the first Zionist Congress in Basle, in 1897, which elected him as President of the World Zionist Organization. The foundation of a Jewish state, for which he campaigned energetically, was not to become a reality for more than forty years after his death.

Mór Jókai (1825–1904)

Folk Storyteller The great folk storyteller is one of the most-read authors of Hungarian literature. His novels, stories and novellas, which are among the best creations of romantic Hungarian prose, are characterized by lively action, the extreme characteristics of the protagonists, and dramatic plots, but also by robust humour, an anecdotal style and magnificent invention. He took an active part in the 1848 revolution, alongside Petöfi, and was forced underground until his pardon in 1852. He founded the newspaper »Hon« in 1863. He was still an active writer in his last years, but the quality of his late works does not match that of his early ones.

János Kádár (1912–1989)

Politician János Kádár dominated Hungarian politics as the head of the Communist Party for over thirty years. Due to the relatively high standard of living and the small political freedoms that Kádár's careful reforms made possible, Hungary was also known as the »happiest hut in the camp«. From 1948 to 1950 Kádár was interior minister and a member of the revolutionary government of Imre Nagy. He took power after the quashing of the 1956 uprising. The aging government leader Kádár clung to the Party's claim to power right up to the end, and was thus forced to give way to younger reformers before the final ending of the old system.

Imre Kertész (born 1929)

Writer In 2002 the Nobel Prize for Literature went to **Imre Kertész** (born 1929), for »a literary work that upholds the fragile experience of the individual against the barbaric arbitrariness of history«. The author was initially deported to Auschwitz, and later to Buchenwald, at the age of 15, due to his Jewish roots. Later, he became a journalist and then lived as an independent author in Budapest, and wrote musicals and drama; he earned his living through his work as a translator. He began work on his autobiographical *Fatelessness* as early as 1960. Today it is one of the most important works of contemporary European literature, but it only found recognition after a long time, and helped Kertész gain an international breakthrough in 1995.

Hungary's most recent Nobel prize winner: the novelist Imre Kertész

Mihály Kertész (Michael Curtis) (1888–1962)

Film director

The movie *Casablanca*, filmed in 1943, with Ingrid Bergman and Humphrey Bogart, made the Hungarian-born Michael Curtis famous and gave him the highest American film honour, an Oscar. Curtis already made his first film in 1912, at the age of 24. After periods in Vienna and Berlin he arrived in Hollywood in 1927, where he was already working in colour in 1930. His most famous films are *Robin Hood* (1938), *Virginia City* (1940), *Yankee Doodle* (1942), *Mission to Moscow* (1943) and *The Life of Francis of Assisi* (1961).

Zoltán Kodály (1882–1967)

Composer

The composer and musician, who was born in Kecskemét, became famous above all for his systematic research of Hungarian folk music, whose special characteristics he worked out by a comparison with the folk music of other Finno-Ugrian peoples. After completion of his studies at the Budapest School of Music, he taught theory of music and composition there from 1907 and, from 1937, folk music as well. His compositions, which reflect his detailed work with Hungarian folk music, were popularized abroad as well, by Toscanini and Furtwängler. Beginning in the 1920s, but especially after the Second World War, his focus was on the reform of music teaching in schools. The system of music teaching developed by him is today well-known throughout the world.

György Konrád (born 1933)

Writer

György Konrád is among the leading representatives of the intellectual opposition in Hungary which from the 1970s fought for the democratization process in the country. Until the political changes at the end of the 1980s, the writer could only publish his work abroad, or in the underground press. His first novel *Látogató* (*The Case Worker*, 1969) evolved from the experiences of this former philosophy student when working at the youth protection unit of a Budapest government organization. In this and his later novels, among them *The City Builder* from 1975, *The Loser* (1980) and *A Feast in the Garden* (1986), the social and political problems in a socialist society are portrayed.

Lajos Kossuth (1802–1894)

Freedom fighter Kossuth was one of the leading figures in the battle for Hungarian independence and civil rights in the 19th century. He campaigned for secession from Austria, social reforms, the abolition of feudal privileges, taxation for all, and the establishment of representative bodies. In April 1849, the Hungarian Parliament under his leadership voted for independence, as well as the abdication of the House of Habsburg, electing him as regent. After the revolution Kossuth fled to Turkey and then through Europe, where he continued the fight for Hungarian independence. Even though he was granted amnesty in 1867, he never returned to Hungary. His work of several volumes entitled *My Writings in Exile* was published in 1880–1882. Already a national hero in Hungary during his lifetime, the revolutionary died in his elective home of Turin, in 1894.

Ferenc (Franz) Liszt (1811–1886)

Composer Franz Liszt, who is now considered one of the country's greatest sons, was born in present-day Raiding, in the Austrian Burgenland, which at that time was Hungarian. The concert virtuoso lived in Paris from 1823 to 1835, where he was influenced by Berlioz, Paganini and Chopin. He enjoyed a life-long friendship with Richard Wagner. In Weimar, where Liszt was engaged as director of music at the court of the grand duke, he composed, among other things, various piano pieces, with which he founded the so-called New German School. Between 1861 and 1869 he lived, at various times, in Rome, Weimar and Budapest. In Budapest he took over the leadership of the Academy of Music whose foundation was inspired by him. His close relationship with Hungary is particularly evident in his *Hungarian Rhapsodies*. The composer was ennobled by the Duke of Sachsen-Weimar in 1859 and died in Bayreuth in 1886.

Composer of the Hungarian Rhapsodies

György Lukács (1885–1971)

Philosopher and Historian of Literature György Lukács, a philosopher and historian of literature was born in Budapest, and became a member of the Communist Party in 1918. After the collapse of the People's Republic, he emigrated via Vienna to Moscow. His writings, in which he outlined the core themes of

Marxist aesthetics and artistic philosophy, had a permanent influence on left-wing European intellectuals.In the 1930s Lukács concentrated on working with European literature of the 19th century, especially the realistic novel. After the end of the war he returned to Hungary and taught aesthetics and philosophy of culture in Budapest from 1945 to 1958. As one of the main movers of the Hungarian uprising in 1956, he suffered great discrimination after it was crushed and was relieved of all his posts. Lukács withdrew into internal exile for some years and his books were published abroad. He re-emerged into Hungarian intellectual life in the mid-1960s, but did not live to complete his planned final work on ethics.

László Moholy-Nagy (1895–1946)

Artist

The multi-talented artist, painter, sculptor, graphic artist and photographer, born in the north-eastern town of Bácsborsod, is widely known as an influential teacher at the Bauhaus in Weimar, where he taught from 1923 to 1928. After Hitler took power, he initially emigrated to England, and then to the USA in 1937. He founded the »New Bauhaus« in Chicago. Moholy-Nagy embodies the modern artist of the early 20th century, who liberated himself from traditional forms and single tracks of expression and experimented with new materials, media and techniques, touching on and influencing various contemporary trends, such as Dadaism, Constructivism and de Stijl. His extensive repertoire included abstract compositions, collage, stage sets and photo montage.

Imre Nagy (1896–1958)

Politician

Nagy, a locksmith from Kaposvár joined the Russian Bolsheviks towards the end of the First World War. He became a member of the newly founded Hungarian Socialist Workers Party in the 1920s. He qualified as an agrarian specialist in Moscow in the 1930s. He returned to Hungary with the Russian troops in 1944 and, as Minister for Agriculture, oversaw the dispossession of the large landowners without compensation. Nagy, who held important party posts, was forced to work with Stalinist trends. He was elected as Hungarian prime minister in 1953, as representative of the »new course«, but was already forced to resign under pressure from the Stalinists by 1955. Imre Nagy became prime minister once more at the beginning of the Hungarian uprising in 1956. He took the lead in the uprising and proclaimed Hungary's neutrality in the Cold War. After the suppression of the uprising by Soviet troops Nagy was carried off to neighbouring Communist Rumania. He was returned to Hungary in 1958, and sentenced to death in a secret court, along with several fellow activists. In 1989, Nagy and his comrades were officially rehabilitated by a formal act of state. His mortal remains were buried at the new city cemetery (Új köztemetö).

Sándor Petöfi (1823–1849)

Poet

Sándor Petöfi is honoured as Hungary's greatest national poet. The characteristics of his poetry are unpretentious language and a confession of personal feelings, which is particularly evident in his love poems, but also in other genres. In his heroic epics, fairy tales and songs – his hero »János« (1845) was particularly famous – he portrayed the traditions and landscapes of the great Hungarian plain in the daily lives of the farmers and cowherds. His revolutionary tendencies made him a leading figure of the freedom movement, and on 15 March 1848, Petöfi led Pest's youth and recited his revolutionary *National Song* on the steps of the National Museum. Convinced of the need for armed resistance, he took part in the Hungarian War of Independence as a captain in the revolutionary army, and is believed to have fallen at the Battle of Segesvár (today Sighisoara in Rumania).

Ferenc Puskas (1927–2006)

Football legend

The career of the great Hungarian footballer Ferenc Puskas began in 1943, in his birthplace of Kispest, a suburb of Budapest. The short and stocky Puskas gave his debut performance in the Hungarian national team aged 18, against Austria. After four Hungarian championship titles with Kispest Honved, Puskas moved abroad in reaction to the political events in Hungary in 1956. He signed for Real Madrid in 1958 and, along with Alfredo di Stefano, he became part of the most feared international pair of strikers of his time. While at Real Madrid, he won the Spanish championship six times, was European Footballer of the Year and World Footballer of the Year twice. His performance at the European Cup Final in 1960 remains unforgettable: he scored four goals in the home match at the Bernabéu Stadium, which led to a 7:3 victory against Eintracht Frankfurt. As captain of the Hungarian national team between 1950 and 1956 he only suffered one defeat, against Germany at the World Championships in Berne. In 84 games for the Hungarian team Puskas scored 83 goals, and it would have been more had he not taken Spanish nationality so that he could work for the Spanish national team. Ferenc Puskas was elected as Hungary's Footballer of the Century in 1998. He died of Alzheimer's in Budapest, aged 79, in 2006.

Ignác Semmelweis (1818–1865)

Doctor

The doctor from Buda went down in medical history as »the saviour of mothers«. During his work as a birthing assistant he discovered that dirty hands, instruments and bandages could cause an infection at childbirth that was usually fatal. He therefore advised doctors to disinfect these with chlorine water before beginning treatment. He returned to Budapest from Vienna in 1850, and became consultant gynaecologist at the Rókus Hospital. From 1855 onwards, he taught at the Medical University that today carries his name. Even though his method, which paved the way for the antiseptic treatment of wounds, had great success, he was denied international recognition beyond Hungary during his lifetime.

Mephisto made him world-famous

István Szabó (born 1938)

Director

István Szabó began his film studies in Budapest, in 1956, the year of the Hungarian uprising, and already achieved international recognition in 1963, with his short film *Concert*. His first full-length movie, *The Age of Dreams*, followed in 1964. Since then he has numbered among the most creative and artistically influential filmmakers in Europe. His early films reflect the political trauma of the suppression of the Hungarian uprising in allegorical, deeply poetic and melancholy visual language. Szabó began his European career in the 1980s, with his film *Mephisto* (1981). To this day he continues to work on his theme of the relationship of artists to political power, and the damage done to the individual by social circumstances. István Szabó was born in Budapest in 1938. Between 1956 and 1961 he studied film direction under Félix Máriássy at the Theatre and Film School. In 1959, he was a founding member of the Béla Balázs Studio; his first short films were created there in 1961–62 (*Variations on a Theme*, 1961; *You*, 1962). He was a founding member of the literary and artistic academy Széchenyi, and became an honorary citizen of Budapest in 1996. Szabó teaches at the Theatre and Film School in Budapest, and is also a visiting lecturer at the London and Berlin film academies.

Raoul Wallenberg (1911–?)

Diplomat

Raoul Wallenberg, the son of a successful Swedish banking family, resided in the Hungarian capital of Budapest as a member of the Swedish Legation during the Nazi era. Diplomatic skill in the relationship with the fascist powers enabled him to save numerous Hungarian Jews from certain death(► Baedeker Special p 184). After the liberation of Budapest by Russian troops at the beginning of 1945, Raoul Wallenberg was kidnapped by the Red Army and presumably died in a Soviet camp.

Practicalities

WHERE'S THE BEST PLACE TO GO SWIMMING? HOW DO YOU BUY CONCERT TICKETS AND SAY »THANK YOU« IN HUNGARIAN? READ UP ON IT HERE – IDEALLY BEFORE YOU GO!

Accommodation

Categories Budapest's hotels are categorized according to their facilities. The scale goes from five stars (luxury) to one star (lowest category has rooms with hot and cold water). However, there are considerable differences within each category in terms of price, facilities and service. Tourist information offices have the most up-to-date listings for hotels (►Information).

Pensions, private rooms In Budapest there are many small pensions and numerous private rooms, which are often indistinguishable from hotels in the lower categories in terms of comfort, yet charge a lot less.

Seasonal accommodation During the summer months there is additional accommodation in student halls of residence. Rooms can be booked via the accommodation booths at the three large railway stations and via Tourinform offices

Accommodation service In general, it is not difficult to find a room in Budapest. However, it can still be hard to find acceptable accommodation during the summer high season, as well as at Whitsun, Corpus Christi, Ascension Day, and especially during the Formula One Grand Prix at the Hungaroring in mid-August. Mid-priced rooms, in particular, are often booked up at that time. Those who arrive without reservations are offered help at the room service counters at the three large railway stations, as well as at the bus terminal at Erzsébet tér.

Prices As a rule, hotel prices within each category can vary greatly, though overall they have gradually adjusted to the levels of other central European capitals. It is often worthwhile booking via internet, and asking for weekly rates.

ACCOMMODATION INFORMATION

BOOKING SERVICES

► **Non-Stop Hotel Service**
Tribus
V, Apáczai Csere János u. 1, tel. 266–80 42, 318–57 76, fax 266–81 59, www.tribus.hu

► **Booking service for pensions**
Panzió Centrum
XII, Szarvas Gábor u. 24, tel. 200–88 70, fax 200–88 69
pansiocentrum@mail.matav.hu

► **Booking service for private rooms and apartments**
Maria & István, IX, Ferenc körút 39, tel. / fax 216–07 68

► **Hotels via internet**
www.travelport.hu
www.budapestinfo.hu

RECOMMENDED HOTELS

► **① etc. see map on p.88/89**
No number: outside the map

LUXURY: OVER 32,000 Ft

▸ ⑬ Budapest Marriott Hotel

Apáczai Csere János u. 4
H-1052 Budapest, tel. 266–70 00, fax 266–50 00
www.marriott.com
Thanks to its location on the Pest Danube Corso, this hotel ranks among the most desirable choices in Hungary's capital. Many of the 362 luxury rooms enjoy a superb view of the Castle District opposite.

▸ Corinthia Aquincum

Árpád fejedelem útja 94
H-1036 Budapest, tel. 436–41 00, fax 436–41 56
www.corinthia.com
On the banks of the Danube at Óbuda, not far from the Árpád Bridge and Margaret Island, this superbly equipped spa hotel is a tempting place for an extended stay. The hotel has 312 rooms and suites. It not only has its own thermal bath with sauna and gym, but also offers a wide range of medicinal treatments.

▸ ⑧ Danubius Hotel Gellért

Szent Gellért tér 1
H-1111 Budapest, tel. 385–22 00, fax 466–66 31
www.danubiusgroup.com/danubius/gellert.html
The »mother of all hotels« in Budapest, so to speak, is the Gellért spa hotel, with its 234 rooms and suites. The hotel and attached thermal bath were built in art nouveau splendour from 1911 to 1918, immediately adjacent to the generously flowing thermal springs at the foot of Gellért Hill. Unfortunately, this traditional hotel has lost something of its shine in terms of standards and service.

▸ ① Hilton Budapest

Hess András tér 1–3
H-1014 Budapest
Tel. 488–66 00, fax 488–66 44
www.budapest.hilton.com
This modern luxury hotel in the heart of the Castle District, close to the Fishermen's Bastion, was built during the era of »goulash communism«. The architects incorporated architectural remains of the Gothic Dominican monastery. The Hilton has 322 comfortable rooms and suites, and the restaurant is one of the city's best.

▸ ⑭ Inter-Continental Budapest

Apáczai Csere János u. 12–14
H-1052 Budapest
Tel. 327–63 33, fax 327–63 57
www.interconti.com
Built in 1981 and extensively modernized in 1998, the Budapest Inter-Conti stands on the Danube Corso on the Pest side. This hotel, with its 398 rooms and suites is mainly frequented by business travellers.

! *Baedeker* TIP

Gresham Palace

Adjacent to the Chain Bridge, with view of Castle Hill, lies the Gresham Palace Hotel, reopened in 2003 after restoration work that cost 85 million US dollars. Even if you cannot afford a room at the hotel where Sophia Loren stays, at least take a look at the entrance hall: wonderful art nouveau windows, intricate mosaics of Murano glass, and silk wallpaper from Belgium. The palace is a breath-taking spectacle, especially at night. (Roosevelt tér 5-7, tel. 268-60 00, fax 268-50 00, www.fourseasons.com)

▶ ⑯ **Kempinski Hotel Corvinus**
Erzsébet tér 7–8
H-1051 Budapest
Tel. 429–37 77, fax 429–47 77
www.kempinski.budapest.com
The Budapest Kempinski in the Pest city centre, close to the lively Váci utca, opened in 1992 and is considered a post-modern architectural highlight to this day. The luxury hotel has 369 extremely comfortable rooms and suites.

▶ ⑱ **Radisson SAS Béke**
Teréz krt. 43
H-1067 Budapest
Tel. 301–16 00, fax 301–16 15
www.danubiusgroup.com/hungarhotels/radisson.html
This hotel, which has a long tradition and 239 somewhat small rooms, is located quite centrally on the Great Ring, near the West Railway Station and the opera. Along with »Zsolnay«, it is home to one of the city's best café-restaurants.

▶ ⑮ **Sofitel Atrium Budapest**
Roosevelt tér 2
H-1051 Budapest
Tel. 266–12 34, fax 266–91 01
www.accorhotels.com
This luxury hotel stands on the Pest side of the Danube, near the Chain Bridge. The 355 rooms and suites are ranged around an inner courtyard with piano bar. Of course the hotel also has a swimming pool, as well as a gym with sauna and solarium.

▶ ⑫ **Taverna**
Váci utca 20
H-1052 Budapest
Tel. 485–31 00, fax 485–31 11
www.hoteltaverna.hu
This modern city hotel is located on Budapest's busy shopping street. The 226 rooms have functional interiors, and the atmosphere is described by many guests as decidedly friendly.

MID-RANGE: 17 000–32 000 Ft

▶ ② **Carlton Hotel Budapest**
Apor Péter u. 3
H-1011 Budapest, tel. 224–09 99, fax 224–09 90
www.carltonhotel.hu
Guests at the Carlton can stay in 95 attractively decorated rooms, at the foot of Castle Hill and near the Chain Bridge.

▶ ㉑ **Astoria Szálloda**
Kossuth Lajos u. 19–21
H-1053 Budapest, tel. 317–34 11, fax 318–67 98
www.danubiusgroup.com/hungarhotels/astoria.html
Things are friendly and familiar in this hotel in the centre of Pest. It has over 129 nicely decorated rooms. Connoisseurs of art history will enjoy the unadulterated Empire style here.

▶ **Budapest**
Szilágyi Erzsébet fasor 47

H-1026 Budapest
Tel. 488–98 00, fax 488–98 08
www.danubiusgroup.com/
Budapest
The 289 rooms are contained in a 15-storey cylindrical building which has great views the upper floors.

► **Danubius Grand Hotel Margitsziget**
Margitsziget
H-1138 Budapest
Tel. 452–62 00, fax 452–62 64
www.danubiusgroup.com/
danubius/grand.html
Guests taking a cure feel most at home here, in the 164 rooms on Margaret Island. The spa facilities of the neighbouring Danubius Thermal Hotel Margitsziget can be reached by underground tunnel.

► **Danubius Thermal Hotel Helia**
Kárpát u. 62–64,
H-1133 Budapest
Tel. 452–58 00, fax 452–58 01
www.danubiusgroup.com/
danubius/helia.html
This modern spa hotel with all necessary medical facilities lies on the Pest side of the Danube, opposite Margaret Island. The 262 rooms and suites are well equipped. The hotel's own thermal bath is fed by the medicinal waters of the springs on Margaret Island.

► **Danubius Thermal Hotel Margitsziget**
Margitsziget, H-1138 Budapest
Tel. 452–62 00, fax 452–62 61
www.danubiusgroup.com/
danubius/thermal.html
Those who want to relax in an attractive environment away from city noise are well served by this spa hotel with its 248 comfortable rooms.

► ⑳ **Hungária**
Rákóczi út 90, H-1074 Budapest
Tel. 478–11 00, fax 478–11 11
www.danubiusgroup.com/
This reasonably comfortable 1000-bed hotel is very centrally located by a major road junction and opposite the East Railway Station. Short-stay guests are well-provided for here.

► ⑰ **k + k Hotel Opera**
Révay u. 24, H-1065 Budapest
Tel. 269–02 22, fax 269–02 30
www.kkhotels.com
This modern and well-run hotel lies in a quiet side street behind the opera, and contains over 200 tastefully decorated rooms. The service is first rate.

► ⑨ **Mercure Korona**
Kecskeméti u. 14
H-1053 Budapest
Tel. 317–41 11, fax 318–38 67
www.mercure-korona.hu
This hotel, one of the Hungarian capital's large establishments with its 424 rooms, has a very central location on the Little Ring. The rooms are relatively small, but nevertheless quite comfortable.

► ③ **Novotel Budapest Congress**
Alkotás u. 63–67
H-1123 Budapest
Tel. 372–57 00, fax 466–56 36
www.novotel-bud-congress.hu
Business travellers especially, but tourists too, appreciate this hotel with its 324 rooms situated on the Buda side, in the neighbourhood of the Congress Centre.

► **Park Hotel Flamenco**
Tas vezér u. 7, H-1113 Budapest
Tel. 372–20 00, fax 365–80 07
www.danubiusgroup.com/
hungarhotels/flamenco.html

The Park Hotel Flamenco, in a small park, was built during the socialist era. The 348 rooms are modern and the service is exemplary. The bustling centre of Pest is just a few minutes' walk from the hotel.

BUDGET: 7000–17 000 Ft

▶ **Agro**
Normafa u. 54
H-1121 Budapest
Tel. 375–40 11, fax 375–61 64
h.agro.budapest@mail.matav.hu
This hotel with a personable service is hidden in the middle of a wood on the Szabadsag-hegy (hill) and provides a relaxing stay. The 149 rooms have a contemporary interior.

▶ ⑤ **Bara**
Hegyalja út 34–36
H-1118 Budapest
Tel. 385–34 45, fax 385–09 95
This small and fairly basic hotel with 36 rooms lies at the foot of Gellért Hill and near the road to Vienna. The Gellért Bath is also just a few minutes' walk away.

▶ ⑲ **Benczúr**
Benczúr u. 35
H-1068 Budapest
Tel. 342–79 70, fax 342–15 58
hotel@hotelbenczur.hu
www.hotelbenczur.hu
This hotel is situated in a more or less peaceful location near Heroes' Square and Városliget woods. The exterior is not very appealing, but the 93 rooms are OK.

▶ ⑪ **City Panzió Pilvax**
Pilvax köz 1–3
H-1052 Budapest
Tel. 266–76 60, fax 317–63 96
www.taverna.hu
The modern City Hotel with 32 rooms occupies a historic site. Hungarian writers and revolutionaries once met in the Pilvax restaurant.

▶ ⑩ **Erzsébet**
Károlyi Mihály u. 11–15
H-1053 Budapest
Tel. 328–57 00, fax 328–57 63
buderz@euroweb.hu
www.danubiusgroup.com/hungarhotels/erzsebet.html
Not far from the Elizabeth Bridge, this hotel with its 123 rooms is especially favoured by price-conscious business travellers, who can eat well for a good price in the hotel restaurant. The hotel bar is always lively.

▶ ④ **Kristal**
Társ u. 9
H-1118 Budapest
Tel. / fax 466–90 43
www.kristal.hu
Small bijou hotel in a quiet location, about 20 minutes' walk from the city centre.

▶ **Normafa**
Eötvös út 52–54
H-1121 Budapest
Tel. 395–65 05, fax 395–65 04
This well-run hotel is idyllically situated on Szabadsag-hegy (hill). It has 70 comfortable rooms; guests can also play tennis up here.

▶ ⑦ **Queen Mary**
Béla király út 47, H-1121 Budapest
Tel. 274–40 00, fax 395–83 77
This small but elegant hotel has 22 clean and quiet rooms. The service is impeccable.

▶ **Híd**
Szobránc u. 10, H-1143 Budapest
Tel. 363–16 33, fax 252–70 64
hid.hotel@ntk.hu
Simple hotel with 32 rooms near the Nép Stadium.

▶ **Omnibusz**
Üllooï út 108, H-1101 Budapest
Tel. 263–07 94, fax 263–11 63
Hotel with 23 rooms by the Népliget forest, 15 minutes' drive from the city centre.

PENSIONS

▶ ⑥ **Panzió Ábel**
Ábel Jenoö u. 9, H-1113 Budapest,
Tel. / fax 209–25 37
Pension Ábel is one of the prettiest and best-run little establishments in the Hungarian capital. Its ten clean rooms are housed in a beautiful villa.

▶ **Panzió Beatrix**
Széher út 3
H-1021 Budapest
Tel. / fax 394–37 30
www.1-800-travel.com/beatrix
This small pension with its 15 rooms is well known for its familiar atmosphere.

▶ **Panzió Gizella**
Arató u. 42/b, H-1121 Budapest
Tel. / fax 249–22 81
This cosy pension with 12 rooms lies in a good neighbourhood on the edge of the Buda hills.

▶ **Panzió Molnar**
Fodor u. 143, H-1124 Budapest
Tel. 395–18 75, fax 395–18 73
23 clean and comfortable rooms in the XII district; the pension is very quiet and the service is very helpful.

YOUTH HOSTELS

▶ **Information**
Hungarian Youth Hostel Association
Tel. / Fax 343–51 67
www.youthhostels.hu

▶ **Hostel Bánki**
Podmaniczky u. 8,
H-1065 Budapest, tel. 413–20 62
www.backpackers.hu
Hostel with 80 beds located in the middle of a shopping centre.

▶ **Diáksport**
Dózsa György út 152
H-1134 Budapest
Tel. 340–85 85, fax 320–84 25
www.youthhostels.hu
One of Budapest's most popular hostels; the 138 beds are in demand all year round so making a reservation is good time is recommended.

▶ **Landler Universum Hostels**
Bartók Béla út 17,
H-1114 Budapest
Tel. 463–36 21, fax 275–70 46
universumhostels@
mail.matav.hu
250-bed hostel on the Buda side.

Arrival • Before the Journey

Travel Options

By air

There are direct flights from destinations around the world, including the USA, to Budapest . The Hungarian national carrier Malev serves a large number of routes, sometimes via Amsterdam, Madrid or Prague. Direct connections within Europe are operated by low-cost airlines such as easyjet (e.g. from London Gatwick, flight time 2.5 hrs, www.easyjet.com), Ryanair (from Liverpool and Dublin, flight time 3 hrs, www.ryanair.com) and Wizzair (from London Luton, www.wizzair.com). Budapest's international Ferihegy airport lies around 24km/15mi from the city centre. It has three terminals: terminal 2A is reserved for the Hungarian airline **Malév** and its partners; **Terminal 2B** is designated for foreign airlines. **The low-cost airlines** use **Terminal 1**, which is around 5km/3mi west of Terminal 2 and not as modern as Ferihegy 1. To avoid time problems on the return flight, it is most advisable to check the exact departure terminal, as it is often not cited on the ticket!

Malev is the national airline of Hungary, based at Budapest

City transfers ►

Those who rely on a traditional **taxi** should ensure the meter is set back to the minimum fee at the outset, and also agree a price before beginning the journey. Several taxi firms have set fixed prices for airport transfers to and from the city. At present, depending on your destination in Buda or Pest, the price for a city transfer lies at around 4500 to 6000 Ft (forints). Unofficial taxi drivers, who pester passengers in the arrivals hall, are definitely the most expensive option for travelling the route into the city, which takes at least half an hour.
The **minibus service** takes flight passengers to their hotel for around 2300 Ft (one way). If there are several passengers, this is therefore cheaper. Tickets are purchased at the booth in the arrivals hall. The return transfer must be booked 24 hrs in advance (► Baedeker Tip p.61)

The cheapest option is to travel into the city by **city bus** and the **underground**. First take bus no. 93 from terminal 1 or 2 to the Kőbánya-Kispest underground station, where there is a fast metro link to the city centre.

Desks of the car hire firms (► car hire) can be found in the airport terminals.

By train

The most direct rail journey from London to Budapest goes via Paris and Munich. Other routes from western and central Europe are via Nuremberg, Passau, Linz and Vienna; or via Berlin, Dresden, Prague and Bratislava. Connections from the east (Moscow) and south (Rome) are also often routed through Bratislava. Most international trains arrive at Budapest's East Railway Station (Keleti pu.).

Coach tours

Many bus companies offer round trips from other European countries to Budapest. Information is available from travel agencies. Volánbusz AG in cooperation with Eurolines has an all-year-round service to Budapest to regular time-table from many European cities, though the number of direct connections is limited. Journey time from London to Budapest is around 24 hrs.

By car

The easiest way to reach Budapest from western Europe is via Austria. From Vienna, the Austrian motorway leads to the Nickelsdorf/Hegyeshalom border crossing, and from there it's the Hungarian M 1 motorway, for which you need a vignette. From the north, the best route is via the Czech motorway D 1 (Prague to Brno) and then the Slovak motorway D 2 (Brno to Bratislava), crossing the Hungarian border for Budapest at Rajka.

By boat

From the beginning of April to the beginning of November, there are daily hydrofoils between Vienna (landing stage: Reichsbrücke/Mexikoplatz) and Budapest (landing stage: Belgrád rakpart). Journey time from Vienna to Budapest is about five hours heading downstream and around six hours heading upstream. Information available at: Mahart Tours Budapest, V, Belgrád rakpart, tel. 318–17 04, fax 318–77 40, www.mahart.hu

River cruises

Between the middle of March and the end of October, as well as during Christmas and New Year, several very comfortable cruise ships travel from Germany and Vienna to the Hungarian capital. Information available from any travel agent.

Travel Regulations

Travel documents

Citizens of the European Union, USA, Canada, Australia and New Zealand need a valid passport or identity card for visits to Hungary. South African citizens need a visa. Children now require their own passport.

◄ Vehicle documents

Car drivers must carry their driving licence and vehicle registration documents, and insurance is recommended. Damaged cars can enter or leave Hungary only with the relevant documentation issued at the border or at the accident site in Hungary.

FLIGHT INFORMATION

AIRLINES

▶ **Malév**
V, Dorottya utca 2,
Tel. 235–35 65, fax 266–27 84

Ferihegy Airport
Terminal 2A: tel. 296–71 79
Terminal 2B: tel. 296–7544
www.malev.hu

! Baedeker TIP

Shared taxis into the city

Minibuses take visitors directly from the airport to their address in metropolitan Budapest much cheaper than traditional taxis but with almost the same comfort and speed. Buy tickets at the minibus ticket booth, which you can't miss, in the arrivals hall. A route for several travellers sharing is put together after no more than 30 minutes. The minibuses can be booked by telephone for the return journey to the airport. (Tel. 296–85 55; tel. / fax 296–89 93). They operate daily between 5am and 10pm, or until the last arrival or departure.

▶ **Air France**
Tel. 483 88 00
www.airfrance.com

▶ **British Airways**
Tel. 411 55 55
www.ba.com

▶ **Lufthansa**
Tel. 266–45 11
www.lufthansa.com

LOW-COST FLIGHTS

▶ **easyjet**
www.easyjet.com

▶ **Ryanair**
www.ryanair.com

▶ **Wizzair**
www.wizzair.com

FERIHEGY AIRPORT

▶ **Information**
Information: tel. 296–80 00
Departures: tel. 296–70 00

RAILWAY INFORMATION

▶ **National**
Tel. 461–54 00

▶ **International**
Tel. 461–55 00

▶ **Internet journey planning**
elvira.mavinformatika.hu

RAILWAY STATIONS

▶ **East Railway Station (Keleti pu.)**
VIII, Baross tér. Long distance trains to Austria, Switzerland, southern and western Germany, France, Belgium and the Netherlands, as well as to the Czech and Slovak Republics depart from here. National routes to Miskolc and Békéscsaba.

▶ **West Railway Station (Nyugati pu.)**
VI, Nyugati tér. Trains depart to the Slovak and Czech Republics, as well as to eastern and northern Germany from here. National routes to Debrecen und Szeged.

▶ **South Railway Station (Déli pályaudvar)**
I, Alkotás út. Trains for Slovenia,

Croatia, Serbia and Bosnia depart from here, as well as some for Austria. National routes to Lake Balaton, and trains to Pécs, Tapolca, Szombathely und Györ.

RAIL INFORMATION IN LONDON

Rail Europe Travel Centre
178 Piccadilly
London W1V 0BA
Tel. 0870 8 37 13 71
www.raileurope.co.uk

BY BUS

▸ **Népliget Bus station**
IX Üllöi út 131
Underground line 3
Népliget
Tel. 219 80 00

▸ **Volánbusz**
Reservations in Budapest
Volánbusz
V, Erszsébet tér
Tel. 117–25 62
www.volan.hu

▸ **Reservations international**
In UK through National Express
Tel. 087 05 80 80 80
www.eurolines.com and
www.nationalexpress.com

Animals

The importation of animals to Hungary is only permitted with an official veterinary certificate that may not be more than eight days old at the time of entry. A rabies vaccination certificate must be produced and, in addition, dogs require a vaccination for canine distemper. Dog owners must bring a lead and muzzle; the import of so-called dangerous fighting dogs is prohibited.

Customs regulations

◂ Arrival

Since 2004 Hungary has been a member of the European Union. Movement of goods for private purposes is largely duty free within the area of the European Union. Certain restrictions on quantities apply (e. g. for visitors over 17, 800 cigarettes, 10 litres of spirits, and 90 litres of wine). In the case of spot checks by the authorities, confirmation is required that the commodities are truly for private use only. The duty-free allowances for passengers arriving from outside the EU are: 200 cigarettes or 50 cigars or 250g of tobacco; one litre of wine and 0.25 litres of spirits; one kilo of coffee, tea, cocoa or spices (not paprika!) respectively; 250ml of eau de toilette and 100ml of perfume. Tobacco, wine and spirits may only be carried by individuals over the age of 16. Presents up to a value of 19,000 Ft per person per year can also be imported. Video cameras must be registered on arrival. Non-pasteurized meat and milk products are prohibited.

◂ Departure

All personal items may be taken out duty free, as well as presents and souvenirs to a maximum total value of 100,000 Ft.

◂ Export of valuable items

The export of artefacts, precious metals and precious metal products, as well as of stamps, is only possible with special permission. Precise information is available from the customs authorities.

Baths and Spas

Thermal baths

Europe's most important thermal and mineral springs are found in the metropolitan area of Budapest: 123 registered thermal springs supply over thirty baths, of which ten are medicinal baths with state recognition. The most productive thermal baths, with water temperatures of up to 76° Celsius (169 °F), occur along a geological fault that runs north from Gellért Hill and onwards beyond Margaret Island.

BUDAPEST'S MEDICINAL BATHS

Current opening times
The official opening times of individual departments can vary from the general bath opening times
Infos: www.spasbudapest.com

Császár Komjádi fürdö
II, Frankel Leó út 35
Treatments for chronic mobility and joint conditions; rehabilitation. Services: thermal indoor and outdoor pools, baths, inhalations, drinking cures. (Opening times: Mon–Sat, 6am–9pm, Sun, 6am–7pm).

Dagály fürdö
XIII, Népfürdö utca 36
Treatments for orthopaedic diseases, arthritis, joint diseases, sciatic problems and neuralgia. Services: thermal exercise bath, indoor and outdoor pool. (Opening times: daily, 6am–8.30pm).

Gellért fürdö (Gellért Bath)
XI, Kelenhegy út 4–6
Treatments for joint disease and back problems, inflammations, blocked arteries, cardiovascular disease and gynaecological problems. Services: thermal, steam and hot tub baths, as well as carbonated and iodine baths; physiotherapy and electric therapy, massage, exercise pools, and several saunas and solariums. (Opening times: May–Sept, daily, 6am–7pm; Oct–April, Mon–Fri, 6am–7pm, Sat–Sun, 6am–5pm).

Király fürdö
II, Fö utca 84
Offers convalescence and physical conditioning. Services: thermal, steam and hot tub baths; iodine baths, massage and sauna. (Opening times: men only Tue, Thu and Sat, 9am–7pm; women only Mon, Wed, and Fri, 7am–5pm).

Lukács fürdö
II, Frankel Leó út 25–29
Treatments for joint diseases, back problems, skeletal calcium deficiency, stomach and intestinal diseases, gall bladder problems and lung disease. Services: thermal, steam and hot tub baths, as well as mud baths, carbonated and iodine baths, as well as massage, gymnastics, physiotherapy and electric therapy, drinking cures and exercise pools. (Opening times: Mon–Sat, 6am–7pm, Sun, 6am–5pm).

Palatinus fürdö
XIII, Margitsziget
Treatments for rheumatic and gynaecological diseases. Services: thermal and outdoor pool. (Opening times: May–mid Sept, daily 6am–7pm).

Rác fürdö (Raitzenbad)
I, Hadnagy utca 8–10
Treatments for chronic joint problems, and muscle and nerve inflammation. Services: thermal and hot tub baths, massage, solarium, and physical conditioning. (Opening times: for women on Mon, Wed, and Fri, 6.30am–7pm; for men on Tue, Thu and Sat, 6.30am–7pm).

Rudas fürdö
I, Döbrentei tér 9
Treatments for joint problems, skeletal calcium deficiency, cardiovascular complications, stomach lining inflammations, gall bladder problems, and lung disease. Services: thermal, hot tub and steam baths, irrigation and massage; physiotherapy and electric therapy, exercise pool and drinking cures. (Opening times for the thermal spa: for men Mon and Wed–Fri 6am–8pm; for women Tue 6am–8pm, mixed sexes Fri 10pm–4am; Sat 6am–5pm and 10pm–4am; Sun 6am–5pm. Swimming pool, Mon–Fri, 6am–6pm; Sat–Sun, 6am–2pm).

Széchenyi fürdö
XIV, Állatkerti krt. 11
Treatments for orthopaedic illnesses and injuries, stomach and intestinal problems, gall bladder disease and lung disease. Services: thermal, hot tub and steam baths, mud treatments, carbonated and iodine baths, massage, gymnastics, physiotherapy and electric therapy, as well as solarium, sauna, drinking fountain and thermal exercise pool. (Opening times: May–Sept, daily, 6am–10pm; Oct–April, Mon–Fri, 6am–7pm, Sat–Sun, 6am–5pm).

Hotel Thermal
XIII, Margitsziget
Treatments for cardiovascular irregularities, impaired mobility, nervous diseases, gynaecological illnesses, therapy for age-related ailments; treatments for stomach and intestinal problems, gall bladder problems and asthma and allergy-related illnesses. Services: thermal and hot tub baths, massage, mud treatments, physiotherapy and electric therapy, gymnastics, colonic irrigation and sauna. (Opening times: daily 7am–8pm).

Thermal Hotel Hélia
XIII, Kárpát utca 62–64
Treatments for cardiovascular irregularities, impaired mobility, nervous diseases, gynaecological illnesses, therapy for age-related ailments, stomach and intestinal problems, gall bladder problems, asthma and allergy-related illnesses. Services: thermal and hot tub baths, massage, mud treatments, physiotherapy and electric therapy, gymnastics, colonic irrigation and sauna. (Opening times: daily 7am–10pm).

The Széchenyi Bath in Városliget is the Budapest locals' favourite. Even in the depths of winter, chess players meet in the hottest pools of the neo-Baroque bath for a game in the warm water.

IN BALNEIS SALUS... (Bathing is health...)

Spring water at a temperature of between 22 and 77 degrees Celsius (72–170°F), highly rich in minerals and trace elements, bubbles out of the earth in over 120 places in the metropolitan area of the Hungarian capital.

Its health-promoting properties were probably already known during the earliest period of settlement in the Pannonian basin. The Celts had already developed a bathing culture, and the Romans were also delighted by this natural treasure. They used the thermal springs at their settlement of Aquincum, whose name can be traced to the Celtic expression of »ak ink«, meaning »lots of water«.

Ottoman Relics

At the springs on the south-eastern slope of Gellért Hill, which were famed for their health-giving properties, a thermal bath was built as early as the 13th century and enjoyed great renown throughout the Magyar empire from then onwards. This was not the only installation that was extended in the 16th and 17th centuries by the Turkish occupiers, who were otherwise not very popular. In the area of Buda alone, they maintained at least five so-called hamams with copper domes crowned by the Mohammedan sickle, which survive as thermal baths to this day: Rác fürdö, Rudas fürdö, Király fürdö (king's bath), Császár fürdö (emperor's bath), and Gellért fürdö. During Turkish rule these previously rather simple baths were turned into magnificent sites of a luxuriant bathing culture.

Bathing Temples of the Austro-Hungarian Monarchy

Of course Budapest also experienced a magnificent renaissance during the time of the Austro-Hungarian monarchy. During this era, veritable temples to bathing were created, such as the neo-Baroque Széchenyi Bath in Városliget and the Lukács Bath, which originated in the Turkish era but was redeveloped in the classical style in the 19th century, when it became a meeting place for artists and intellectuals. A bathing boom occurred in 1807, when powerfully streaming thermal springs were discovered in the middle of the Danube close to Margaret Island. The culmination of this era can be seen in the magnificent building of the Gellért Bath, designed in the Secessionist style in 1918. The Hungarian writer Ferenc Katinthy wrote about a visit to the Gellért steam baths thus: Everyone receives a

The Gellért Bath is a treat for lovers of art nouveau.

small white apron; the old and the young, the fat and skinny wander about in this African uniform. Bathing takes place according to centuries-old ceremonies. First stop is the »dry air«: three chambers, ever hotter, with the innermost between 65 and 70 degrees Celsius hot. The visitor sits down dry in this desert heat, but the skin is soon bathed in sweat … a quick shower follows, then warm water to recover. Afterwards, those who dare dive quickly into the thimble-sized cold pool and once all slough has been washed away in this manner, one is permitted to enter the inner sanctum, the »damp steam«. It is a confined chamber. One sees nothing but white seething clouds of steam that sting the eye, provoke the throat into coughing, and prick the skin with heated needles. Steps rise into the steamy, mysterious heights, but the geometry of this place is the opposite of Dante's inferno: here, the higher up the condemned souls do penance, the more the heat exhausts them.

Development of the Baths

People also came to Budapest for bathing between the two world wars, and the city has been the seat of the international association of thermal baths since 1937. Bathing culture in Budapest was further developed after the Second World War, with the main focus on the installations on Margaret Island and at the neighbouring south-western bank of the Danube. In recent times, several new and luxurious spa hotels have been built according to the latest balneological knowledge on Margaret Island and near the Roman ruins of Aquincum. Budapest's medicinal baths primarily focus on the treatment of diseases impairing mobility, but they also successfully cure nervous ailments, skin diseases and metabolic irregularities.

Children in Budapest

Visiting Budapest with toddlers in strollers can be exhausting: steps onto buses and trams are often very high and there are not yet many elevators at metro stations. Escalators are long and the main trams and buses are constantly overcrowded. If children are a bit more mobile, however, it is not difficult to arrange a visit to the city in such a way that both offspring and parents have a good time. Kids under the age of six go free on public transport; after that they pay full price. There are, however, reduced weekend tickets for families, or you can choose to buy a »Budapest Card« from the outset (►Prices and Discounts). Almost all museums and sights offer significant child discounts, and hotels very often even offer free additional children's beds in parents' rooms. A friendly request for a child's portion is normally acceptable should restaurants not offer a specific children's menu.

Discounts ►

Excursions with kids

The ►Vàrosliget woods is one of the most favoured destinations for families with children, as there are a host of »child-friendly« attractions very close together: you can go boating on the small lake in the summer, the zoo is a great destination for a family afternoon, and right next door is the large metropolitan circus with guest performances by famous circuses from all over the world. The theme park nearby is an alternative, full of attractions like a giant wheel, roller coaster and shooting galleries. In bad weather, you can make for the Transport Museum, and in winter the ice-skating rink is fun. A ride on the cable car to the ► Royal Palace is a must, and a trip to the ►Buda hills to take a ride on the children's railway should not be missed on any account. Rides on the funicular railway and on chairlifts will also be a popular alternative if the younger generation is not keen on going for walks. On ► Margaret Island children can really run around: there is almost no traffic, but playgrounds and broad meadows. At the Palatinus Bath, with slides and a wave pool, it is easy to spend an entire summer day. A ride on the bicycle carriages (for 2–6 people) can also be fun. They can be rented at the northern end of the island, at the »Bringó-vár«, opposite the hotels along the Danube quay. Outside the open-air swimming pool season, a visit to the ►Gellért Bath is highly recommended. The large pool has artificial waves and small children are happy in the warm water of the

! *Baedeker* TIP

Central Europe's largest oceanic aquarium

What could be more beautiful and exciting on a rainy day than, for example, eye-balling a shark? The Tropicarium in the south of the city, opened in the year 2000, offers a global tour of discovery through the underwater world of our planet, through rainforests and the tropics. (Opening times: daily 10am–8pm, Nagytétényi út 37–45, tel. 424–30 53, www.tropicarium.hu).

City holidays don't have to be boring: excursion to the Sculpture Park

paddling pool. And when your legs won't carry you any further after a long day in the city, a relaxing boat cruise on the Danube (►Transport, ►City tours, Sightseeing) or a tour of the ►Castle District in a horse-drawn carriage are good options. This is also the site of the underground labyrinth, which is fascinating and just a little scary to explore by oil lamp. In bad weather, a puppet theatre performance can while away the time, though language problems might be unavoidable. The Palace of Wonders (►Tip Great Ring p. 108) can enthuse the whole family or you can sink into seats at the Planetarium.

ATTRACTIONS FOR CHILDREN

THEATRE

► **Puppet Theatre Budapest, Bábszínház**
Andrássy út 69, tel. 321–52 00

► **Youth Theatre Kolibri Színház**
Jókai tér 10, tel. 311–08 70

PLANETARIUM

Népliget, tel. 263–18 11

PALACE OF WONDERS

Feny utca 20-22
www.csodapalota.hu

Electricity

The Hungarian electricity grid has 220-volt AC.

Emergency

► **Emergency call**
Tel. 112

► **Police**
Tel. 107

► **Tourist police**
Tel. 438-80 80
(German, English)

► **Ambulance**
Tel. 104

► **Fire brigade**
Tel. 105

► **Emergency dentist**
SOS Dental Service
VI, Király utca 14
Tel. 267–96 02

Entertainment

nightlife

As far as is concerned, Budapest deserves its reputation as the »Paris of the East«. In the evenings, gipsy and folk groups, always popular with visitors, perform in many restaurants – especially in those in the touristy Castle District – and countless nightclubs offer revue and variety shows, as well as cabaret programmes. Trendy and modern bars, smoky jazz cellars, nightclubs of every kind, as well as numerous dance clubs are open into the small hours of the morning. Information on the many bars and clubs with a predominantly gay clientele can be found on the internet at: www.gayguide.net/europe/Hungary/budapest

ADDRESSES FOR GOING OUT

REVUE

► **Moulin Rouge**
VI, Nagymezö utca 17, revue cabaret, restaurant and café; the »Moulin Rouge« programme that begins at midnight does its name proud.

NIGHTCLUBS AND COOL PLACES

► **A 38**
IX, Danube bank, 150m south of the Petöfi Bridge on the Buda. side An unusual location: underground music, bar, artists' lounge, art and

exhibitions on a decommissioned Ukrainian stone freighter. For the latest programme see: www.a38.hu (Hungarian).

▶ **Angyal Bár**
VII, Szövetség u. 33
Gay bar with restaurant, dance floor in the cellar and occasional transvestite shows; more mixed clientele on Fri and Sun.

▶ **Railway Budapest Music Club**
VI, West Railway Station, by the car park
Funk, rock, alternative club with two dance floors; occasional live gigs.

▶ **Bamboo Music Club**
VI, Dessewffy u. 44
Disco, Latin nights, 1980s music and often Techno and House.

▶ **Capella**
V, Belgrád rkp. 23
Tue and Thu predominantly gay; dance club every night except Mon.

▶ **Chaos**
VII, Dohány u. 38
Gay music pub with a large cellar bar.

▶ **Club 7**
VII, Akácfa u. 7
Café, restaurant, cocktail bar and nightclub in one; live music every night.

▶ **Eklektika**
V, Semmelweis u. 21
Male and female gay-friendly café; women-only parties every second Saturday of the month.

▶ **E-Klub**
X, Népligeti út 2
www.e-klub.hu
Huge nightclub with male and female go-go dancers, as well as entertainment programmes typical of these giant places.

▶ **Fat Mo's**
V, Nyáry Pál u. 11
Well-frequented music club with live concerts or DJ music, with an impressively long bar; occasional jazz.

A buzzing place in the evenings: bars on Jokai utca

▶ **Janis Pub**
V, Király Pál u. 8
Cool live music daily from 9pm.

▶ **Old Man's**
VII, Akácfa u. 13
Legendary music bar with live music every night, followed by DJ sounds: blues, jazz, swing and soul.

▶ **Supersonic Technikum**
III, Pacsirtamezö u. 41
Techno nightclub, only open on Sat.

▶ **Süss fel nap**
V, Honved u./Szt. István krt.
One of the most popular music clubs in Budapest; live concerts on Mon and Tue.

ROCK AND ROLL

▶ **Buddy Holly Club**
IX, Könyves Kálmán krt. 12–14
Rock-and-roll party every Fri from 9pm.

▶ **Café Rolling Rock**
XI, Bartók Béla út 76
DJ music every night, with occasional rock and roll parties and Latin Combo performances

JAZZ

▶ **Hades Jazztaurant**
VI, Vörösmarty u. 31
Piano jazz on Wed and Thu.

▶ **Jazz Garden**
V, Veress Pálne u. 44
Famous Hungarian and international artists play jazz here every night, which makes a visit very worthwhile.

CASINOS

▶ **Las Vegas**
V, Roosevelt tér 2
In the large casino with the highly original name of »Las Vegas«, within Hotel Sofitel Atrium, American roulette is played, as well as blackjack, baccarat and various variations of poker.

▶ **Tropicana**
V, Vigadó u. 2
American roulette, variations of blackjack, baccarat and poker.

CINEMAS

▶ **Corvin Filmpalota**
Corvin köz 1, tel. 317–93 38

▶ **Hollywood Multiplex Duna Plaza**
Váci út 178, tel. 467–42 67

▶ **Palace West End**
Váci út, 1–3, tel. 238–72 22

NIGHTLIFE ON THE INTERNET

www.budapestparty.com
www.est.hu

Etiquette and Customs

Hungary from the outside Hussars galloping across the puszta plains to the sound of passionate gypsy music; later »goulash communism« or »the happiest hut in the camp«: these are the clichés that come to mind when speaking of

Hungary. Beyond that, the impossible, unintelligible language with its unbelievably long words might come to mind – or the famously beautiful Hungarian women. It is true that Hungary's communist state was a lot more relaxed and colourful than its fellows behind the grim Iron Curtain. However, privately, Hungarians reject the other clichés, without wanting to constantly deny them either. After all, it is these – predominantly positive – clichés that year on year draw many millions of visitors to their state on the Danube. For a country without significant reserves in primary products, tourism is an essential economic factor. It is therefore not beyond the realms of possibility that when a western tourist sees a genuine-looking rider with a whip in his hand on the legendary plains of the Hungarian Puszta Hortobágy, he is actually watching a philosophy student from the University of Debrecen earning money in the summer holidays to finance a trip to Majorca.

Hungarian self-image

Loneliness and tragic pathos – always spiced with a positively insistent hope that good will triumph –are the sentiments that make the Hungarian soul come alive. This small nation feels alone, surrounded by great and important nationalities, and its thousand-year history seems a tragic chain of disasters. Of course, no one, much less a nation, can endure only sadness, and therefore the positive milestones are noted with great pride: 1456, when Marshal János Hunyadi expelled the Turks from Belgrade; 1848–49 when the country flew the flag of the European revolution to the last; or October 1956, when the uprising temporarily toppled the communist dictatorship. Despite the ultimately tragic outcome of all these events, despair and hope lie very close together in Hungary. Apart from this, Hungarians in the 21st century appreciate the same values as in the rest of Europe: independence, a united family, education, security, property and holidays abroad.

Drinking

It is said that »the Magyar amuses himself crying«. Crying, but never without wine. Hungarian drinking was and is a defiant expression of a love of life. In hardly any other literature is there so much and such passionate boozing, and so it is at parties and festivals in real life as well. Hungarians are friendly hosts and like to spoil their guests with their national dishes. Small presents for the host, such as flowers, chocolates or wine are always welcome.

Greetings

As a rule, people introduce themselves by their surname, occasionally followed by their first name (Kovács Sándor). Adults normally greet each other with a firm handshake, good friends embrace each other and offer a kiss on the cheek, to the left and right. It counts as especially polite to address people by their title (Doctor, Professor ...), followed by their surname. Colloquial greetings include, among others, Szervusz oder Szia. And when you say good-bye, you say Viszontlátásrá or simply Viszlát.

Festivals • Holidays • Events

Events programme

The city information booths (►Information) often have quite extensive monthly events programmes available, such as »Budapest Panorama« (► Media). Dates for events can also be found in the daily press and in publicity from the Hungarian Tourist Office. An up-to-date events calendar can also be found on the internet at www.budapestinfo.hu

HOLIDAYS AND EVENTS

HOLIDAYS

1 January: New Year
15 March: National holiday in remembrance of the Liberation War of 1848
Easter Monday
1 May: Labour Day
Whitsun Monday
20 August: St Stephen's Day, state holiday with big fireworks display on the banks of the Danube
23 October: Day of the Republic (day of the 1956 uprising and establishment of the republic in 1989)
1 November: All Hallows
25/26 December: Christmas

EVENTS IN JANUARY

► **Opera Gala**
Gala performance for the New Year in the Vigadó concert hall in Pest (1 Jan)

IN FEBRUARY

► **Carnival**
Budapest »Carnival« is comprised of dance events, concerts and various other performances (end of Feb/early March).

IN MARCH / APRIL

► **Opera Ball**
Traditional Hungarian ball: the similarity with the Viennese Opera Ball is obvious (beginning of March).

► **Budapest Spring Festival**
Extensive series of cultural events over a period of several weeks, with opera and operetta performances, concerts and folklore (mid-March to early/mid-April; www.festivalcity.hu)

IN MAY

► **Operetta concerts in the Vigadó**
Beginning of the operetta season in Vigadó in Pest (May to Oct)

IN JUNE / JULY

► **International Danube Carnival**
Folklore ensembles present Hungarian musical and dance tradition, for example on Vörösmarty tér and Margaret Island

► **Budapest Church Day**
An event lasting several days with open-air concerts and street processions (end of June to beginning of July)

IN AUGUST

► **Pepsi Island Festival**
Rock and cultural festival on the Danube island Hajógyári-sziget; especially popular with the young

(beginning of Aug; www.diaksziget.com)

▶ **BudaFest of the Hungarian State Opera**
Opera and ballet festival in the opera house on Andrássy út (early to mid-Aug)

▶ **Hungarian Grand Prix**
Formula One Grand Prix on the Hungaroring (mid-Aug; information and tickets: www.datanet.hu/formula1)

▶ **International Festival of Crafts**
Folk art market in and around the Royal Palace, with music and comedians; craftsmen from all over the world demonstrate traditional production methods (mid-Aug).

▶ **National Day**
Concerts, markets and a fireworks finale celebrate the foundation of the state (20 Aug).

▶ **St Stephen's Day**
St Stephen's Procession is held on the same day, when the saint's right hand – the famous relic in St Stephen's Basilica – is carried through the streets of Budapest (20 Aug)

▶ **Jewish Summer Festival**
Concerts, film and book days, and exhibitions on Herzl Square, in the synagogue on Dohány utca, and at various other places (end of Aug/beginning of Sept)

IN SEPTEMBER

▶ **International Wine Festival**
Hungarian wine regions present themselves in the Castle District (early/mid-Sept).

At the heart of the procession on St Stephens Day: the reliquary shrine containing the saint's right hand

IN OCTOBER AND NOVEMBER

▶ **Budapest Autumn Festival**
Dance, film, and theatre performances, photo exhibitions and much more at various venues: a festival of experimental contemporary art (mid-Oct to beginning of Nov; www.festivalcity.hu)

▶ **Supermarathon Vienna–Budapest**
Substantially longer than the usual 42,195 km/26 miles; untrained runners should content themselves with watching the event (mid-Oct).

IN DECEMBER

▶ **Christmas Markets**
Christmas markets are held at several places around the city in December.

▶ **Gipsy Orchestra Concerts**
The famous gipsy orchestra of the Hungarian State Folk Ensemble, comprising 100 musicians, plays dramatically at the Congress Centre each year (30 Dec).

▶ **New Year's Eve Gala and Ball**
Performance by the State Opera's ballet and orchestra ensembles and ball lasting into the New Year (31 Dec)

Food and Drink

Hungarian cooking is hearty, heavy and down-to-earth. Nourishing meat and pastry dishes predominate. Traditional recipes characterized by a generous use of fat and spices – especially paprika – are popular. Freshwater fish are also often eaten, especially carp, catfish and pike perch.

Typical Dishes

Gulyás and pörkölt

Gulyás is not the same as goulash! Bitter disappointment results when the culinary novice visits Hungary for the first time, hoping to eat meat chunks sautéed in lard, with onions, paprika, tomatoes, garlic, caraway and marjoram served in a hearty sauce, usually with dumplings on the side, only to be served with a well-spiced stew of beef and potato cubes, with paprika, onions, tomatoes, garlic and caraway. The former dish is called **pörkölt** and most closely resembles what we consider to be goulash, the latter is called **gulyás** in Hungary.

Tokány, a dish very similar to pörkölt, is steamed beef in a thick spiced sauce, finished off with a shot of wine. Both dishes are normally prepared with sour cream, which gives the sauce a creamy character. Nourishing, calorie-heavy meals spiced with paprika and flavoured with sour cream, such as pörkölt und tokány, can collectively be called **paprikás**.

Halászlé are soups carefully spiced with hot paprika, often containing more than one type of fish, such as carp or catfish, with the addition of a variety of vegetables, onions, croutons and a little sour cream. The Hungarian version of French bouillabaisse tastes very spicy here! **Paprika chicken** with pasta is a simple, but classic Hungarian dish (paprikás csirke galuskával). An equally delicious attack on the figure is baked **goose liver** (libamáj rántva); and then there is the **Hungarian salami** (szalámi), spicy and regular travel companion on the return journey from Hungarian holidays, though they say that szalámi only tastes really good in Hungary. Try it!

! *Baedeker* TIP

Pancakes à la Gundel

Undoubtedly one of the most famous recipes from Budapest. The only question is: to flambé or not to flambé? The magical show of flames is supposedly only put on for tourists. The dough mixture requires 120g flour, 4–5 eggs, 250ml milk, and a pinch of salt, which should be left for 30 min and then formed into eight pancakes. The filling is made from 100ml of milk heated up with 3 tablespoons of sugar and 100g of ground walnuts, together with two teaspoons of orange peel, 40g of raisins and two tablespoons of rum. The sauce for these filled pancakes is made from 250ml whipping cream into which 150g of dark chocolate and 100g of milk chocolate has been melted. To flambé, sprinkle three to four tablespoons of rum over the hot pancakes and light before serving.

Hungarian cuisine is hearty, spicy and not exactly low on calories.

Sweet dishes

The sweetest temptations of Hungarian cuisine are undoubtedly the various strudels, and pancakes filled with quark and dusted in icing sugar; or Gundel pancake with nut filling and chocolate sauce, as well as Schomlau dumplings. Budapest's coffee houses and pastry shops complement the repertoire of sweet dishes with their own artful cake creations.

- ... that paprika, today almost synonymous with Hungarian cuisine, was used only as medicine for a high temperature until the middle of the 19th century?

Drinks

Wine (bor)

Wine-growing enjoys a long tradition in Hungary, going right back to Roman times, and the selection of good wines has increased rapidly in recent years. Dry wines are also increasingly being cultivated these days, and a many local wines can be tasted in many Budapest wine cellars.

◄ Tokaj wine

The region around Tokaj produces the Tokaj dessert wine from Furmint and Hárslevelü grapes. The grapes are prone to the »noble rot« botrytis, which has a positive effect on sugar content and taste. Tokaj comes in three quality levels: furmint (light and dry), szamorodni (mild and sweet), and aszu (from selected grapes with three, four or five stars; only limited stocks).

Spirits

Hungarian fruit liqueurs are famous and popular, especially barack, an apricot schnapps, szilva (plum schnapps) and cherry schnapps.

Beer (sör)

In Budapest, foreign beers – especially Austrian and German ones – are increasingly available alongside local beers.

Coffee houses and cake shops

For Budapest tourists a visit to a coffee house is almost compulsory! And the Hungarian capital offers countless stylish old cake shops and cafés. **Some of the best and most famous are described in more detail in ▸Baedeker Special, p. 248**. Here follows an **additional** selection of pleasant coffee houses:

COFFEE HOUSES

▸ **Angelika**
I, Batthyány tér 1
Literary café: in addition to poetry readings, there are also various musical events.

Sweet temptations

▸ **Astoria**
V, Kossuth Lajos u. 19
Pleasant and elegant café in the Hotel Astoria

▸ **Auguszt**
V, Kossuth Lajos u. 14–16
Small romantic café with antique interior that serves up delicious cream cakes and choice pastries. Mmmh, delicious!

▸ **Fröhlich**
VII, Dob u. 22
Koscher pastry shop in the former Jewish quarter of the Hungarian capital. Worth a visit!

▸ **Miró**
I, Úri utca 30
It is as if the Spanish artist had created the interior himself; a modern contrast to the many traditional cafés.

▸ **Mozart**
VII, Erzsébet körút 36

The interior and the staff's uniform recall Mozart's era. No prizes for guessing what kind of music plays in the background here?

► **Pierrot**
I, Fortuna u. 14
Evening piano music at the Pierrot makes for a nostalgic meeting place.

► **Zsolnay**
VI, Teréz krt. 43
Atmospheric café in the Radisson SAS Béke Hotel, with discreet piano music in the afternoons.

► **Gerbeaud, Ruszwurm, Lukácz, Müvesz, New York, Central**
►see p.248, Baedeker Special »Cukrászdas in Budapest«

Restaurants

Multi-faceted gastronomy

The gastronomic palette in Budapest is pretty varied. The selection ranges from simple self-service restaurants to cosy wine bars, and all the way to fine restaurants, but the basic preference is for hearty fare.

Csárdás

Csárdás, hostelries that often have their origin in old country road taverns in which the csárdás was danced, are typically Hungarian. Rustic interiors and gipsy music revive memories of »the good old days«, even today. Generally speaking, csárdás serve typically Hungarian dishes.

Goulash, pörkölt, paprika

Budapest likes it calorie-rich: dumplings, beef and pork, goose lard, heavy sauces, and sweet pancakes for dessert – that's what you get in the traditional restaurants. But international cuisine has also long established itself in the Hungarian capital and makes its contribution to the culinary variety on offer.

RECOMMENDED RESTAURANTS

► **① etc. ►See mapp.88/89**
No number: beyond the map

► **Price categories**
Expensive (Cat. I): over 5000 Ft,
Moderate (Cat. II): 3000–5000 Ft,
Inexpensive (Cat. III): up to 3000 Ft

TOP RESTAURANTS

► **Gundel (Cat. I)**
XIV, Állatkerti út 2
Tel. 468–40 40, fax 363–19 17
In terms of renown at least, the top address in the Hungarian capital is Gundel (table reservations essential) near the Budapest Zoo. Founded by Ferenc Wampetics in 1894, it was taken over by the great master of modern Hungarian cuisine, Károly Gundel, in 1910. Today, the master chef and his team conjure up almost all delicacies of Hungarian and inter-

national cuisine here, including of course the legendary Gundel pancakes with raisin and nut filling.

▸ **Kisbuda Gyöngye (Cat. I)**
III, Kenyeres u. 34
Tel. 368–64 02, fax 368–92 27
Since the political changes of 1989, this restaurant has developed into a fashionable meeting place, especially for the younger generation. In addition to international dishes, excellent Hungarian specialties are served here.

▸ **Mágnáskert (Cat. I)**
II, Csatárka út 58
Tel. 325–99 67, fax 325–99 72
This luxury restaurant favours a traditional classic cooking style.

▸ **Vadrózsa (Cat. I)**
II, Pentelei Molnár u. 15
Tel. 326–58 17, fax 326–58 09
A fine restaurant with a pretty seating area in the garden with a lovely location on Rose Hill, where many classy villas stand proud once again. Food and service are unmatched.

HUNGARIAN CUISINE

▸ ⑨ **Costes Restobar (Cat. II)**
1092 Ráday utca 4
Tel. 219 06 96
costes@axelero.hu
Modern Hungarian restaurant with a very appealing art nouveau ambience; friendly service and unpretentious atmosphere.

▸ **Kéhli Vendéglö (Cat. II)**
III, Mókus u. 22
Tel. 250–42 41, fax 387–60 49
Lovers of exquisitely prepared game and fish dishes get their money's worth at Kéhli Vendéglö. The inn has a long tradition – you can even still catch a whiff of the Austro-Hungarian monarchy.

▸ ② **Király (Cat. I)**
I, Táncics Mihály u. 25
Tel. 212–98 91, fax 212–85 66
Something hearty from the land of the Magyars can be enjoyed in this restaurant in the Castle District, even if the interior seems over the top. Good news for wine lovers: really excellent Tokaj can be enjoyed here.

▸ ⑩ **Mátyás pince (Cat. II)**
V, Március 15. tér 7
Tel. 318–16 93, fax 318–16 50
The interior of this long-famous restaurant, established since 1904 on the Pest side of the Elizabeth Bridge, has a preservation order. Paprikás in all variations are served here, accompanied by gipsy music.

HUNGARIAN AND INTERNATIONAL CUISINE

▸ ③ **Aranyhíd Étterem Pub (Cat. III)**
I, Hegyalja út 64
Tel. / fax 209–66 66
Meals are substantially cheaper

here than in the city centre; the Hungarian drivers' habit of ignoring red lights can be observed from the terrace next to the busy road.

▶ **Aranymókus (Cat. III)**
XII, Istenhegyi út 25
Tel. 355–67 28, fax 355–95 94
On the Buda side of the Danube, on Orbán tér, this establishment welcomes visitors who enjoy original game dishes. Apart from the best of stag, wild boar and deer, you can also savour pheasant and quail.

▶ **Bagolyvár (Cat. III)**
XIV, Állatkerti út 2
Tel. 343–02 17, fax 342–29 17
This offshoot of the neighbouring world-famous Gundel is called Bagolyvár; this lively tavern serves goulash soup and pikeperch of Gundel quality, but for half the price.

▶ ⑥ **Belcanto (Cat. II)**
VI, Dalszínház u. 8, tel. 269–27 86, fax 311–95 47
A special tip for opera buffs: in the VI district, right next to the opera. Top European and Hungarian cuisine in close proximity to the occasional diva or opera star – what more could you want?

▶ ④ **Biarritz (Cat. III)**
V, Kossuth Lajos tér 18, tel. 302–39 43, fax 311–44 13
A kitchen team that delights in experimentation wields the culinary wand here, right next to Parliament, and to such effect that many parliamentary members well-known for their gourmet tastes meet here before and after sessions.

▶ **Chicago Rib Shack (Cat. III)**
V, Szent István krt. 13, tel. 302–31 12, fax 302–31 01
Visitors are transported to the

»Gundel« is Budapest's most famous address for moneyed gourmets.

Budapest Hotels and Restaurants

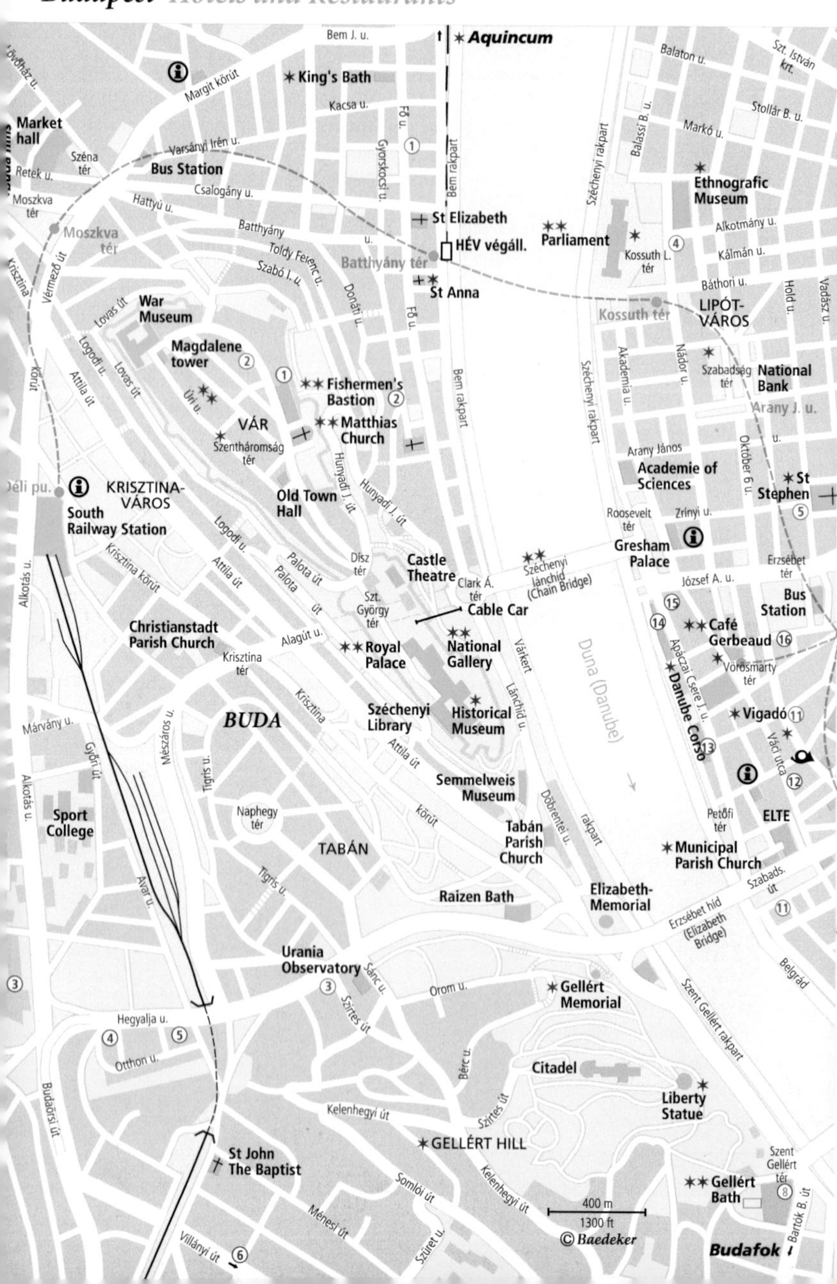

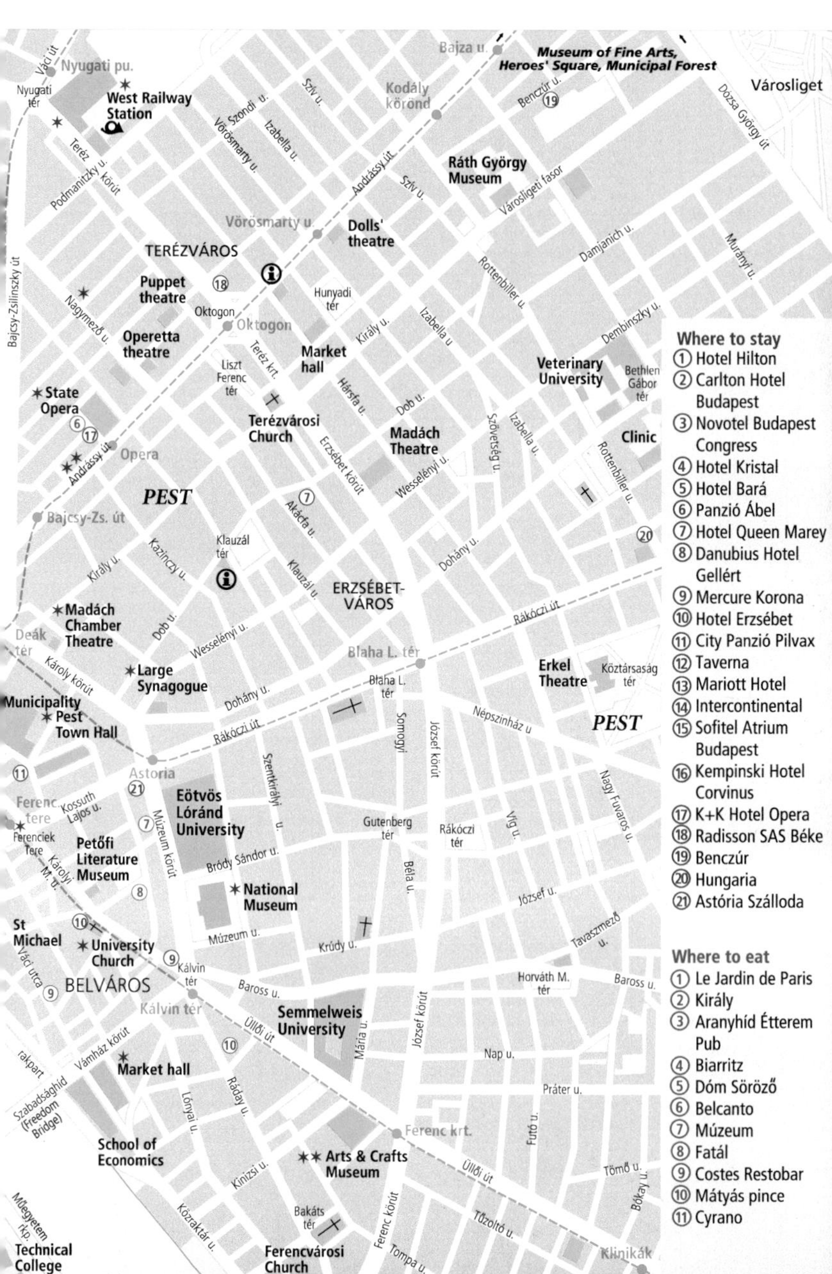
Museum of Fine Arts, Heroes' Square, Municipal Forest
Városliget
Nyugati pu.
Nyugati tér
West Railway Station
Kodály körönd
Bajza u.
Benczúr u.
Dózsa György út
Ráth György Museum
Városligeti fasor
Vörösmarty u.
Dolls' theatre
TERÉZVÁROS
Puppet theatre
Oktogon
Hunyadi tér
Operetta theatre
Market hall
Liszt Ferenc tér
State Opera
Opera
Terézvárosi Church
Madách Theatre
Veterinary University
Bethlen Gábor tér
Clinic
PEST
Bajcsy-Zs. út
Klauzál tér
ERZSÉBET-VÁROS
Madách Chamber Theatre
Deák tér
Large Synagogue
Blaha L. tér
Erkel Theatre
Köztársaság tér
Municipality Pest Town Hall
Astoria
Eötvös Lóránd University
Ferenc tere
Ferenciek Tere
Petőfi Literature Museum
National Museum
Gutenberg tér
Rákóczi tér
St Michael
University Church
BELVÁROS
Kálvin tér
Horváth M. tér
Semmelweis University
Market hall
Szabadsághíd (Freedom Bridge)
School of Economics
Arts & Crafts Museum
Ferenc krt.
Bakáts tér
Technical College
Ferencvárosi Church
Klinikák
Where to stay
① Hotel Hilton
② Carlton Hotel Budapest
③ Novotel Budapest Congress
④ Hotel Kristal
⑤ Hotel Bará
⑥ Panzió Ábel
⑦ Hotel Queen Marey
⑧ Danubius Hotel Gellért
⑨ Mercure Korona
⑩ Hotel Erzsébet
⑪ City Panzió Pilvax
⑫ Taverna
⑬ Mariott Hotel
⑭ Intercontinental
⑮ Sofitel Atrium Budapest
⑯ Kempinski Hotel Corvinus
⑰ K+K Hotel Opera
⑱ Radisson SAS Béke
⑲ Benczúr
⑳ Hungaria
㉑ Astória Szálloda
Where to eat
① Le Jardin de Paris
② Király
③ Aranyhíd Étterem Pub
④ Biarritz
⑤ Dóm Söröző
⑥ Belcanto
⑦ Múzeum
⑧ Fatál
⑨ Costes Restobar
⑩ Mátyás pince
⑪ Cyrano

If it has to be fast food, then at least in this ambience next to the West Train Station.

American Mid-West in this restaurant, where beer from the New World, spare ribs, hamburgers and, of course, Caesar salad can be had at relatively affordable prices.

▶ ⑪ **Cyrano (Cat. III)**
V, Kristóf tér 7–8
Tel. 266–30 96, fax 266–68 18
A young clientele, young management, youthful décor and kitchen team are the characteristics of Cyrano, a fashionable venue near Váci utca. Fresh and vitamin-rich salads are served here, as well as uncommon dishes from international cuisine.

▶ ⑤ **Dóm Sörözö (Cat. III)**
V, Szent István tér 2
Tel. 317–25 06
A beer tavern decorated in classical style near St Stephen's Basilica. Grilled dishes and a large selection of salads are among its specialties.

▶ ⑧ **Fatál (Cat. III)**
V, Váci u. 67
Tel. 266–26 07
Restaurant under the cellar arches; large, positively giant portions are served by the staff here, who make little effort to be friendly.

▶ **Hong Kong Pearl Garden (Cat. III)**
II, Margit krt. 2
Tel. 212–31 31, fax 212–55 24
A variety of Chinese specialties can be tried at this restaurant on the Buda side of the Margit híd bridgehead.

▶ ① **Le Jardin de Paris (Cat. III)**
I, Fö utca 20
Tel. / fax 201–00 47

If you don't want to do without French cuisine in the »Paris of the East«, then your best bet is Jardin de Paris in Watertown. Fresh ingredients and variety are the hallmark of this creative kitchen. In the summer, the neighbouring garden café is an oasis of peace and quiet.

► ⑦ **Múzeum (Cat. II)**
VIII, Múzeum krt. 12
Tel. 338–42 21
This tavern with a classical interior offers excellently prepared Hungarian and international dishes at moderate prices.

► **Karma Café & Restaurant (Cat. II)**
VI, Liszt ferenc tér 11
Tel. 413–67 64
A tasteful oriental interior and an international menu on which Thai dishes and Indian Tandoori predominate. The duck breast in apple and mustard sauce is delicious!

► **Tiroli (Cat. III)**
II, Lajos utca 33
Tel. / fax 335–23 79
Restaurant in Óbuda with Austrian cuisine: beef olives and Tyrolean apple strudel are accompanied by traditional music in the evenings.

Baedeker recommendation

► **Robinson Rest. & Café (Cat. II)**
XIV, Városligeti-tó
Tel. 343–09 55, fax 343–37 76
Robinson Cafè is built in original style and has a beautiful location on the lake in Városliget. You can eat very well here and, in addition to the international dishes, we recommend the authentic »Hungarian recipes«. In summer months, there is idyllic seating on the terrace.

Health

First aid is always provided free of charge. European tourists in Hungary are entitled to the same care as in other European Union countries. The cost of repatriation is generally not carried by medical insurance, and it is therefore usually best to arrange private travel insurance.

EMERGENCY SERVICE NUMBERS

► **Ambulance**
Tel. 104

► **Duty doctor**
Falck SOS Hungary
II, Kapy utca 49/B, tel. 200–01 00

► **Emergency dentist**
SOS Dental Service
VI, Király utca 14
Tel. 267–96 02

Pharmacies Each municipal district has at least one pharmacy (Patika, Gyógyszertár) each day with a 24-hour service, usually on a rota basis. Every pharmacy has a notice displaying the address of the nearest pharmacy offering a night service; several are always open around the clock.

Information

USEFUL ADDRESSES

IN UK

► **Hungarian National Tourist Office**
46 Eaton Place
London SW1X 8AL
Tel. 00800 36 000 000
(free of charge)
www.gotohungary.co.uk

IN USA

► **Hungarian National Tourist Office**
350 Fifth Avenue, Suite 7107
New York, NY 10118
Tel. (212) 6 95 12 21 www.gotohungary.com

IN BUDAPEST

► **Hungarian Tourism Office**
Magyar Turizmus Rt.
PO Box 215, 1364 Budapest, fax 266–74 77
info@budapestinfo.hu
www.hungarytourism.hu
www.budapestinfo.hu
(only for written queries)

► **Tourinform main office**
V, Sütö utca 2 (Pest), tel. 438–80 80, fax 317–96 56
www.tourinform.hu

► **Tourinform branch office**
Liszt Ferenc Square 11,
(Pest, near Oktogon)
Tel. 322-40 98
fax 342-9390

► **Tourinform branch office, Castle Hill**
Szentháromság Square (Buda)
Tel. 488-04 75, fax 488-04 74

► **Tourinform Call Centre**
Tel. 438–80 80 (24 h)
Fax 356–19 64
hungary@tourinform.hu

► **Touchscreen information**
Electronic information pillars can be found spread all over the city. They provide information, for example, on sights, museums, opening hours, local transport and accommodation options

INTERNET

► **www.budapestinfo.hu**
Website for the Budapest Tourist Office with information on sights, the Budapest Card, shopping, excursions and much more

► **http://hotels.hu**
Hotels, restaurants, holiday rental properties

► **http://english.budapest.hu**
The Budapest portal, internet presentation of the city in English

▸ **www.visitorsguide.hu**
Online information from the Budapest Sun

EMBASSIES IN BUDAPEST

▸ **Australia**
XII, Királyhágó tér 8–9
Tel. 457–97 77
www.hungary.embassy.gov.au

▸ **Canada**
II, Ganz utca 12–14
Tel. 392–33 60
http://geo.international.gc.ca/canada-europa/hungary/

▸ **Ireland**
Bank Center, Granite Tower, V Szabadság tér 7
Tel. 301–49 60

▸ **United Kingdom**
V, Harmincad utca 6
Tel. 266–28 88
www.britishembassy.gov.uk/hungary

▸ **USA**
V Szabadság tér 12
Tel. 475–41 64
http://hungary.usembassy.gov/

HUNGARIAN EMBASSIES AND CONSULATES

▸ **Australia**
Suite 405, Edgecliff Centre, 203-233 New South Head Road
Edgecliff, Sydney, NSW 2027
Tel. 02 / 93 28 78 59
Fax 93 27 18 29

▸ **Canada**
299 Waverley Street
Ottawa, Ontario K2P OV9
Tel. 613 / 230 27 17, fax 230 75 60

▸ **Ireland**
2 Fitzwilliam Place, Dublin 2
Tel. 01 / 661 29 02 00, fax 6 61 28 80

▸ **UK**
35 Eaton Place
London SW1X 8BY
Tel. 02 07 / 235 52 18, fax 823 13 48

▸ **USA**
223 East 52nd Street
New York, N.Y.10022
Tel. 212 / 752 06 69, fax 755 59 86

Language

Foreign languages It is rarely difficult to communicate in Budapest, as most young people speak English.

Hungarian The Hungarian language belongs to the Finno-Ugrian family of languages and therefore holds a special place in Europe. Foreigners have difficulties with the difference in the pronunciation of consonants and vowels. In Hungarian the first syllable of a word is always stressed.

HUNGARIAN LANGUAGE GUIDE

Pronunciation

Vowels

a	as in »pot«
á	as in »father«
e	as in »pet«
é	as in »air«
i	as in »pit«
í	as in »peat«
o	as in »saw«, but short
ó	as in »shawl«
ö	as in »curt«, but short with no »r« sounded
u	as in »hull«
ú	as in »rule«
ü	as in French »tu«

Consonants

c	as »ts«in »pits«
cs	as »ch« in »chips«
dz	as in »adze«
dzs	as »j«in »jump«
gy	as »du« in »duel« (British)
j/ly	as in »yes«
ny	as in »canyon«
r	rolled
s	as in »shut«
sz	as in »sit«
ty	as »tu« in »tune« (British)
zs	as »s« in »leisure«

At a glance

Yes / No	Igen / Nem.
Maybe	Talán.
Please	Kérem.
Thank you	Köszönöm.
It's a pleasure	Szívesen.
Sorry!	Bocsánat!
What did you say?	Tessék?
I don't understand you	Nem értem.
I only speak a little ...	Csak egy kicsit beszélek ...
Do you speak ...	Beszél ...
... English?	... angolul?

Please write it down for me	Kérem írja fel!
Can you please help me?	Tudna nekem segíteni kérem?
I want	Szeretnék
I (don't) like that	Ez (nem) tetszik.
Do you have ...?	Van ...?
How much is it?	Mennyibe kerül?
What time is it?	Hány óra (van)?

Greetings

Good morning!	Jó reggelt!
Good day!	Jó napot!
Good evening!	Jó estét!
Hello! / Hello!	Szia! / Sziasztok!
How are you?	Hogy van / vagy?
Thank you. And you?	Köszönöm. És Ön / te?
Good bye!	Viszontlátásra!
Bye!	Szia / Sziasztok!
See you soon! / See you later!	Viszlát!

Out and About

left / right	balra / jobbra
straight ahead	egyenes(en)
near / far	közel / messze
Excuse me, where is... ?	Hol van kérem a(z) ... ?
How far is it?	Milyen messze van?
You can take...	Mehet ...
... the bus ...	... busszal.
... the tram ...	... villamossal.
... the metro ...	... metróval.

Breakdowns

My car has broken down	Defektem van.
Could you please send me a towing vehicle?	Tudna nekem egy vontatókocsit küldeni?
Where is there a garage near here?	Hol van itt a közelben egy muhely?

Petrol station

Where is the next petrol station please?	Hol (van) a legközelebbi benzinkút?

I want ... litres ...	... liter ... kérek.
... leaded petrol.	... normálbenzint
... super.	... szupert.
... diesel.	... dízelt.
... unleaded.	... ólommenteset
Fill it up please.	Tele kérem.

Accident

Help!	Segítség!
Careful!	Figyelem!
Watch out!	Vigyázat!
Please quickly call ...	Hívjon gyorsan ...
... an ambulance.	... mentot.
... the police.	...a rendorséget.
... the fire brigade.	... a tuzoltókat.
It was my fault.	Ön vagyok a hibás.
It was your fault.	Ön a hibás.
Please give me your name and address.	Adja meg kérem a nevét és a címét!

Eating

Where can I find ...	Hol van itt ...
... a good restaurant?	... egy jó étterem?
... a not too expensive restaurant?	... egy nem túl drága étterem?
Is there a cosy tavern here?	Van itt valahol egy nyugodt, hangulatos kocsma?
Please reserve a table for us for this evening.	Foglaljon kérem nekünk ma estére egy asztalt.
The meal was excellent.	Az étel kituno volt.

Accommodation

Can you recommend ...	Tudna ajánlani egy ...
... a good hotel ...	... jó szállodát?
... a pension ...	... panziót?
Do you have a room available?	Van még szabad szobájuk?
a single	egy egyágyas szobát
a double	egy kétágyas szobát
with bathroom	fürdoszobával
for one night	egy éjszakára
for one week	egy hétre
What does the room with ... cost?	Mennyibe kerül a szoba ...?

... breakfast	... reggelivel
... half-board	... félpanzióval

Numbers

0	nulla	1	egy
2	ketto két	3	három
4	négy	5	öt
6	hat	7	hét
8	nyolc	9	kilenc
10	tíz	11	tizenegy
12	tizenketto/tizenkét	13	tizenhárom
14	tizennégy	15	tizenöt
16	tizenhat	17	tizenhét
18	tizennyolc	19	tizenkilenc
20	húsz	21	huszonegy
22	huszonketto/ huszonkét	30	harminc
40	negyven	50	ötven
60	hatvan	70	hetven
80	nyolcvan	90	kilencven
100	száz	101	százegy
200	kétszáz	300	háromszáz
1000	ezer	2000	kétezer
10,000	tízezer	1/2	fél
1/3	harmad	1/4	egy negyed
3/4	háromnegyed		

Doctor

Can you recommend a good doctor?	Tud nekem egy jó orvost ajánlani?
It hurts here.	Itt fáj.

Bank

Where is there a bank here?	Hol van itt kérem egy bank?
I want to change ... euros (pounds/dollars) into forint.	Szeretnék ... Euro (svájci frankot) forintra átváltani.

Post

What does it cost to send ...?	Mibe kerül ...?

... a letter ...	... egy levél ...
... a post card ...	... egy levelezolap ...
stamp	bélyeg

Étlap (menu)

Reggeli	**Breakfast**
feketekávé	black coffee
tejeskávé	white coffee
tea tejjel	tea with milk
tea citrommal	tea with lemon
lágytojás	soft egg
rántotta	scrambled egg
szalonnás rántotta	egg and bacon
kenyér / zsemle / pirítós	bread / rolls / toast
kifli	croissant
vaj	butter
sajt	cheese
kolbász	sausage
sonka	ham
méz	honey
lekvár	jam
müzli	muesli
joghurt	yogurt
gyümölcs	fruit

Eloöételek ès Levesek	**Starters and soups**
bableves	bean soup
burgonyaleves	potato soup
eroleves	bouillon
hortobágyi palacsinta	pancake with meat filling
libamájpástétom	goose liver paté
májgombócleves	liver dumpling soup
töltött paradicsom	stuffed tomatoes
zöldségleves	vegetable soup

Húsételek és Szárnyas	**Meat and poultry**
báránypaprikás	paprika lamb with sour cream
bécsi szelet	Viennese Schnitzel
bélszínjava	steak
birkapörkölt	mutton goulash
borjúpaprikás	veal goulash with cream
csirke	chicken
fott marhahús	stewed beef

hagymás rostélyos	onion roast meat
(vad)kacsa	(wild) duck
(vad)liba	(wild) goose
naturszelet	schnitzel without breadcrumbs
pirított máj	chopped liver
pulyka	turkey
sertéskaraj	pork cutlet
sült kolbász	bratwurst
vagdalt	minced meat

Nemzeti Ételek	**National dishes**
bográcsgulyás	goulash
csirkepaprikás	paprika chicken with sour cream
gulyásleves	goulash soup
Gundel palacsinta	pancake with nut filling and chocolate sauce
halászlé	spicy fish soup
hideg meggyleves	cold sour cherry soup
káposztás kocka	cabbage
kapros-túrós rétes	quark strudel with dill
lecsó	cooked whole paprika, tomatoes and onions
máglyarakás	bread pudding with apples
somlói galuska	Schomlau dumplings
töltött káposzta	meat-filled cabbage
töltött paprika	stuffed paprika
túrós csusza pirított szalonnával	noodles with sour cream and lard

Halak	**Fish**
angolna	eel
csuka	pike
fogas / süllo	pikeperch
lazac	salmon
pisztráng	trout
ponty	carp
tonhal	tuna

Zöldség és Köretek	**Vegetables and side dishes**
bab	beans
borsó	peas
fejes saláta	lettuce
fokhagyma	garlic
fott burgonya	boiled potatoes
galuska	dumplings

gomba ... mushrooms
(zsemle)gombóc ... (bread dumplings
hagyma ... onion
hasábburgonya ... French fries
karfiol ... red cabbage
kelbimbó ... cabbage
kelkáposzta ... curled lettuce
lencse ... lentils
paradicsom ... tomatoes
paprika ... paprika
póréhagyma ... mashed potatoes
rizs ... rice
sárgarépa ... carrots
spagetti ... spaghetti
sparga ... asparagus
sült burgonya ... sautéed potatoes
vegyes saláta ... mixed salad

szpresszó ... **Coffee**
dobostorta ... Dobos gateau (six layers of pastry with chocolate cream and caramel icing)
fagyaltkehely ... ice cream
kávé ... coffee
sütemény ... cake
teasütemény ... biscuits
tejszínhab ... cream

Itallap (drinks menu)

Borok ... **Wine**
asztali bor ... table wine
különleges minöségü bor ... premium-quality wine
evjarat ... vintage
édes ... sweet
fröccs ... mixed with mineral water
könnyu ... light
fehér ... white
vörös ... red
száraz / fanyar ... dry
fèlédes ... semi-sweet
fèlszáras ... semi-dry
pezsgo ... champagne, sparkling wine

Szeszes Italok	**Alcoholic Drinks**
sör	beer
pohár	glass
korsó	small jar
üveg	bottle
gyomorkeseru	schnaps (digestif)
pálinka	schnaps

Alkoholmentes Italok	**Soft Drinks**
almalé	apple juice
(ásvány)víz	(mineral) water
gyümölclé	fruit juice
narancslé	orange juice
szódavíz	soda water

Literature

Attila József, »Selected Poems«, iUniverse.com 2005. Moving collection of poems. József (1905–37) grew up in the poor working-class district of Ferencváros.

Imre Kertész, »Fateless« Vintage Books 2006. The Nobel prize-winner for literature in 2002 (▸ Famous People) attempts the demystification of Auschwitz in this great book; it is the semi-autobiographical tale of a young man's journey to the concentration camp.

Imre Kertész, »Liquidation« Vintage Books 2007. Set in Budapest after the end of communism, this book explores the attempts of a man to come to terms with the suicide of a friend.

Arthur Phillips, »Prague« Duckworth 2006. No, the title is not a

Keeping informed

mistake. In this novel about life in Budapest during the post-communist years, many of the characters find the Czech capital more attractive than their own.

Giorgio and Nicola Pressburger, »Homage to the Eighth District: Tales from Budapest«, Readers International 1990. Tales of life and survival in the Jewish quarter during the Nazi era and Stalinism.

Betty Schimmel / Joyce Gabriel, »To See You Again: the Betty Schimmel Story«, Simon & Schuster 1999. The tragic love story between Betty and Richie during the Second World War is shattering, and not just for its authenticity.

Bryan Cartledge, »The Will to Survive: A History of Hungary«, Timewell Press 2006. Detailed history, well written and researched, by a former British ambassador to Hungary.

John Lukacs, »Budapest 1900: A Historical Portrait of a City and its Culture«, Grove Press 1988. This classic description of Budapest portrays the city in its golden age.

Sándor Márai, »Memoir of Hungary: 1944–48« Central European University Press 1996. The playwright Márai was forced to flee Hungary in 1948. Here he tells of the destruction of Budapest in the war and the post-war establishment of communism.

Kriztián Ungváry, »The Siege of Budapest: 100 Days in World War II«, Yale University Press 2006. Details of the battle that resulted in the loss of 25,000 civilian lives and the destruction of or severe damage to most of the city's historic buildings.

i Budapest in the Movies

- **A song of Love and Death – Gloomy Sunday:** Wonderful, melancholy story about a lover's triangle in German occupied Budapest during the Nazi era with Joachim Król and Ben Becker, directed by Rolf Schübels (1999).
- **Budapest Tales:** In the bombed Budapest after World War II, there is an incredibly strong will to rebuild and start over. Director: István Szábo (1976)
- **The Lord's Lantern in Budapest** Gravediggers and thieves, bankrupt businessmen and lawyers, life, death, success and failure, humour and satire – this successful film of episodes combines everything into an enjoyable mixture. Director: Miklós Jancsó (1999)

Lost Property (Talált tárgyak osztálya)

In Budapest all transport companies, including the airport, have their own lost property offices. Items found in public places, shops or department stores are handed to the relevant municipal district lost property office.

▶ **Ferihegy Airport**
Terminal 2A
Tel. 296–81 08 or 296–72 17

Terminal 2B
Tel. 295–34 80 or 296–76 90

▶ **Rail (MÁV)**
VI, West Railway Station
Tel. 349–01 15

▶ **Metropolitan Transport BKV**
VII, Akácfa u. 18, tel. 267–52 99
(lost on the same day)

Money

Currency

The Hungarian currency is the forint (Ft or HUF). Coins in circulation are to the value of 1, 2, 5, 10, 20, 50 und 100 forint, and notes are to the values of 200, 500, 1000, 2000, 5000 and 10 000 forint.

Currency regulations

Foreign currency over the equivalent of one million forint has to be declared; other than that there are no import restrictions.

Foreign exchange

Changing money anywhere other than hotels, foreign exchange booths and banks is extremely inadvisable. It is preferable not to buy Hungarian forint until you are in Hungary, as the rate of exchange is significantly better there. Similarly, it is best to change back from forint in Hungary and to compare rates of exchange at the different banks and foreign exchange booths before changing money. Rates in the city centre are noticeably better. Foreign exchange receipts for buying forint must be retained and produced for customs if required. Since Hungary plans on introducing the Euro by 2012/2013 at the latest, it would be wise to change all forints back before leaving Hungary.
Banks, the larger hotels, up-market restaurants, car hire firms, as well as shops and department stores predominantly frequented by tourists accept standard **credit cards**, such as Eurocard, Mastercard, Visa, American Express, Diners or Carte Blanche. **Cash machines** (ATMs) can be found all over the city, in which the standard cards, plus use of your personal security number, can be used to withdraw cash. The machines have multi-lingual service instructions.

Exchange Rates

- 100 forint = 0.41 euros
- 1 euro = 246 forint
- 100 forint = 0.,28 GBP (£)
- 1 GBP (£) = 358 forint
- 100 forint = 0.55 US$
- 1 US$ = 190 Forint

Bank opening times

Opening times for branches of the Hungarian banks and savings institutions are normally Mon–Fri 8am–3pm. Some banks already close at 1pm on Fridays. On Castle Hill there are foreign exchange booths that are also open on Sundays.

Museums and Exhibitions

General Budapest's large museums are described in detail under »Sights from A to Z«. Most museums are open Tue–Sun 10am–6pm (in the winter until 4pm). Smaller museums often have different opening times, and it is best to ask locally. It is common for museums to close temporarily for renovations; up-to-date information can be found at tourist information offices (►Information).
Unfortunately, information leaflets and notice boards in many of the smaller museums are normally produced only in Hungarian, though the larger museums also have them in English.

MUSEUMS IN BUDAPEST

HISTORY/CULTURAL HISTORY

Apothecary Museum
►Castle District

Bank notes and coin collection
V, Szabadság tér 8; opening times: Tue, 9am–2pm
The Hungarian National Bank's display of national coins and banknotes.

Bible Museum
IX, Ráday u. 28; opening times: Tue–Sun 10am–5pm
Comprehensive exhibition on the history of the Bible in the Hungarian and international context.

Church History Collection
►Matthias Church

Crime Museum
VIII, Mosonyi u. 7; opening times: Tue–Sun 10am–5pm
Police items and evidence from criminal cases since the mid-1960s.

Emergency Services Museum
V, Markó u. 22; opening times: daily, 9am–1pm
History and development of the emergency services in Hungary.

Ernst Museum
VI, Nagymezö u. 8; opening times: Tue–Sun 11am–7pm
Changing exhibitions on the culture and art of the 20th century.

Ethnographic Museum
p.177

Fire Services Museum
X, Martinovics tér 12
Opening times: Tue–Sat 9am–4pm, Sun 9am–1pm
The history of fire-fighting since Roman times.

Flag Museum
VIII, József krt. 68; opening times: Tue–Sun 11am–6pm
Official flags from countries and provinces, mostly donated by the relevant state presidents or rulers.

Gül Baba Türbe
►Rose Hill

Historical Museum
►Royal Palace

- **House of Terror**
  ►Andrássy út 60
- **Jewish Museum**
  ►Great Synagogue
- **Kiscelli Museum**
  ►Óbuda
- **Medieval Jewish prayer-house**
  ►Castle District
- **Nagytétény Palace Museum**
  ►Nagytétény, Palace
- **National Museum**
  ►p.211
- **Post Museum**
  ►Andrássy út
- **Protestant Museum**
  ►Little Ring
- **Stamp Museum**
  VII, Hársfa u. 47; opening times April–Oct: Tue–Sun 10am–6pm; Nov–Mar: Tue–Sun 10am–4pm

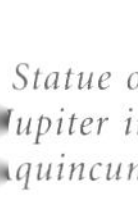
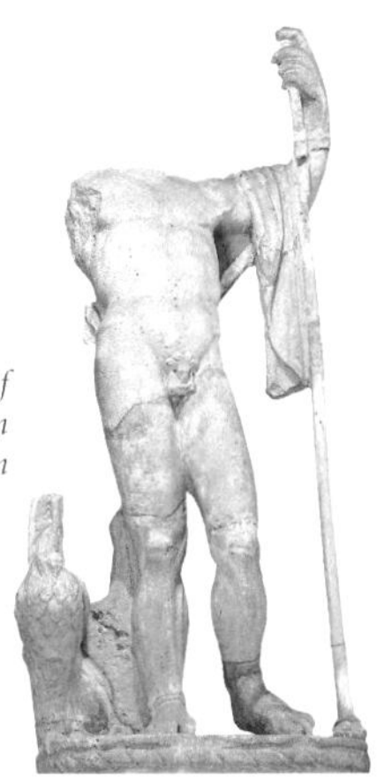

Statue of upiter in quincum

Turkish tent in the National Museum

All Hungarian stamps as well as numerous international ones.

- **Szentendre Open Air Museum**
  ►Szentendre
- **Trade and Gastronomy Museum**
  ►Castle District
- **Treasury of**
  ►St Stephen's Basilica

ART AND ARCHAEOLOGY

- **Aquincum**
  p.146
- **Exhibition of the national monuments authority**
  ►Castle District

Poultry Market by L. Déak-Ebner in the National Gallery

Arts and Crafts Museum
►p.148

Budapest Exhibition Hall
V, Szabadsjtó út 5; opening times: Tue–Sun 10am–6pm
Painting, sculpture, photography and more from all over the world

Budapest Gallery exhibition hall
III, Lajos u. 158; opening times: Tue–Sun 10am–6pm
Contemporary national and foreign art.

Contra Aquincum
►Március 15. tér

Dorottya-Gallery
V, Dorottya u. 8; opening times: Mon–Thu 1–7pm, Fri–Sun 11am–7pm
Exhibition on contemporary Hungarian artists.

Ferenc Hopp Museum for East Asian Art
VI, Andrássy út 103; opening times: April–Oct 10am to 6pm, Nov–March 10am–4pm
Miniature carvings (netsuke) from Japan.

György Ráth Museum
VI, Városligeti fasor 12; opening times: April–Oct: Tue–Sun 10am–6pm; Nov–March: Tue–Sun 10am–4pm
Collection of oriental and East Asian art.

Hercules Villa
►Óbuda

House of Hungarian Photography
VI, Nagymezö u. 20
Opening times: Mon–Fri 2pm–6pm; Sat and Sun 10am–6pm
Exhibition of contemporary photographs.

Imre Varga Museum
►Óbuda

Ludwig Museum – Museum for Contemporary Art
►Royal Palace

Miksa Róth Memorial House
VII, Nefelejcs u. 26
Opening times: Tue–Sun 2pm–6pm

Museum of Fine Arts
►p.202

National Gallery
►Royal Palace

Pál Molnár Museum
XI, Ménesi út 65

Opening times: Nov–March: Tue–Thu 3pm–6pm; April– Oct: Tue–Thu 3–6pm, Sun 10am–1pm
Work by the artist Pál Molnár (1894–1981), who belonged to the »Rome School«, in his former studio.

▸ **Palace of Art**
►Heroes' Square

▸ **Roman Bath Museum – Fürdö-Museum**
►Óbuda

▸ **Roman Garrison**
►Óbuda

▸ **Sculpture Park**
►p.237

▸ **Vasarély Museum**
►Óbuda

LITERATURE, THEATRE AND MUSIC

▸ **Béla Bartók House**
►Rose Hill

▸ **Endre Ady Memorial**
V, Veres Pálné u. 4–6
Opening times: March–Oct: Wed–Sun 10am–6pm; Nov–Feb: Wed–Sun, 10am–4pm
The poet Endre Ady's last place of residence (1877–1919)

▸ **Franz Liszt Museum**
►Andrássy út

▸ **Josef Attila Museum**
IX, Gát u. 3
Opening times: Tue–Sun 10am–6pm (closed July and August)
Documents and letters in the poet's former apartment

▸ **Lajos Kassák Museum**
►Óbuda

▸ **Mór Jókai Museum**
XII, Költö u. 21
Opening times: March–Oct Wed–Sun 10am–6pm
Personal items of the writer (1825–1904)

▸ **History of Music Museum**
►Castle District

▸ **Petöfi Museum**
►Palais Károlyi

▸ **Gizi Bajor Theatre Museum**
XII, Stromfeld Aurél u. 16
Opening times: Sept–June, Thu and Fri 2pm–6pm, Sat and Sun 10am–6pm
Items belonging to Hungarian actors at the former villa of the actress Gizi Bajor (1893–1951).

▸ **Zoltán Kodály Museum**
►Andrássy út

NATURE UND TECHNOLOGY

▸ **Agricultural Museum**
►Városliget

▸ **Electro-technical Museum**
VII, Kazinczy u. 21
Opening times: Tue–Sat 11am–5pm
Historical presentation on the use and production of electrical energy, including experiment installations

▸ **Flight Museumin the Petöfi Exhibition Hall**
XIV, Zichy Mihály u. 14
Opening times: mid-May–mid Oct Tue–Fri 10am–5pm; Sat and Sun, 10am–6pm

Passenger aircraft, as well as a space capsule, models, and gliders.

► **Foundry Museum**
►Víziváros

► **Geological Museum**
XIV, Stefánia út 14
Opening times: Thu, Sat, Sun. 10am–4pm (closed during the Christmas holidays)
The art nouveau building houses Hungarian minerals and fossils.

► **Mill Museum**
IX, Soroksári út 24; opening times: Mon–Thu, 9am–2pm
Milling and sifting utensils, as well as items from water, wind and electric mills.

! *Baedeker* TIP

Palace of Wonders

The Palace of Wonders (Csodák palotája) offers young and old the chance to discover technology and natural science in a playful and inter-active way. Opening times: Tue–Fri 9am–5pm, Sat and Sun 10am–6pm; II, Feny utca 20–22 (in a former factory building by the Millenaris Park, north-west of Castle Hill, www.csodapalota.hu)

► **Natural Science Museum**
VIII, Ludovika tér 2
www.nhmus.hu
Opening times April–Sep: Mon and Wed–Sun 10am–6pm; Oct–March: Mon and Wed–Sun 10am–5pm
An introduction to the natural history of the Carpathian basin, with many fossils, minerals, plants and animals, as well as human remains and artefacts.

► **Railway Museum Park**
XIV, Tatai út 95
www.miwo.hu/old_trains
Opening times: April–Oct: Tue–Sun 10am–6pm; Nov–March: Tue–Sun, 10am–5pm
Almost 100 carriages and trains from days gone by.

► **Semmelweis Museum for Medical History**
►Tabán

► **Telephone Museum**
► Castle District

► **Textile Museum**
III, Lajos u. 138
Opening times: Tue–Sun 10am–2pm
Old machines as well as a complete interior of a former shoe factory introduce the history of the textile industry in Hungary.

► **Underground Museum**
►Baedeker Tipp.192

► **Transport Museum**
►Városliget

MILITARY

► **War Museum**
►Castle District

SPORT

► **Sport Museum**
XIV, Dózsa György út 3
Opening times: daily except Fri, 10am–4pm
Documents, medals, photos and film of famous Hungarian sportsmen and women from the past and present.

Newspapers and Listings

International Press

International newspapers and magazines can be found at many newspaper kiosks in the city centre, as well as at the airport, at the three major railway stations, and at the newspaper stands of the large hotels.

Hungarian Press

Two English-language newspapers are published weekly: the tabloid »Budapest Sun« (www.budapestsun.com) on Thursdays, with a useful arts and events section, and the »Budapest Times« (www.budapesttimes.hu) on Mondays with reviews of what's on in the city. »Budapest Week« (www.budapestweek.hu). For serious reading on Hungary, its culture and current issues, read the high-brow »Hungarian Quarterly« (www.hungarianquarterly.com)

Brochures, listings magazines

Apart from the above papers and the information available frree of charge from the tourist offices and hotels in »Budapest Panorama« and »Budapest City Magazine«, it is worth consulting the English-language brochures »Budapest In Your Pocket« (www.inyourpocket.-com) and »Budapest Pocket Guide« (www.budpocketguide.com), which are updated four or five times a year and contain relevant information for tourists, including addresses, opening times and an events calendar.

Personal Safety

Car theft

Crime against tourists in Hungary does not exceed the average of other European holiday destinations. The number of car thefts has declined drastically, although valuable new cars continue to be objects of desire among professional car thieves. Budapest visitors are well-advised to park their cars at supervised car parks and not to leave any items in the car that are even slightly valuable.

The places in Budapest with a strong tourist presence are naturally an Eldorado for **pick-pockets**. Their activities can be noted everywhere, especially in the Castle District, on Váci utca, Heroes' Square and in the large market hall by the Freedom Bridge. Take care at ticket booths for metro and tram tickets too!

In many places around Budapest, but especially near railway, bus, tram and underground stations, as well as by taxi stands, luxury hotels and on the Danube bridges, dubious **black-market money changers** and fraudsters try to trick naïve tourists.

Tourist police

- During the tourist high season, from 1 June to 1 September, specially trained tourist police accompanied by translators are present on all streets and squares heavily frequented by tourists. These law-enforcers are entitled to see your passport on request, but they are not allowed to ask for money or credit cards.
- The tourist police have established a phone number for tourist victims of crime: the Budapest number is 438-80-80 (area code if calling from outside Budapest is 06-1-). Victims of crime can get help and information in English, French, German or Spanish. The hotline is operational around the clock.

A few brazen **taxi gangs** have specialized in tricking uncertain and inexperienced visitors. Inattentive tourists can already fall into the hands of such gangs during arrival at the airport or at one of the Budapest train stations. It is therefore highly recommended to establish clearly at the outset of a journey that the taxi meter is not only switched on, but also clearly shows the price per kilometre.

Prostitution especially, but also **drug-related crime** pose a significant problem for the Budapest police. Often posing as beggars, prostitutes or gays, members of highly organized gangs try to proposition tourists with drugs, black-market money or sexual services. Violent attacks are not uncommon. Trading in, owning or using drugs (including hashish and marihuana) are punished with jail terms in Hungary!

Post and Telecommunications

Post

Post offices

Budapest post offices open Mon–Fri, 8am–6pm, Sat 8am – 1pm; post office at the East Railway Station (Keleti pályaudvar), Mon–Sat, 7am–9pm; post office at the West Railway Station (Nyugati pályaudvar), Mon–Sat 7am–9pm, Sun 8am–8pm.

Postal rates

Postcards within Europe cost 120 Ft, to the rest of the world 140 Ft; airmail up to 20g within Europe costs 185 Ft, 210 Ft to the rest of the world. Stamps are available from post offices and almost everywhere that sells post cards. Hungarian post boxes are red, decorated with a post horn.

Telephones

Long-distance calls

For public long-distance calls you need 10-, 20-, 50- or 100-forint coins, or a telephone card that you can buy at post offices, kiosks, petrol stations and tobacco shops.

National and international calls

For local calls just dial the number; for long-distance calls within Hungary, dial 06, wait for a tone and then dial the area code and number you require. For international calls, dial 00, wait for a tone and then dial the area codes for the relevant country and location, plus the actual telephone number you require. Telephone booths for international calls are marked with a relevant sign.

Mobile phones

Hungarian mobile phone numbers have eleven digits. The first four are unique to the relevant service provider, being06 20, 06 30, 06 60 and 06 70. All eleven numbers must be dialled if calling from a landline or a mobile phone with a non-Hungarian service provider. If calling a mobile phone with the same service provider, the first four numbers can be dropped. If calling between different Hungarian service providers, the initial 06 can be left out.

TELEPHONE INFORMATION

CODES AND SERVICE NUMBERS

- **Within Hungary to Budapest**
  Tel. 06-1
- **From other countries**
  Tel. 00 36-1
- **From Budapest to other countries:**
  First 00, then country code, e.g. to UK 00 44, to USA 00 1
- **Operator services (international)**
  Tel. 190
- **National enquiries**
  Tel. 198
- **International enquiries**
  Tel. 199

Prices • Discounts

A broad spectrum

Prices are rising in Budapest. In the top restaurants and hotel chains they are on a par with those in western Europe, and naturally shops and restaurants in the tourist districts adapt their prices to the financial resources of their international customers. Nevertheless, it is possible to eat and drink well for little money in most cafés and restaurants. Souvenirs, CDs and local specialties remain good value even today, and high-quality Hungarian wine and spirits are available at low prices.

Hungarian Tourist Card

For exploring the environs of Budapest, it is worth taking advantage of the reductions offered by the Hungarian Tourist Card. It is valid for 13 months and provides discounts on rail and boat tickets, in many taxis, and in hotels and restaurants.

WHAT DOES IT COST?

Three-course menu
From 1500 Ft

Hamburger
From 250 Ft

Cup of coffee
From 200 Ft

Litre of petrol
From 245 Ft

Basic double room
From 7000 Ft

Single ticket
From 106 Ft

Budapest Card The discount card of the Budapest tourist authorities offers free public transport in the metropolitan area (except on the cable car up Castle Hill), and free entry to around 60 museums and sights. Many shops, restaurants, spas and car rental firms also grant significant discounts to card holders. The card (valid for one adult and one child under 14) can be purchased at tourist offices and travel agents, hotel receptions or at the larger metro stations; 6450 forint for two days, and 7950 forint for three days. As many museums are free anyway, and public transport is cheap (free from age 65), it is worth checking to see if the card is worthwhile.

Tipping 10–15% of the bill is standard and in the classier establishments the head waiter and wine waiter also expect a tip. A 20% service charge is often already listed on the bill, in which case no tip is necessary. Taxi drivers get 10–15% of the bill, and wardrobe staff get a few forint. Self-employed gipsy bands play in many establishments and the musicians request a contribution from patrons. 500 forint is normal.

Shopping

Shopping streets Even though Budapest cannot quite match London, Milan or Paris as a shoppers' paradise, the Hungarian capital offers the widest choice and the greatest range of products in all of central eastern Europe. The main shopping streets are in the city centre area of Pest. They are Váci utca, Petöfi Sándor utca, Régisposta utca, Páriszi utca, Andrassy ut and Kigyó utca. There are also wonderful shops on Kossuth Lajos utca, Rákóczi út, Múzeum körút, Károly körút, Erzsébet körút, Szent István körút and József körút. Nor should the many little shops in the Castle District be overlooked.

VAT refunds

Foreigners can have value added tax (ÁFA) refunded on departure, as long as the value of products is at least 50,000 Ft. The original bill and a refund form filled in by the relevant shop are required. The money is refunded at departure by the IBUSZ travel agents at Ferihegy Airport, at the West Railway Station, as well as at all road border crossings.

Souvenirs

Souvenirs of varying quality are offered at all tourist hot spots. Dolls in folk costume and bulky wine jars are popular. Hand-made textiles such as blouses, dresses, table cloths and bedding are often exquisitely embroidered and make pretty, unique holiday gifts. Kalocs blouses, Matyó embroideries, jackets with colourful cloth decorations and woven country ware find just as many buyers as Herend porcelain, Pécs ceramics, pottery after the style of puszta shepherds, and cutlery and vessels carved from different types of wood. Glass, leatherwear, elegant ladies' handbags, shoes, cravats, belts and natural remedies – especially flower pollen, propolis, honey and medicinal herbs – are very popular with tourists as they are relatively cheap. Popular holiday gifts are Hungarian salami, Barack apricot schnapps, and the popular Szilva damson schnapps, spirits made by Peter Zwack, wines from the various wine-growing regions – especially Eger and Tokaj – as well as creatively packaged paprika and garlic.

Made-to-measure clothing and shoes

Those who value the personal touch can have value-for-money clothes and shoes made to measure from high-quality materials by excellent craft workers in Budapest.

Opening hours

Shops are generally open Mon–Fri 10am–6pm, Sat 9am–1pm. In the Pest pedestrian zone shops often stay open till the evening, and shopping malls till 9pm. Market halls and markets operate weekdays from 6am to 5pm.

SHOPPING ADDRESSES

ANTIQUES • GALLERIES

► **Antik Bazár**
V, Váci utca 67
Large selection of antiques, especially dolls, jewellery and clothes.

► **Belvárosi Aukcióház**
V, Váci utca 36
Auction house which sells valuable furniture, jewellery, art works and more every Monday from 5pm; previews are possible daily from 10am.

► **BÁV (Bizományi Áruház Vállalat)**
V, Bécsi utca 1–3 (jewellery, paintings and gift items)
V, Párizsi u. 2 (furniture and art)
V, Kossuth Lajos u. 1 (especially

porcelain and paintings)
V, Semmelweis u. 15 (weapons)
VII, Károly krt. 3/A (coins)
The numerous shops of the state auction house BÁV are a good place for all kinds of antiques and great for bargain hunters

▶ **Csók István Galéria**
V, Váci utca 5
Old and contemporary Hungarian art, also sculptures, prints and jewellery.

▶ **Nagyházi Galéria**
V, Balaton utca 8
Budapest's largest gallery offers, next to its extensive selection of paintings, also furniture, porcelain and jewellery

▶ **Style Antique**
VII, Király u. 25
Very beautiful restored antique pine furniture

BOOKS • SECOND-HAND BOOKSHOPS

▶ **Atlantisz Könyvsziget**
V, Piarista köz 1
Literature about Hungarian culture and history

▶ **Írók Boltja**
VI, Andrássy út 45
Bookshop with regular readings by authors and a café; those who haven't mastered Hungarian should head for the foreign language department

▶ **Központi Antikvárium**
V, Múzeum krt. 17
Hungary's largest antiquarian bookshop has been trading since 1881, and also sells foreign language books and maps.

▶ **Párisi Udvar**
V, Petőfi Sándor u. 2
Large selection of travel books, illustrated books and maps.

▶ **Sós Antiquárium**
V, Váci utca 73
In addition to books, there is a large selection of prints, maps and postcards.

CDs

▶ **Fotex Records**
V, Szervita tér 2
Centrally located music shop with a broad selection from pop to classical.

▶ **INDIeGO**
VIII, Krúdy Gyula u. 7
Alternative rock and indie music not dictated by commercial hit lists.

▶ **MCD Amadeus**
V, Szende Pál utca 1
Large selection of classical and jazz.

▶ **Virgin Mega store**
XIII, Váci út 178 (Duna Plaza)
Impressive selection of pop and rock, jazz, world music, classical music and other genres.

DEPARTMENT STORES• SHOPPING CENTRES

▶ **Corvin**
VIII, Blaha Lujza tér 1–2
You can get just about anything here, and for a good price too; this once state-owned chain still has something of the socialist era about it.

▶ **Duna Plaza**
XIII, Váci út 178
Shopping mall and multiplex cin-

ema, with restaurants, ice skating rink and bowling alley, along with over 150 shops

► **Europark**
XIX, Üllöi út 201
In the Europark you can concentrate on shopping without distractions: there is no cinema or other entertainment to stop you from shopping till you drop

► **Luxury**
V, Vörösmarty tér 5
A collection of small boutiques for the elegant lady; the privileged already bought their imported Western fashions here during socialist times.

► **Mammut**
II, Széna tér 1–3
Popular shopping centre on Moszkva tér; the original weekly market has been integrated.

► **Westend City Centre**
VI, Váci út 1–3
Central Europe's largest shopping, commercial and leisure centre: over 400 shops in an area of 90,000 sq m (100,000 sq ft). The triangular building with sloping glass roof is worth a visit alone.

FASHION

► **Artista**
VI, Jókai tér 8
Loud and youthful designer gear.

► **Clara-Liska**
V, Váci utca 12
Exclusive ladies' fashions with prices to match.

► **Gréti**
V, Bárczy István utca 3
Elegant designer boutique.

► **Imagine Moda**
V, Vitkovits Mihály utca 3–5
Young fashion for him and her.

► **Kaláka Stúdió**
V, Haris köz 2
Clothing and shoes in Hungarian style at affordable prices.

► **V-50 Design Art Studio**
V, Belgrád rakpart 16
Classic designer fashion, linen dresses, and hats for brave ladies.

FLEA MARKETS

► **Ecseri flea market**
XIX, Nagykörösi út 156
Huge flea market at which the bargain hunter can find virtually anything that the heart desires: watches, furniture, clothes, porcelain. Prices are always negotiable! (Opening times: Mon–Fri, 8am–4pm, Sat, 7am–3pm)

► **Flea market in Városliget**
On the area around the Petöfi Hall (XIV district)
Significantly smaller than the Ecseri flea market, but still worth a visit. (Opening times: Sat–Sun, 7am–2pm).

FOLKLORE • FOLK ART

► **Folk Art Centre**
V, Váci utca 14
Hungarian folk art, especially embroidery, clothes, ceramics, but also a lot of kitsch

► **Vali Folklore Souvenir**
V, Váci utca 23
There is a very fine line between Hungarian folk art and mass-produced kitsch sold as folk art – here you stand a very good chance of finding something hand-made.

A stroll along Váci utca should be part of every visit to Budapest.

GLASS • PORCELAIN

▶ **Haas & Czjzek**
VI, Bajcsy-Zsilinszky út 23
Large selection of Hungarian porcelain.

▶ **Herend**
V, József Nádor tér 11
V, Kígyó utca 5
I, Szentháromság utca 5
High-class Herend table ware.

▶ **Zsolnay**
V, Kígyó utca 4
V, Kristóf tér 1
Zsolnay porcelain is no less famous than Herend porcelain, but not as delicate, more in the rustic and bourgeois tradition.

BUTTONS

▶ **Dénes Vandorffy**
V, Váci utca 75
Amazing selection of ladies' buttons.

MARKET HALLS

▶ **Central Market Hall**
IX, Fövám körút 1-3
A much-visited and unique century-old Budapest institution; Hungarian specialties and folklore goods (opening times: Mon 6am–5pm, Tue–Fri 6am–6pm, Sat 6am–2pm).

▶ **Market on Lehel tér**
XIII district
This traditional market has been held in an architecturally pleasing hall since 2002 (opening times: Mon–Fri 6am–6pm, during winter till 5pm, Sat 6am–noon).

▶ **Additional market halls**
Just as the central market hall, the following were also founded in the late 19th century and offer similar products:
V, Hold u. 13
VI, Hunyadi tér 4

VII, Klauzál tér 11
VIII, Rákóczi tér 7–9
IX, Vámház krt. 1–3

OPEN-AIR MARKETS

Market square on Közraktár utca (IX district)
I, Batthyány tér
II, Fény utca
XI, Fehérvári út

SHOES

► **Vass**
V, Haris köz 2
Made-to-measure shoes for those with plenty of time; the rest will have to buy the standard goods on offer.

Sport and Outdoors

Spectator sports

Football is still the most popular game among Hungarian sports fans, even if the days of great international success, such as reaching the finals of the 1954 World Cup, are long gone. Hungarians continue to be a nation of horse lovers, as before, and the **horse-racing season** runs from April to October.

Sports events

Fixed major sports events are the Budapest International **Marathon** in October, and the Vienna–Budapest **Supermarathon**, as well as the **Formula One Grand Prix** (►Festivals and Events) in August.

Cycling

Budapest's cycle tracks encompass a total of around 100km/65mi. Margaret Island, Városliget woods, the Népliget forest and the Buda hills offer ideal cycling terrain, and mountain bikers find their Eldorado at János-hegy. Cycling maps are available at tourist information centres (►Information) and bookshops.

SPORTS FACILITIES

STADIUMS

► **Budapest Aréna**
Rákoczi út 42

► **Volksstadion**
Stéfania út 3–5

ICE SKATING

►Baedeker Tipp.250

AIR SPORTS

► **Pannon Air Service**
Budakeszi-Farkas-hegy Airport (5 km/3mi west of Budapest), tel. 23/452–000
Flight tours, hang gliding, and gliding at weekends

GOLF

► **Budapest Golf Park & Country Club**
Kisoroszi (35km/22mi north of Budapest), tel. 317–60 25

► **Pannonia Golf & Country Club**
Alcsútdoboz

(40km/25mi west of Budapest)
Tel. 266–55 80

RIDING

► **Akadémia Lovarda**
XVII, Régi Vám köz 37–40,
Tel. 20/912–20 24

► **Aranypatkó Lovarda**
III, Aranyhegyi út 18
Tel. 387–71 52

► **Budapesti Lovas Klub**
VIII, Kerepesi út 7, tel. 313–52 10

► **Petneházy Lovasiskola**
II, Feketefej utca 2–4
Tel. 397–50 48

ROWING

► **Csepel Sport Club**
XXI, Gubacsi hídfoö
Tel. 420–38 11

► **Danubius Nemzeti Hajós Egylet**
XIII, Margitsziget
Hajós Alfréd sétány 2
Tel. 329–31 42

► **Ganz Evezoös Club**
III, Királyok útja 286
Tel. 20/940–07 90

► **Vízügy Sport Club**
III, Kossuth Lajos
üdüloöpart 70–71, tel. 210–10 90

SWIMMING

►Baths

SPORTS CENTRES

► **Lido Szabadidoöközpont**
III, Nánási út 67
Tel. 242–43 86
Squash, bowling, tennis, keep fit, boat hire

A highlight of spectator sport in Hungary: Formula One Grand Prix on the Hungaroring

▶ **Margitszigeti Atlétikai Centre**
XIII, Margitsziget, tel. 329–34 06
Jogging, athletics, tennis, streetball, handball and volleyball

SQUASH

▶ **City Squash Club**
II, Marcibányi tér 13
Tel. 325–00 82

▶ **Griff Squash és Fitness Club**
XI, Bartók Béla út 152
Tel. 206–40 65

▶ **Top Squash**
II, Lövoöház utca 2–6
Mammut Shopping Centre, tel. 345–81 93

TENNIS

▶ **Budapesti Spartacus SC**
I, Dózsa tér, tel. 202–43 76

▶ **MTK Tenisz Szakosztály**
XI, Bartók Béla út 63, tel. 209–15 95

▶ **Római Teniszakadémia**
III, Királyok útja 105, tel. 240–38 94

▶ **Városmajori Teniszakadémia**
XII, Városmajor utca 63–69
Tel. 202–53 37

POOL

▶ **Black Pool**
IX, Vámhaz körút 15
Tel. 218–93 79

▶ **MC Monte Carlo Biliárd Club**
II, Török utca 4, tel. 212–10 13

▶ **Noiret Biliárdszalon**
VI, Desewffy utca 8–10
Tel. 331–61 03

▶ **WEGA Biliárdterem**
IV, Árpád út 81, tel. 370–42 66

BOWLING

▶ **Bowling Centrum**
XIII, Váci utca 178
(Duna Plaza), tel. 239–38 29

▶ **Bowling Pub – Novotel Budapest Congress**
XII, Alkotás utca 63–67
Tel. 209–19 80

▶ **Lido Szabadidoöközpont**
XI, Nánási út 67, tel. 242–19 37

▶ **Strike Bowling Club**
XI, Budafoki út 111–113
Tel. 206–27 54

▶ **Taverna Bowling Bar**
V, Váci utca 20, tel. 485–31 71

Theatre • Concerts • Musicals

Booking offices

Theatre, opera, and concert tickets should be bought in advance at the ticket desks of the relevant theatres or from advance booking offices. The tourist information offices (►Information) also sell tickets for various events.

Theatre

Over forty theatres vie for an audience in Budapest. Most performances are in Hungarian and only a small number of international productions are intelligible to non-native speakers. The following selection of theatre venues concentrates on those that include foreign-language productions in their programme. Information on the relevant programmes at individual stages can be found in the monthly free **»Budapest Panorama«** (► Newspapers and Listings), available from hotels, tourist information offices and travel agents, and also from the free listings in **»Budapest City Magazine«**. Tickets are available from advance booking offices and the evening ticket booths.

Concerts

Hungarian music enjoys world renown and its heritage is especially well tended in Budapest. In addition to Franz Liszt (► Famous People), its fame is especially based on the compositions by Ferenc Erkel, Béla Bartók (► Famous People) and Zoltán Kodály. Budapest's musical life offers something for every taste, from symphony concerts, opera and operetta to bold productions of modern musical theatre. Those who enjoy folk music can find programmes in many places or dance to the lively »csárdás« gipsy music. And Budapest also caters for fans of rock and pop, as famous bands regularly perform here.

Music taverns

► Nightlife

Budapest Spring Festival

Fans of music should visit the city during the annual Budapest Spring Festival in March. Musicians from all over the world perform at almost all the city's venues.

THEATRE & MUSIC INFORMATION

BOOKING OFFICES

► **Central Booking Office**
VI, Andrássy út 18, tel. 312–00 00, fax 322–61 36

► **Ticketexpress**
XIII, Szent István krt. 16, tel. 329–34 08, fax 329–35 93
www.ticketexpress.hu

► **Vigadó Ticket Service**
V, Vörösmarty tér 1, tel. 327–43 22, fax 327–43 21

THEATRES

► **International Buda Stage**
II, Tárogató út 2–4, tel. 391–25
Theatre performances in English; musical shows and film premieres.

► **József Katona Theatre**
V, Petoöfi Sándor utca 6
Tel. 318–37 25
The world-famous theatre is almost always sold out; its repertoire includes drama by Shakespeare.

► **Korona Podium**
I, Dísz tér, tel. 318–85 17
Literary and chanson evenings.

► **Madách Theatre**
VII, Erzsébet körút 29–33
Tel. 478–20 41
www.madachszinhaz.hu
Musicals and classical theatre productions.

► **Merlin Theatre**
V, Gerlóczy utca 4

Tel. 317–93 38
Comedies and tragedies in English.

▶ **Pesti Theatre**
V, Váci utca 9, tel. 266–55 57
Small theatre in the city centre, well-known for its excellent comedies.

▶ **Trafó**
IX, Liliom utca 41, tel. 456–20 50
Modern productions by foreign theatre groups: bizarre, irrational and avant garde.

▶ **Víg Theatre**
XIII, Pannónia utca 1, tel. 329–23 40
Classics, including modern interpretations, in a building that is well worth seeing.

CONCERT HALLS

▶ **Béla Bartók Memorial House**
II, Csalán út 29, tel. 342–21 00
Occasional chamber music performances.

▶ **Budapest Congress Centre**
XII, Jagelló út 1–3, tel. 361–28 69
Classical concerts, opera and ballet galas, but also performances by international jazz and soul greats.

▶ **Danube Palace**
V, Zrínyi utca 5, tel. 317–27 54
Concerts by the Danube Symphonic Orchestra and annual venue of the opera gala.

▶ **Academy of Music**
VI, Liszt Ferenc tér 8, tel. 341–47 88
Symphony concerts / solo evenings

▶ **Pest Redoute (Vigadó)**
V, Vigadó tér 2, tel. 317–50 67
Especially liked for its operettas.

CHURCH CONCERTS

▶ **St Michael's Church**
V, Váci utca 47
Works by Bach, Bartók and Kodály, among others, are performed on Budapest's oldest organ.

▶ **Matthias Church**
I, Szentháromság tér
Organ concert pieces are performed on Fridays, and oratorios on Saturdays.

▶ **St Anna Church**
I, Batthyány tér
Organ concerts of works by Bach, Kodály and Bartók every now and then.

▶ **St Stephen's Basilica**
V, Szent István tér
Organ concerts underneath the basilica's beautiful dome.

OPERA • BALLET

▶ **Erkel Theatre**
VIII, Köztársaság tér 30, tel. 333–05 40
Varied programme of operas and ballet from works by various artists, but with a special emphasis on works by the composer of the Hungarian national anthem, Ferenc Erkel.

▶ **Hungarian State Opera**
VI, Andrássy út 22, tel. 331–25 50
Superb productions of ballet and opera performances; book early!

OPERETTA

▶ **Budapest Operetta**
VI, Nagymezoö utca 17, tel. 353–21 72
Well-known operettas by Hungarian composers such as Lehár and Kálmán.

Cultural institution: the Operetta

- **Pest Redoute (Vigadó)**
  ►see concert halls

FOLKLORE

- **Buda Redoute**
  I, Corvin tér 8, tel. 317–27 54, 317–13 77
  The Hungarian State Folk Ensemble, with its famous gipsy orchestra, performs gipsy music, folk dances and folk music.

- **Danube Palace**
  see ►concert halls
  The Danube Folk Ensemble is well known for its excellent performances: top quality folk dances and music. The Gipsy Orchestra and the Rajkó Folk Ensemble also perform.

- **Folk Theatre**
  XI, Fehérvári út 47, tel. 203–38 73
  Performances by folk musicians and folk dance troupes.

- **Puppet Theatre**
  VI, Andrássy út 69, tel. 317–27 54
  Regular appearances by the Rajkó Folk Ensemble

OPEN AIR STAGES

The three open-air stages on Szabad Tér Színhaz present operettas, cabaret, pop concerts and folk programmes; information at tel. 375–59 22, fax 356–09 98

- **Open-air stage on Margaret Island**
  XIII, Margitsziget

- **Park stage**
  XI, Kosztolány tér

- **Városmajor Open-Air Stage**
  XII, Városmajor park

MUSICALS

- **Madách Theatre**
  VII, Erzsébet krt. 29–33, tel. 478–20 41
  Internationally famous commercial musicals, such as Andrew Lloyd Webber's »Cats«, are performed at the Madách Theatre

POP AND ROCK

- **Laser Theatre**
  IX, Népliget, tel. 263–08 71
  Laser shows to the sounds, for example, of Pink Floyd, Vangelis or Madonna.

- **SAP Event Hall/Round Hall**
  XIV, Istvánmezei út 3–5
  A suitable setting for concerts by famous musicians.

Tours • Guides

Organized tours

There is extensive information material on city tours by bus, as well as on boat cruises on the Danube, air tours and, of course, walks around particular districts, at the tourist information offices, as well as at hotel receptions.

Tram tour

For holders of the Budapest Card (►Prices, Discounts), tram lines 2, 4 and 6 are a cost-effective way of getting an overview of sights around the Pest side of the city: a recommended tour begins at the Margaret Bridge, south of ►Margaret Island. Tram lines 4 and 6 travel along the ► Great Ring, past the West Railway Station, the Oktogon (►Andrássy út) and Café New York to the Petöfi Bridge, where you change to tram line 2 or 2A heading north. From here the journey goes along the Danube, with views of ► Fövám tér and the Central Market Hall, the ► Chain Bridge and ►Parliament, as well as ►Gellért Hill and the ►Gellért Bath, before ending back at the starting point. Not recommended during the rush hour (5–7pm) because of the crowded trams!

! *Baedeker* TIP

Bird's-eye view

Close to the Westend City Centre, at the Honvéd Sports ground on Dózsa György út, a giant red hot-air balloon, anchored to the ground and visible from far and wide, rises 150m/500ft into the air several times a day. For the maximum of thirty passengers on board, it is definitely the most effective and original way to see as much of the city as possible in the shortest of time (info: tel. 06 30 / 377–89 39).

SIGHTSEEING INFORMATION

CITY WALKS

Information on the wide choice of escorted walking tours around the city can be found at tourist offices (►Information) and hotel receptions. Travel agents offering city tours include:

▶ **Paul Street Tours**
Rozsahegy u. 8
Tel. (06 20) 933 52 40
www.firsteuropean-shipping.com

▶ **Absolute Walking Tours**
Tel. (06 30) 2 11 88 61
www.absolutetours.com

BUS TOURS

▶ **Budatours**
VI, Andrássy út 2
Tel. 353–05 58
www.budatours.hu

▶ **Cityrama**
Báthori utca 22
Tel. 302–43 82
www.cityrama.hu

▶ **Ibusz**
V, Erzsébet tér
Tel. 318–75 85
www.ibusz.hu

► **Program Centrum**
V, Vörösmarty tér 1, tel. 318–44 46
www.programcentrum.hu

► **Queenybus**
XI, Törökbálinti út 28
Tel. 247–71 59

DANUBE CRUISES

► **Legenda Ltd.**
XI, Fraknó utca 4, tel. 317–22 03
www.legenda.hu

► **Mahart Tours**
V, Belgrád rakpart, tel. 318–15 86
www.mahartpassnave.hu

AIR TOURS

► **Indicator Rt.**
Budaörs Airport
XI, Koöérberki út 36, tel: 249–98 24

► **Sup-Air Ballon Club**
Tel. 322–00

Transport

Public Transport

www.bkv.hu

Urban public transport in Budapest is run by **BKV**. This includes **suburban trains HÉV**, the **metro** (underground), **trams**, **trolley buses** and ordinary **buses** which, as a rule, operate between 4am and 11pm, with a 24-hour service on some routes.

HÉV

The four routes of the suburban rail service HÉV provide rapid transport between the city centre and suburbs, as well as to the neighbouring towns of Gödöllö, Csepel, Ráckeve and Szentendre.

Metro

The underground consists of three lines. Line 1 was inaugurated in 1896 and is therefore the oldest underground on the European mainland; it was incorporated in the UNESCO World Heritage list in 2002. An east-west connection was opened in 1973, and a north-south route in 1979. The metro network is still being expanded.

Other city transport

The narrow-gauge railway on Széchenyi-hegy (hill), the chairlift up János-hegy (hill), the cable car onto Castle Hill, the Danube boats and the mini bus operating on Margaret Island, are all leisure and excursion transport, as is the children's railway on Szabadság-hegy (hill), which is 11km/7mi long.

Tickets

Tickets for all public transport can be bought at ticket booths at all underground stations, at all tram and suburban train (HÉV) terminals, as well as at bus terminals, and at many newspaper kiosks and hotel receptions. Tickets must be validated on entering the relevant transport. Travelling without a valid ticket is punished by heavy fines. Single tickets are not valid for changing to another vehicle.

Budapest Underground Plan

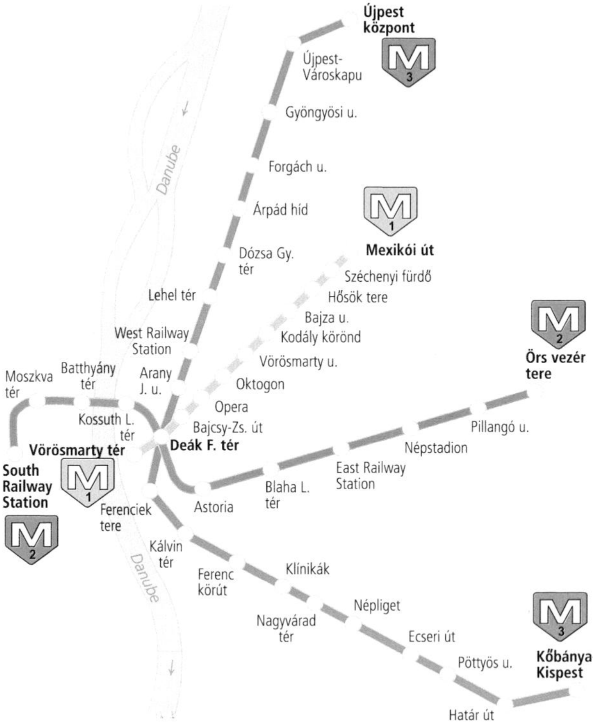

Újpest központ
Újpest-Városkapu
Gyöngyösi u.
Forgách u.
Árpád híd
Dózsa Gy. tér
Lehel tér
West Railway Station
Arany J. u.
Mexikói út
Széchenyi fürdő
Hősök tere
Bajza u.
Kodály körönd
Vörösmarty u.
Oktogon
Opera
Bajcsy-Zs. út
Deák F. tér
Vörösmarty tér
Örs vezér tere
Pillangó u.
Népstadion
East Railway Station
Blaha L. tér
Astoria
Moszkva tér
Batthyány tér
Kossuth L. tér
South Railway Station
Ferenciek tere
Kálvin tér
Ferenc körút
Klinikák
Nagyvárad tér
Népliget
Ecseri út
Pöttyös u.
Határ út
Kőbánya-Kispest
Danube

Line 1

Line 2

Line 3

There are single tickets, books of ten and twenty tickets, multi-line tickets for the metro, day tickets, as well as 3-day and 7-day tourist tickets. Furthermore, there are 14-day and 30-day passes that require a passport photo. Holders of the Budapest Card **Budapest Kártya** (► Prices, Discounts) can use the entire urban public transport network for free.

Narrow gauge railway, chairlift, cable car, local boats

The narrow-gauge railway up Szabadság-hegy (hill)), the chairlift up János-hegy (hill), the cable car on Castle Hill and the local boats on the Danube are also all run by the Budapest transport authority. Passenger boats operate from 1 May to 31 August between Boráros tér and Római fürdo (daily, 9am–4pm).

Regional transport

The rail and bus network plays an important role in regional transport. In the Budapest/Danube Bend area, passenger boats and car ferries run by the Mahart Shipping Company are also in service.

Taxi

Taxis have yellow number plates in Budapest. They are best ordered by phone. They normally arrive at the requested location within ten minutes. Many taxi drivers have at least basic knowledge of English. Every taxi has to have a taxi meter installed, and visitors should make sure it is switched on.

TAXI FIRMS

► **Budataxi**
Tel. 233–33 33

► **City-Taxi**
Tel. 211–11 11

► **Foötaxi**
Tel. 222–22 22, toll-free number:
tel. 06 80/22 22 22

► **Rádiótaxi**
Tel. 377–77 77

► **Taxi 2000**
Tel. 200–00 00

► **Tele 5**
355–55 55

► **6 x 6 Volántaxi**
Tel. 266–66 66

Railway

Budapest is an important national and international transport hub. Rail transport is served by three major railway stations. There are daily trains from Budapest to a wide range of destinations in other European countries (► Arrival). Express trains provide connections between Budapest and all other important Hungarian cities.

Airport

Located 16km/10mi south east of the city centre, Ferihegy airport is Hungary's only international airport. It is served by many, mostly European, airlines. The national airline Malév and its partners bring visitors from all over the world to the Hungarian capital; an increasing number of airborne visitors are also coming in from Tel Aviv, New York and Montréal.

Ports

One of the largest Danube ports is on the western bank of the Danube island Csepel, at the southern end of the city. It has both an international and national free port. 8% of all imports destined for the Hungarian capital arrive at Csepel. The most important goods are building materials, fuel, oil products, iron ores and animal feed.

Passenger boats

Hydrofoils regularly travel between Budapest and Vienna, from April to October. Furthermore, cruise boats regularly stop in Budapest, travelling between Passau (Germany) and the Black Sea. Numerous tour boats also cover the river route between Esztergom and Budapest (the so-called Danube Bend) during spring, summer and autumn.

Travellers with Disabilities

Despite recent efforts, Hungary falls far short of modern European standards in relation to its public provision of disabled access. People with reduced mobility will find a visit to Budapest is not exactly made easy. Only a few buildings and sights are accessible by wheelchair without help.

USEFUL ADDRESSES

UNITED KINGDOM

► **RADAR**
12 City Forum, 250 City Road,
London EC1V 8AF
Tel. (020) 72 50 32 22
www.radar.org.uk

USA

► **SATH (Society for the Advancement of Travel for the Handicapped**
347 5th Ave., no. 610
New York, NY 10016:
Tel. (21) 4 47 72 84
www.sath.org

When to Go

The best time to travel is between the months April to October. Spring and autumn are especially attractive. It can get very dry and hot in the summer, and not a lot goes on in Budapest in August.

MAGNUM
CALIPPO

Hungary is one of Europe's sunniest countries. It gets quieter in Budapest during the cold time of year, roughly from mid-October, and the tourist trade only revives again during the Christmas holidays and around New Year. Remember that Hungarian winters can be very cold.

← *Paprika in all its forms: hardly a traveller returns home without buying some of the red spice.*

10

Tours

THE HIGHLIGHTS OF BUDAPEST IN THE FOLLOWING TOURS ARE WONDERFUL, BUT DON'T FORGET TO MAKE YOUR OWN DISCOVERIES IN THE QUIET SIDE STREETS.

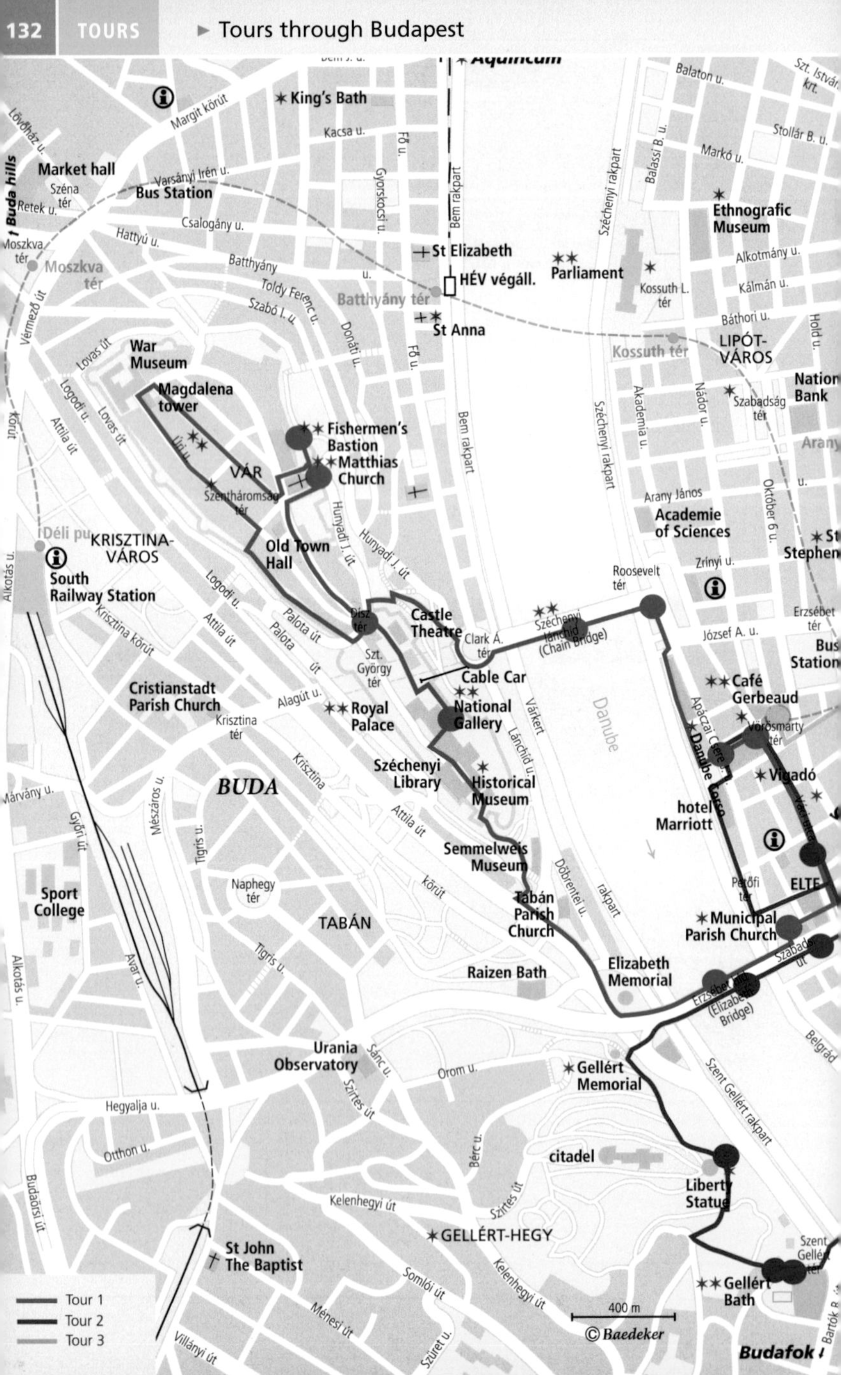
King's Bath
Market hall
Bus Station
War Museum
Magdalena tower
Fishermen's Bastion
Matthias Church
VÁR
Old Town Hall
Castle Theatre
Cable Car
National Gallery
Royal Palace
Széchenyi Library
Historical Museum
Semmelweis Museum
Tabán Parish Church
Raizen Bath
Elizabeth Memorial
St Elizabeth
HÉV végáll.
St Anna
Parliament
Ethnografic Museum
LIPÓTVÁROS
Nation Bank
Academie of Sciences
Café Gerbeaud
Vigadó
hotel Marriott
Danube Corso
ELTE
Municipal Parish Church
KRISZTINAVÁROS
South Railway Station
Cristianstadt Parish Church
BUDA
TABÁN
Sport College
Urania Observatory
Gellért Memorial
citadel
Liberty Statue
GELLÉRT-HEGY
St John The Baptist
Gellért Bath
Danube
Tour 1
Tour 2
Tour 3
400 m
© Baedeker
Budafok

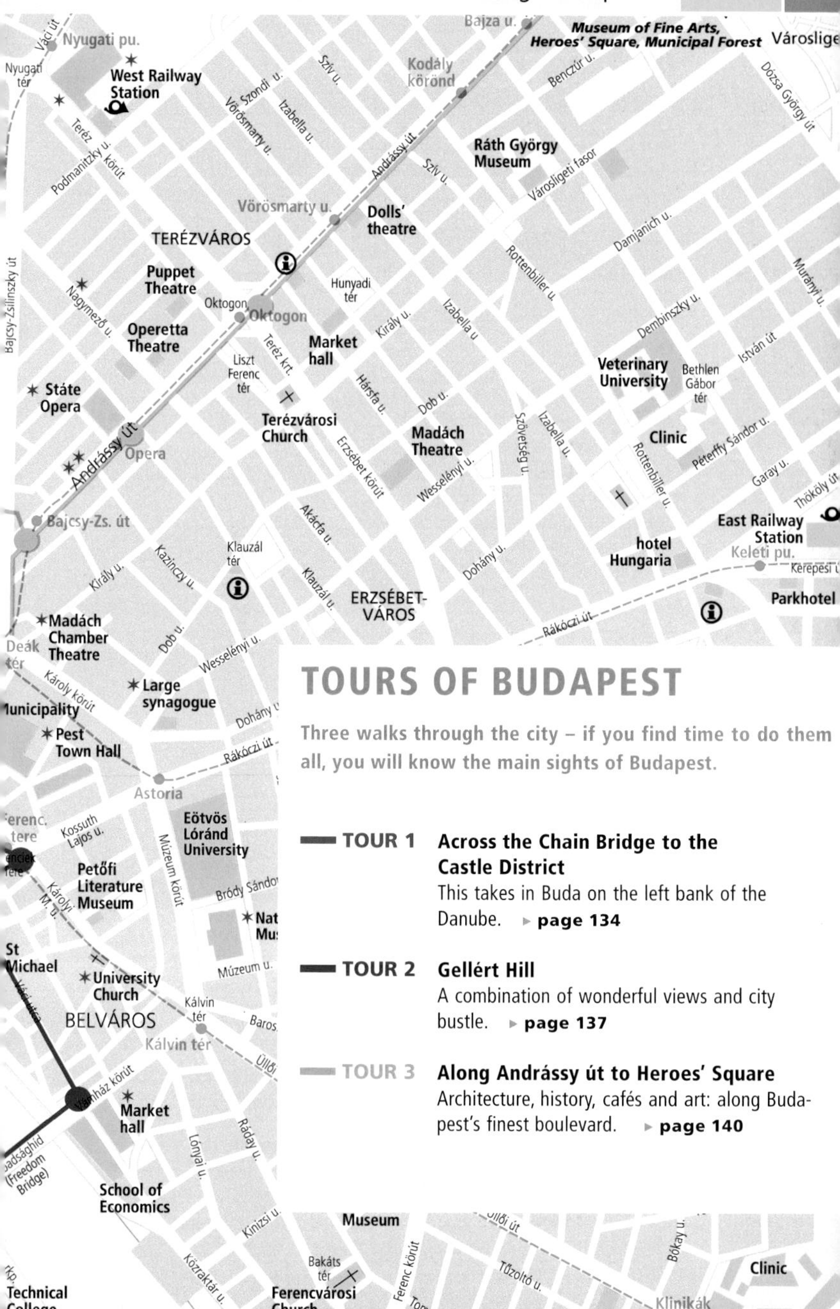

TOURS OF BUDAPEST

Three walks through the city – if you find time to do them all, you will know the main sights of Budapest.

TOUR 1 **Across the Chain Bridge to the Castle District**
This takes in Buda on the left bank of the Danube. ► **page 134**

TOUR 2 **Gellért Hill**
A combination of wonderful views and city bustle. ► **page 137**

TOUR 3 **Along Andrássy út to Heroes' Square**
Architecture, history, cafés and art: along Budapest's finest boulevard. ► **page 140**

Getting Around in Budapest

In the age of cheap flights, it is just a short and inexpensive trip to Budapest from other European countries. In theory, even a day trip is feasible. Nevertheless, this city is so rich in sights that it really deserves at least three days. The good news for weekend visitors is that in Budapest the shops open on Sundays. If you extend the weekend to Monday, however, it would be a good idea to reserve Sunday for museums, since almost all of them are shut on Mondays. Much can be seen on foot in Budapest, but to save energy it is recommended to take a tram occasionally for longer distances. Driving a car in this confusing city is a challenge that non-residents should avoid. Car parks are few and far between, while traffic jams and road works are common! Accommodation in all price categories is available everywhere: due to their central location the fifth and ninth quarters on the Pest side are especially pleasant. On the other side of the Danube it is quieter, though noticeably less convenient. In any event, it is a good idea to consider local transport connections when choosing a base.

! *Baedeker* TIP

Metro, bus and train for free

The cost of public transport in central Budapest is already low compared with other major cities, but those in possession of a Budapest Card (►Practicalities, Prices and Discounts) can travel as the mood takes them, without having the trouble of getting tickets. In addition, entrance fees for many museums and sights are also covered, so it is almost always worth buying the card.

Tour 1 Across the Chain Bridge to the Castle District

Start and finish: Vörösmarty tér **Duration:** One day

This day tour leads along the Danube Corso to the Chain Bridge and over to the Buda side of the Hungarian capital. The Castle District with its numerous sights, including the Matthias Church, Fishermen's Bastion and Royal Palace, can reached either by cable car or on foot, returning via the Elizabeth Bridge.

O On the north-west side of ❶ ✶ **Vörösmarty tér** Vigadó utca leads past the – in comparison with its frontage – drab side of the Vigadó concert hall and ballroom ❷ ✶ **Vigadó** to the Danube Corso, where the bronze princess by Lászlo Marton sits on the railings claiming the admiration due to her. The Danube Corso is Budapest's most popular and best-known promenade, lined by numerous street cafés and several architecturally nondescript five-star hotels on one side, and by the tramline, the busy Belgrád rakpart and the Danube on the other side. Stroll north on the Corso to Gresham Palace on ❸ **Roosevelt tér**, which today houses the Four Seasons, probably the city's most stylish hotel. A peek into the lobby or a coffee in the Gresham Kávéház is highly recommended. From here the ❹ ✶✶ **Chain Bridge** leads over the Danube to Clark Ádam tér on the Buda side, where a cable car (Sikló) covers the short distance up to the ❺ ✶✶ **Castle District.** As an alternative to the Sikló, walk up to Dísz tér via the Royal Steps (Királylépcskö), which are north-west of the cable car's lower terminus. Beyond the square, a rather forlorn statue of a hussar awaits company. Between the bus stop behind the statue and a not particularly attractive café is the start of Tóth Árpad sétány, a pretty tree-lined promenade that leads along the south-west exterior wall of Castle District and offers beautiful views onto the lower Buda quarters of the city. Continue on Szentháromság utca, turning off to the right for a short break at the square that opens out by Café Miró. Friends of the Spanish artist can choose to visit the café designed in his surrealist style, while those with more traditional

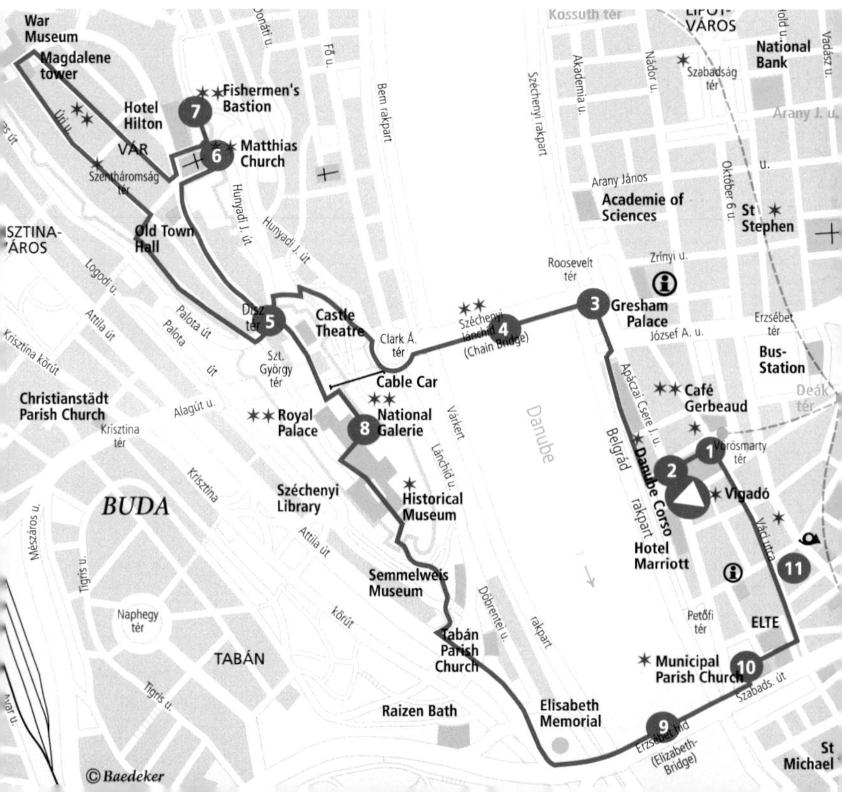

tastes take a few steps further and try to get a seat in Café Ruszwurm. If you have time, follow the atmospheric Úri utca with its Gothic architectural details, heading away from the Matthias Church, all the way to the tower of the Magdalene Church, and then onwards to Szentháromság tér, either via Országház utca or alternatively via Fortuna utca. If you have less time, walk to the end of Szentháromság utca, past the former Buda town hall, directly to Szentháromság tér, where a visit to the ❻ ✶✶ **Matthias Church** constitutes one of the main attractions of Budapest. Immediately next door, the ❼ ✶✶ **Fishermen's Bastion** is a wonderful place for enjoying a view of the city. Return to Dísz tér via Tárnok utca. Cross the square and follow Színház utca, past the Castle Theatre and Sándor Palace all the way to Szent György tér, to reach a neo-Baroque archway on the south-eastern side – eyed suspiciously by the eagle Turul – which gives admittance to the forecourt of the ❽ ✶✶ **Royal Palace** with an equestrian statue of Prince Eugene. A passage leads to another castle forecourt with the Matthias Well Matthias Well and the entrance to the Ludwig Museum. Walk through the Lion Gate to the inner court of the castle, with the main entrances to the Széchenyi National Library and the Budapest Historical Museum, as well as the side entrance to the Hungarian National Gallery. A passage by the Historical Museum leads to the south-facing medieval fortifications of the castle, with the castle tower at their south-western end. From the foot of the tower there is a wonderful view across the Tabán quarter of the city, with its parish church and the Danube flowing behind it, and the Elizabeth and Liberty Bridges. Leave the castle fortifications via the steps at the castle tower. Walk down past the Golden Stag tavern to the bridgehead of Erzsébet híd, with its memorial to the legendary Elizabeth, Empress of Austria and Queen of Hungary, better known as Sisi. Cross the ❾ **Elisabeth Bridge** to the Pest side and pass the ❿ ✶ **inner city parish church** on the left. An archway gives access to the constant melée of ⓫ ✶ **Váci utca,** which leads back to ❶ ✶ **Vörösmarty tér,** where the cakes and coffee of the legendary coffee house Gerbeaud, along with an interesting interior, are a pleasant conclusion to the tour.

Tour 2 Gellért Hill

Start and finish: Vörösmarty tér **Length:** At least six hours

This tour starts from Pest city centre, crossing the Elizabeth Bridge to begin a scenically attractive walk up Gellért Hill with its numerous viewpoints, returning past the Gellért Baths and reaching the Pest side once more via Liberty Bridge.

← *A famous view: particularly photogenic in the evening or morning*

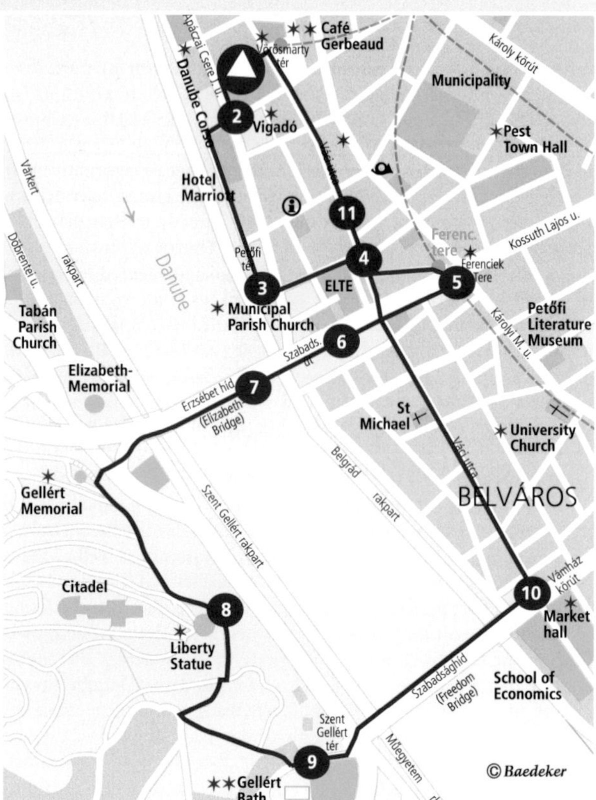

Just as on Tour 1, set off from ❶ ✶ **Vörösmarty tér,** and follow Vigadó utca to the imposing frontage of the ❷ ✶ **Vigadó** concert hall. Beyond Vigadó tér stroll along the Danube Corso in a southerly direction, ignoring the tasteless Marriot Hotel to the left.

A few steps further along the Danube Corso lies ❸ **Petőfi tér** with its bronze statue of the Hungarian poet and the Greek Orthodox Church on its east side. Immediately behind the memorial to Petőfi, take Pesti Barnabás utca to the left all the way to ❹ ✶ **Váci utca**. Leave Március 15th tér on the right and follow Váci utca south for a few paces before turning left onto Kigyó utca, which leads to ❺ ✶ **Ferenciek ter**. It would be a good idea to plan brief stops at Parisi utca shopping arcade and the Franciscan Church. Szabad sajtó út leads back to the Danube and past the Clotilde Palaces and the ❻ ✶ **Inner city parish church** to the ❼ **Elizabeth Bridge**, and the Buda side. From the bridge there is already a great view of the Gellért Memorial and the artificial waterfall beneath. Beautifully designed steps lead to the memorial past both sides of the waterfall. From

Inside Gellért Bath

there choose the path in a south-east direction for wonderful views of the city. After a few minutes of easy walking, the highest point of ❽ ✶ **Gellért Hill** is reached, with its imposing Liberation Monument and Citadella. To get to the famous ❾ ✶✶ **Gellért Bath**, descend through Jubilee Park. A few step along from the Citadella, it is worth visiting the Rock Chapel, a quiet place in a natural cave that is pleasantly cool, even on hot days. Liberty Bridge leads back to Pest and ❿ **Fövám tér**, where the lively scenes of the central market hall await. A variety of spices, fruit and vegetables, meat and sausages, spirits and much more can be found here. Return to the starting point of the tour via the much quieter, though no less attractive southern part of ⓫ ✶ **Váci utca** and then the livelier northern section of the shopping street.

Tour 3 Along Andrássy út to Heroes' Square

Start and finish: Vörösmarty tér – Heroes' Square **Length:** At least three hours

This tour follows the busy Andrássy út, designed as a fine boulevard in 1872, to Heroes' Square and the wooded Városliget park, where there are pedaloes on the lake. Return to Vörösmarty tér and the starting point of this extended walk with the historic underground railway (M 1), a cosy and bumpy version of a city metro line.

Leaving ❶ ✱ **Vörösmarty tér** follow Deák Ferenc utca to Deák Ferenc tér (►Little Ring). Then take Bajcsy-Zsilinszky út in a northerly direction and turn right onto ❷ ✱✱ **Andrássy út**. Before turning off, however, it is worth strolling a bit further along Bajcsy-Zsilinszky út, in order to give ❸ ✱ **St Stephen's Basilica** the attention it deserves. There are several significant sights along Andrássy út. After just a few steps the imposing ❹ ✱ **State Opera House** appears on the left. Drechsler Palace, exactly opposite, is also noteworthy. A few steps further on, the beautiful Müvesz Coffee House (Andrássy út 29) provides an opportunity for a short break with coffee and cake. Alternatively, leave the Oktogon, where the ❺ **Great Ring** crosses Andrássy út, behind you and marvel at the richly decorated interior of the Lukács Coffee House (Andrássy út 70). Once Andrássy út opens onto ❻ ✱ **Heroes' Square**, you have walked the entire length of Budapest's show street. If the pedestrian route along Andrássy út is too far, it is always possible to shorten the distance by taking metro line 1, which runs underneath the street. The ❼ ✱✱ **National Museum of Fine Arts** on the north-west side of Heroes' Square exhibits Budapest's most important art collection, and the entrance steps

Contemplative rest in an autumnal Városliget woods

to this classical building are an ideal place from which to observe life on the square. From the northern end of the square Állatkerti körút leads past Budapest's gourmet restaurant Gundel and the art nouveau entrance of the Zoological and Botanical Gardens to wooded park of 8 ✶ **Városliget**. Immediately behind the Széchenyi Baths a path leads off to the right to Kós Károly sétány, on which a right turn will take you to Vajdahunyad Castle. For the return to Heroes' Square, cross the castle island – not forgetting to take note of the expressive Anonymous Memorial – to the bridge beyond, and take a right turn along the shores of the lake. From the square there is a direct metro connection (line 1) back to Vörösmarty tér.

Sights from A to Z

BUDAPEST'S GOLDEN AGE WAS DURING THE TIME OF THE HABSBURG DUAL MONARCHY, WHEN MOST OF THE SIGHTS WERE BUILT. CASTLE HILL, PARLIAMENT, THE DANUBE PROMENADE: THERE IS MUCH TO DISCOVER ...

★ Andrássy út

C–E 4–6

Location: VI district
Bus: 4, 105

Underground: M 1 (Bajcsy-Zsilinszky út – Hosök tere)

Budapest's glorious boulevard, begun in 1872, has been a UNESCO World Heritage site since 2002. Villas, mansions and important cultural institutions such as the state opera line its majestic course.

Glorious boulevard

Andrássy út runs for a distance of 2.5km/1.5mi in a north-easterly direction out of the city, from ►Erzsébet tér to ► Hosök tere (Heroes' Square), with the Millennium Column as the visual endpoint. Two spacious squares, the Oktogon and Kodály körönd, interrupt its course. **Continental Europe's oldest underground railway**, affectionately called the »Little One« by Budapest's inhabitants, has been running underneath Andrássy út since 1896. The oldest carriages can be seen at the Underground Museum on Deák Ferenc tér (►Baedeker Tip, p.192).

Postal Museum, Saxlehner Mansion

The museum of the Hungarian postal service (Postamúzeum, no. 3) is housed in a mansion that was built for the businessman Saxlehner by Györö Czigler in 1886. The entrance hall and staircase of this former apartment block still has a ceiling fresco by Károly Lotz. The museum on the first floor contains, in addition to documents on the development of the Hungarian postal service, a few items of equipment, including Emperor Franz Joseph I's telephone. (Opening times: April–Oct Tue–Sun 10am–6pm, Nov–March Tue–Sun 10am–4pm).

Drechsler Mansion

Opposite the state opera, the Drechsler Mansion is worth noting. It was built in 1882 by the two leading exponents of Hungarian art nouveau, Ödön Lechner und Gyula Pártos. Today it is home to the state ballet school. Andrássy út passes the ►State Opera House and crosses Nagymezö utca, also known as »Pest's Broadway«, because of its many nightclubs and theatres, and reaches Jókai tér, with its Mór Jókai memorial built by Alajos Stróbl. On the other side of the street, young musicians are trained at the world-famous ►Franz Liszt Academy of Music on Liszt Ferenc tér.

Oktogon

The Great Ring crosses Andrássy út at the Oktogon. Even though this eight-sided square has been re-named several times throughout its history, it has always been the Oktogon for the people of Budapest. It is uniformly lined by tall apartment blocks and businesses in historicist style, which give it both architectural unity and a sense of space. Andrássy út becomes a boulevard after the Oktogon. Narrow streets running parallel, originally riding paths, flank the main traffic artery.

Originally head office for the national socialist Arrow Cross Party and, after the war, seat of the Communist state security services, **Andrássy út no. 60**, with its interrogation rooms and prison cells, was a notorious address in the 1940s and 1950s. Today the »House of Terror« is not so much a museum as a multi-media memorial (unfortunately almost entirely in Hungarian), recalling Hungary's grim era of totalitarian rule.

House of Terror

Opening hours: Tue–Fri, 10am–6pm, Sat–Sun, 10am–7.30pm

The most noteworthy buildings on the section between the Oktogon and the circular Kodály körönd is the magnificent building (no. 67) on the corner of Andrássy út and Vörösmarty utca, built in the style of an Italian Renaissance palace by Alois Lang, in 1879. The Academy of Music founded by Franz Liszt had its original home here, (► Famous People) (► Franz Liszt Academy of Music) and since its restoration in the 1980s the academy has used it once more. The composer's former apartment in this building is now a museum on the first floor (Liszt Ferenc Emlékmúzeum). The reconstructed interior of the three rooms – bedroom and office, dining room, and sitting room – in part with Liszt's own furniture, is augmented by books, scores, memorabilia and a few musical instruments, including the small glass piano in his office, Liszt's favourite Bösendorfer piano, as well as his Chickering concert grand piano. (Entrance: Vörösmarty utca 35).

Liszt Museum

Opening hours: Mon–Fri 10am–6pm Sat 9am–5pm, closed during the first three weeks of August. Internet www.liszt-museum.hu

In the tradition-rich coffeehouses Lukács

At Andrássy út no. 70, **Lukács coffee house** recalls the last years of the 19th century. The original interior has a preservation order, and only the guests have made the transition to the present.

Kodály körönd is a beautifully designed circus, named after the great Hungarian composer Zoltán Kodály (► Famous People). Statues of Hungarian freedom fighters and national heroes decorate its green spaces.

The former **home of the composer Kodály** stands where Kodály körönd leads into the last section of Andrássy út, and is now accessible as a museum (Kodály körönd 1; opening times: Wed 10am–4pm, Thu–Sat 10am–6pm, Sun 10am–2pm). It is easily recognized from the commemorative plaque for Zoltán Kodály outside.

★ Aquincum

Excursion

Location: Óbuda, Szentendrei út 139 **Suburban train HÉV:** Aquincum
Bus: 42, 106

Traces of the Roman past can be found at various places in the Budapest district of Óbuda, but they are especially impressive at Aquincum, where the foundations of a civil settlement have been excavated since the 1870s.

Roman settlement Today the excavation site is open to the public and the most valuable finds are exhibited in a small museum ►(see below). The remains of the garrison, which preceded the civil settlement, lie a little closer to the city centre, near Flórian tér (►Óbuda). The garrison and settlement extended almost all the way to Gellért Hill, and also covered the Danube island at Aquincum, as well as the east bank of the Danube, where the Romans built the fortification Contra-Aquincum close to today's Elizabeth Bridge (►Március 15. tér)
The Romans conquered Transdanubia around the year 10 BC and established the province of Pannonia. A few years after the birth of Christ, they founded a garrison on the terrain of Budapest's present-day district of Óbuda, around which the city of Aquincum soon developed. This flourishing settlement was already the provincial capital of Pannonia Inferior by the beginning of the 2nd century AD. During its heyday in the first half of the 3rd century AD, around 50,000 people lived in Aquincum. Emperor Septimius Severus raised the city to the status of a Colonia in AD 194. Aquincum's decline came after the defeat of the Roman legions at Hadrianopolis and Roman withdrawal from Pannonia in AD 378, and was accelerated by increasingly severe invasions by the Huns.

★★ Archaeological Museum The rooms of the Archaeological Museum, opened in 1894, display items from religious cults, sculptures, fragments of mosaics, tools, containers, coins and jewellery. Among the most valuable exhibits are the famous portable water organ dating from AD 228, the Jupiter column, a marble Diana and Minerva, a Mithras statue, a manuscript dated AD 19, which is the oldest written document so far found in Hungary, and ivory and horn carvings. Several stone artefacts such as altars, tombstones and reliefs stand in the pillar hall and in the lapidarium. (Opening times: 15–30 April and October: Tue–Sun 9am–5pm; May–Sept: Tue–Sun 9am–6pm).

Ruins The ruins around the museum give an idea of the planned Roman city, around 400m x 600m (450yd x 650yd) in size, which in addition to numerous, mostly one-storey private homes, encompassed several baths, a market hall, a Mithras sanctuary and a basilica. The remains of the ancient water and sewage system, including water pipes, canals

Aquincum Plan

and heating installations, are interesting not only for experts. An aqueduct was exposed during the extension of Szentendrei út, a broad arterial road that leads all the way to the small town of Szentendre. Individual sections can still be seen along the side of the road or on the central reservation between traffic lanes.

Amphitheatre Diagonally across from the excavation site, on the other side of Szentendrei út and very close to the HEV Aquincum station, remains of the Roman city's amphitheatre were revealed during excavations in 1880 and 1937. Originally, it measured around 80m x 90m (90yd x 100yd) and could hold 7500 spectators. A restored section of the ancient city walls can also be seen here.

★★ Arts and Crafts Museum

(Iparmüvészeti Múzeum)

D 8

Location: IX district, Üllöi út 33–37
Underground: M 3 (Ferenc körút)
Tram: 4, 6

The Budapest Arts and Crafts Museum is one of the oldest of its kind. Not just the collection, but also the architectural surroundings in which it is presented, make a visit worthwhile.

Art nouveau **Ödön Lechner** (1845–1914), the most important proponent of Hungarian art nouveau, designed the three-storey building at Üllöi út, which opened its doors in 1896. In contrast to his work on the later ►Post Savings Bank building, Lechner still had recourse to past – especially oriental – architectural forms for the Arts and Crafts Museum, and melded them with national elements from Hungarian folk art into a new style. Granite tiles and roof tiles in colourful patterns from the Zsolnay factory in Pécs enliven the façade. To the right of the main entrance stands a statue of the architect, created by Béla Farkas in 1936. The central inner courtyard, which is covered by a glass roof, and the ticket hall in front of it almost appear like a fairy tale with their mixture of Indian and Moorish designs. The construction with its unclad steel supports, similar to the West Railway Station, (►Great Ring) was highly modern at the time.

Exhibition The exhibition on the **ground floor** around the courtyard covers Hungarian domestic culture from the Biedermeier era up to the start of the 20th century (approx. 1850–1900). Furniture, craftwork, carpets and other interior design items are shown in individual rooms that each represent a specific historical style or fashion. On the **first floor**, in similar manner to the rooms on the ground floor, it is possible to get a realistic idea of domestic life from the classical to Bie-

Oriental dream: glass-covered courtyard in the Arts and Crafts Museum

dermeier era (approx. 1800–1850). The dome hall and the east wing accommodate five further departments on the development of Hungarian arts and crafts.

Batthyány tér (Batthyány Square)

B 5

Suburban train HÉV: Batthyány tér
Tram: 19
Underground: M 2 (Batthyány tér)
Bus: 11, 39, 60

This square, named after the first prime minister of the independent Hungarian Republic, Count Lajos Batthyány (1806–1849), has always stood at the heart of Watertown (► Víziváros), the district between Castle Hill and the Danube (I district).

The heart of Watertown

Batthyány tér used to be a marketplace. Today it is the end of the line for the suburban HÉV train coming from ►Szentendre to Budapest, as well as for the Underground and several bus routes. A few of the old houses on the square lie below street level, which emphasizes even further the height of St Anne's Church, on the south side of Batthyány tér, making it appear even taller in relation to its surroundings.

✶ St Anne's Church

Batthyány tér is dominated by the building of St Anne's Church (Szent Anna-templom), whose imposing double-tower frontage oc-

St Anne's Church

cupies the southern side of the square. This church, built between 1740 and 1758 to plans by Christoph Hamom and Matthäus Nepauer, is one of the most beautiful Baroque buildings in Budapest. It was restored in the late 1950s, after severe damage in the 19th century and especially during the Second World War. The three-bay main façade has impressively balanced proportions. St Anne and the Virgin can be seen in the framed niche above the main entrance. The tympanum bears the coat of arms of Buda and a symbol for the Holy Trinity.

The ground plan of the church – typically for Baroque architecture – only becomes apparent in the interior. It consists of an oval nave and choir and two chapels. The tall, extravagantly decorated high altar and the pulpit, which was later redesigned, belong to the original interior of the church and presumably derive from the workshop of the sculptor Carlo Bebo. The marble panelling and the frescoes on the central dome are 20th-century additions by Pál Molnár and Béla Kontuly. The fresco in the choir illustrating the Holy Trinity was done by Gregor Vogl in 1772. The sculptures by Anton Eberhard by the side altars, as well as altar panels by the Viennese painter Franz Wagenschön, are worth seeing.

The White Cross

Compared to St Anne's Church, the other buildings – except for the market hall dating from 1902 to its right – appear rather small. This also goes for the former inn called The White Cross (no. 4), which sinks into the street and now has a less impressive appearance. The house grew out of the combination of two buildings in 1770; while the right half displays Baroque forms, the left one is Rococo in style. Another wing was added between the two courtyards behind the arched gateway in the 19th century. Here theatrical performances and balls were held.

Hickisch House

Hickisch House (Hickisch-ház; no. 3) was built in late Rococo style in 1795 and is named after its former owner, the mason Christoph Hickisch. The relief on the façade represents the four seasons of the year.

Buda Hills (Budai-hegység)

A/B 1–11

Location: Western edge of the city

The Buda hills form a natural western border to the Hungarian capital. The heights, which are mostly wooded, have long been a popular destination for short excursions.

Recreational area

The dense network of footpaths, viewing points and platforms in this pleasant hilly countryside testify to the region's attractions, which include, among others, a train operated by children, a narrow-gauge railway, a chairlift, and inns. The hills consist of dolomite and chalk, as well as clay and marl.

> ! *Baedeker* TIP
>
> **Tour of the Buda Hills**
>
> A pleasant relaxing tour through the Buda Hills begins and ends at Moszkva tér, where numerous bus and rail routes converge. From there walk to the valley station of the narrow-gauge railway at the western edge of Városmajor Park, and ride up Széchenyi-hegy. A few yards from the summit station, can get onto the children's railway, and ride to »János-hegy« station, where a great view can be had by climbing to the top of the hill. The route passes the hill station of the chairlift below János-hegy (John Hill); but to take the chairlift it is first necessary to descend from the summit (daily, 9.30am–4pm, closed every other Monday). Near the valley stop, bus route 158 returns to the starting point.

The **Hármashatár-hegy** (Three Border Hill; 497m/1630ft) rises on the northern border of Budapest and offers a beautiful view of Óbuda from its almost bare summit. Just over one mile north-west of Three Border Hill, as the crow flies, good views are also to be had on Csúcs-hegy (445m/1460ft).

There is an extensive cave system all around Budapest. To the south, in the Paul Valley beneath Hármashatár-hegy, two **dripstone caves** are open to the public. They were discovered in 1904.(Pál-völgy Cave, Szépvölgy út 162, opening times: Tue– Sun 10am–4pm; Szemlö-hegy Cave, Pusztaszeri út 35, opening times: Wed–Mon 10am–4pm). ⏲

János-hegy (John Hill)

John Hill rises to the west of Buda. At 529m/1735ft, it is the Hungarian capital's highest elevation, and from the almost 24m/79ft-tall viewing tower completed in 1910 a magnificent panorama can be enjoyed. John Hill has also become attractive for winter sports enthusiasts since the installation of a **chairlift**, a ski jump and a piste with t-bar lift.

Szabadság-hegy (Freedom Hill)

In the west of the city rises Szabadság-hegy (Freedom Hill). During the age of the Turkish wars there was a garrison here, mostly of soldiers from south-west Germany. In the course of time, wealthy Budapest locals settled on the hillsides. Today it is a sought-after residential area, complete with attractive villas from the late 19th century and architecturally noteworthy modern bungalows.

Széchenyi-hegy

A **narrow gauge railway** runs from Városmajor Park up Szabadság-hegy, and also Széchenyi Hill behind it (439m/1440ft), which is topped by a transmitting station of the Hungarian television company. Several hotels and recreational hostels are also located here in very beautiful surroundings.

★★ Castle District (Buda)

A/B 5–7

Location: Castle Hill
Bus: 5, 16, 78
Cable car: Clark Adám tér–Szent György tér

A stroll along the almost entirely pedestrianized streets and lanes of Castle District is one of the most pleasant experiences the Hungarian capital has to offer.

With its predominantly Baroque buildings, the old centre of Buda on Castle Hill, between Bécsi kapu tér (Viennese Gate) and Szent György tér, has managed to maintain its charm to this day. It is not just the highlights, such as the ► Matthias Church that make the Castle District a prime destination, but also the numerous architectural details, niches and courtyards that can be discovered here.
Buda's Castle Hill, consisting of the Castle District and the ► Royal Palace, is listed as a UNESCO World Heritage site, along with Budapest's Danube panorama, ► Andrássy út and the historic underground railway.

History

The Hungarians recognized the strategic significance of the solitary club-shaped hill (168m/551ft) on the right bank of the Danube in the 13th century, under King Béla IV, and built Buda Castle at its south-eastern tip, which soon became the residence of Hungarian kings. To the north-west, on the Castle Hill plateau, a city developed in tandem and became, for a long time, the glittering heart of the country. It was largely destroyed during the Turkish wars, and the city was rebuilt in the Baroque style during the 17th and 18th centuries. Buda, which rapidly also expanded downwards (► Víziváros), merged with the neighbouring small town of Óbuda to the north, and was amalgamated with Óbuda and Pest in 1873 to become the capital city of Budapest. The Castle District suffered heavy destruction once more during the Second World War. During reconstruction after the war, the medieval foundations and several beautiful details, such as the Gothic seat niches, were revealed in numerous houses.

The picturesque Castle District has no end of charm.

Main Streets and Squares

Tour

The following description of the Castle District is designed as a tour that begins in the north, at the Viennese Gate (which is also where the buses from Moskva tér arrive), and covers the most important sights.

Viennese Gate, Bécsi kapu tér

One of the main access points to Castle District is the northerly Bécsi kapu (Viennese Gate) at the place where the former Szombat kapu (Saturday Gate) once stood. It was built to plans by Jenö Lechner in 1936, on the occasion of the 250th anniversary of Buda's liberation from the Turks in 1686. A memorial tablet on the inside of the gate recalls the event.

Behind the Viennese Gate lies Bécsi kapu tér (Viennese Gate Square), on which the Saturday market was once held.

◄ Lutheran Church

Directly opposite Bécsi kapu square, on the tapering plot of land between Táncsics and Fortuna utca, stands the Lutheran Church (Evangélikus templom) built in 1896, in which organ concerts are held throughout the year.

◄ National Archive

To the right, adjacent to the Viennese Gate, is the neo-Romanesque National Archive (Országos Levéltár), built between 1915 and 1918. Several late Baroque and classical apartment blocks on the western side of Bécsi kapu tér deserve a look, especially the Lobner House (no. 5), with a beautiful stairwell in Hungarian late Rococo style, and the house at no. 7 built around 1800, with a façade adorned by portrait medallions of poets from antiquity.

Anjou Bastion

West of the Viennese Gate, behind the National Archive, is the Anjou Bastion (Anjou-bástya), the north-western section of the castle fortifications, which was fiercely contested during the liberation battles of 1686. There is a wonderful view over the western districts of Budapest and the Buda Hills from the bastion. In 1936, the Hungarians

Castle District Map

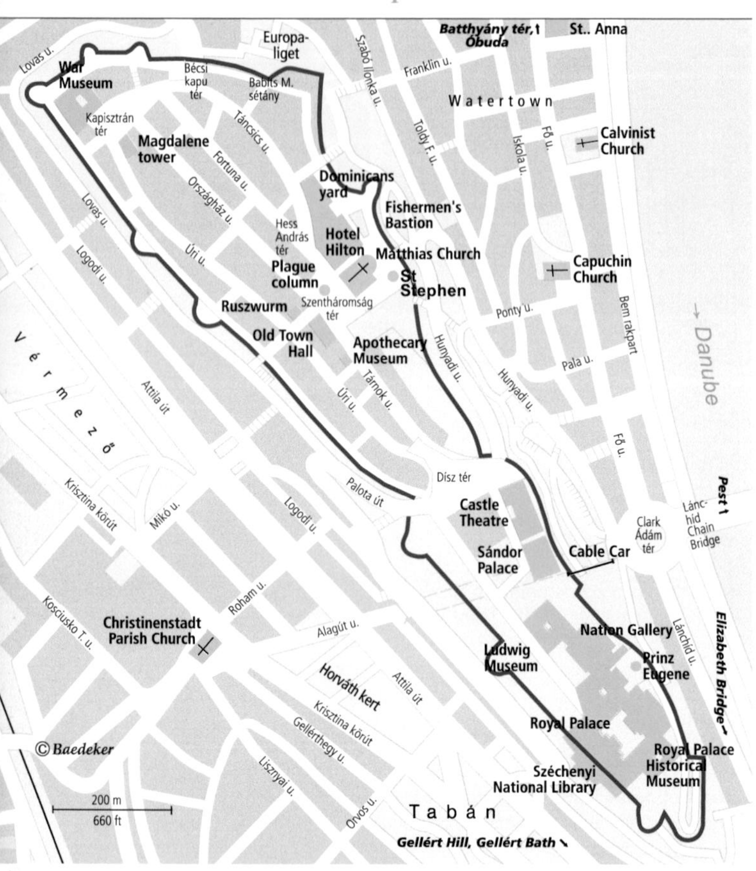

set a memorial to the last Turkish pasha of Buda, who fell here in 1686, on the second semi-circular protrusion of the Anjou Bastion.

Táncsics Mihály utca

From Bécsi kapu tér, Táncsics Mihály utca leads in a southerly direction towards Szentháromság tér (Holy Trinity Square). One of the oldest streets on Castle Hill, it was formerly called the Jewish Lane, but was then renamed after the author Mihály Táncsics.

National Monuments Office ►

The Hungarian National Monuments Office presents a remarkable exhibition in the building at no. 1 Táncsics Mihály utca, where, among other things, illustrations on the life and work of Hungary's most important master builders and architects are shown. (Opening times: daily 9am–4.30pm).

Museum of Music History ► The Museum of Music History has found a worthy home in the house at no. 7, an elegant Baroque mansion built between 1750 and 1769 to plans by Matthäus Nepauer. Musical instruments from different epochs are exhibited here, including those of an entire orchestra from the time of Joseph Haydn (1732–1809). A special exhibition is devoted to the life and work of Béla Bartók (► Famous People). Occasionally top-quality concerts are held in this building (opening times: April–Oct Tue–Sun 10am–6pm).

Medieval Jewish prayer house ► The history of the Jewish community of Buda, which lived in this part of the Castle District from the second half of the 14th century, is recalled in the small exhibition in the Gothic house at Táncsics utca 26. This former Jewish prayer house (Középkori Zsidó Imaház) was restored a few years ago. Fragments from the synagogue built in 1461 are shown in the courtyard, whose foundations were revealed in the garden behind house number 23. (Opening times: May–Oct Tue–Sun 10am–6pm).

Babits Mihály sétány ► From Táncsics Mihály utca, a passage between house numbers 17 and 21 gives access to the north-eastern part of the fortifications, leading to Mihály Babits Promenade, which extends all the way to the Viennese Gate (Bécsi kapu) to the north. There is a beautiful view of the city from here. At the foot of the walls lies the Europa Park (Europa-liget), which was established in 1972 on the occasion of the centenary of the amalgamation of Buda and Pest.

Hess András tér Hess András tér, which was named after the bookbinder Andreas Hess, lies at the junction of Fortuna utca and Táncsics utca. Hess was recalled to Buda in 1472, after having studied in Italy. In 1473, Hungary's first printed book, the *Chronica Hungarium*, was produced in his house at no. 4, now the Fortuna Restaurant. A memorial to Pope Innocent XI, made by József Damkó in 1936, decorates the square in honour of the man who instigated the Holy League against the Turks in 1686.

! *Baedeker* TIP

Carriage tour in the Castle District

The Castle District can be explored in great comfort in a horse-drawn carriage.

The Red Hedgehog ► The house with the red hedgehog as an emblem above its gate (Vörös sün ház) was one of the oldest taverns on Castle Hill. It was built on medieval foundations in the 17th and 18th centuries and was later given a classical façade.

Former Dominican monastery, Hilton Hotel ► The commanding building next to the ► Matthias Church is the luxury Hilton Hotel opened in 1976. Here the Hungarian architect Béla Pinter proved that it is possible for tradition and modernity to exist in close proximity. Fragments of buildings that stood at this spot in the Middle Ages were also incorporated into the new building in such a way that they too come into their own. These sections are parts of a former Dominican monastery, which already existed in Buda in the 13th century. The most significant remnant of the monastery is the late Gothic tower (Miklós-torony) of St Nicholas' Church. On its west wall, a copy of a 15th-century relief of Matthias Corvinus was fixed. It shows the Hungarian king with sceptre and royal orb in an architectural frame.

> ! **Baedeker TIP**
>
> **House of Hungarian Wine**
>
> There is undoubtedly no better opportunity to get to know the numerous wines of Hungary in their entirety (almost) than at the House of Hungarian Wine at Szentháromság tér no. 6. Over 80 wines are available for tasting daily, and over 400 quality and fine wines from 22 wine regions can be purchased (opening times: daily noon–8pm).

The main square of Castle District is **Szentháromság tér** (Holy Trinity Square), which is bordered by the ►Matthias Church to the east and the former Ministry of Finance, built by A. Fellner between 1901 and 1904, to the north.

◄ Plague column

In the middle of the square stands a magnificent Baroque plague column designed in 1714 by Philipp Ungleich from Würzburg to commemorate the epidemic of 1691. A representation of the Holy Trinity forms the tip of this 14m/46ft-high memorial, while the base is surrounded by saints. The emblems and reliefs on the pedestal are the work of the sculptor Antal Hörbinger. This plague column is a copy of the original monument, which was badly damaged during the Second World War.

The wide two-storey Baroque building on the corner of Szentháromság tér and Szentháromság utca was once Buda town hall, recognizable by the beautiful bay on the top floor. Today it is the seat of the language institute of the Hungarian Academy of Science. The Italian architect Venerio Ceresola supplied the plans to which the building was constructed in 1710, incorporating the medieval wall fragments of previous constructions. Later, an extension was built on Úri utca. The courtyard and the stairwell are also architecturally noteworthy. The statue of the Greek goddess Pallas Athene underneath the corner bay displays the coat of arms of Budapest emblem on her shield. The figure, which dates from 1785, is the work of the Italian Carlo Adami.

Café Ruszwurm

On narrow **Szentháromság utca**, which leads west from Holy Trinity Square all the way to the western wall of Castle Hill, a visit to **Café Ruszwurm** (Ruszwurm cukrászda; no. 7) is recommended. In business since 1827, its original Empire interior is still largely intact. The selection of cakes and pastries can certainly match those on offer at the Gerbeaud coffee house on ►Vörösmarty tér.

Tárnok utca The broad Tárnok utca (Treasurer Street), a lively shopping street in the past as well as now, leads from Holy Trinity Square to Dísz tér. Historic buildings mix with modern houses. This is where most foreign exchange booths and souvenir shops, as well as antique shops, taverns and boutiques, are to be found. The house with its eaves facing the street at Tárnok utca no. 14 and a façade covered with colourful geometric patterns is a typical example of the Gothic merchants' houses that once characterized Tárnok utca.

At Tárnok utca 18, the ground floor rooms housed the Arany Saspatika (Golden Eagle Pharmacy) in the 18th century. A merchant's house built in the 15th century, today it is home to the Apothecary Museum. This exhibition on the history of modern pharmacy from the 16th and 17th centuries occupies just four small rooms, but is nevertheless well worth seeing. (Opening times: Tue– Sun 10am–5pm).

Dísz tér At the southern end of the Castle District lies the spacious Dísz tér, once a showpiece square. In the Middle Ages, this square lined by imposing buildings in the Baroque and classical styles, such as the Batthyány Mansion (no. 4), was a marketplace. On the spot where a church burnt down, the Honvéd statue by György Zala has stood since 1893, recalling the liberation battles of 1848–49. The Italian architect Venerio Ceresola built the Kremsmünster House at Dísz tér 4–5, so-called because Kremsmünster Abbey owned the property. The Gothic seating niches dating from the 13th century, over which Ceresola built his new building, can still be seen in the entrance. The post office building next to Café Korona also contains medieval architectural fragments in its Baroque structure.

Decoration on the Apothecary Museum

Színház utca The Castle Theatre is south of Dísz tér, on Színház utca. The long building complex once housed a Carmelite nunnery which was dissolved by decree of the Austrian Emperor Joseph II in 1786. The commission to convert the convent and church into a theatre was given to Farkas Kempelen. The first drama for the stage in the Hungarian language was performed in this theatre on 15 October 1790 – an important event for Hungarian national consciousness.

Sándor Mansion The classical Sándor-palota (Sándor Mansion, with its main façade facing towards György tér, stands next to the Castle Theatre. It was built for Count Vincent Sándor by Mihály Pollack in 1806, and has been home to the Hungarian president since 2003.

Úri utca

Úri utca (Gentleman's Walk), is characterized by Romanesque, Gothic and Baroque buildings whose origins reach back to the 13th century. Nobles and wealthy merchants built their town houses here, in close proximity to the royal castle, in the 14th and 15th centuries. After the devastations of the Turkish wars, Baroque and classical houses were built over the originals. Úri utca is a very atmospheric scene, as the buildings have been carefully renovated in recent years, the colour of their façades carefully matched, and their Baroque decorations restored.

✶

◄ Gothic architectural details of the Úri utca

The most interesting and oldest buildings are to be found in the section north of the junction with Szentháromság utca. Gothic seating niches under pointed arches can be discovered in, for example, the entrances to the buildings at nos. 32, 34, 36, 38 and 40 on Úri utca. The Hölbling House (no. 31), dating mostly from the 15th century, is the only surviving Gothic home. A courtyard surrounded by Gothic arcades opens up beyond the entrance gate. The house at no. 32 contains a cross-vaulted columned arcade between the gate entrance and the courtyard, a typical feature of most buildings. The classical façade of the house at no. 40 conceals the remains of two Gothic residential houses, of whose splendour the cross-vaulting in the gateway and the filigree tracery above the seating niches still testify. Field Marshal András Hadik (1710–90), whose equestrian statue stands at the crossing of Úri utca and Szentháromság utca, lived at house no. 58. The hussar from Buda was made a field marshal by Empress Maria Theresa because of his considerable daring and is remembered for his temporary conquest of Berlin during the Seven Years' War. Touching the gold testicles of the horse is said to bring students luck for imminent exams.

◄ Telephone Museum

The Hungarian Telephone Museum is housed at Úri utca 49, and not without reason: the world's first functional telephone exchange was built in Budapest. The branch exhibited at the museum is still in working order today. (Opening times: Tue–Sun 10am–4pm).

◄ Ruins of the Magdalene Church

The reconstructed west tower of the Church of Mary Magdalene (Mária Magdolna-templom) rises at the northern end of Úri utca. Originally dating from the 13th to 15th centuries, the church was destroyed during the Second World War and the ruins were later removed.

Tóth Árpád sétány

A short detour to Tóth Árpád sétány, which was part of the castle fortifications extended in the 17th century, is worthwhile. Today it makes for a pretty promenade with four bastions as popular viewpoints.

Kapisztrán tér

Kapisztrán tér, at the extreme north-western corner of Castle District, is named after Johannes Capistranus, an Italian Franciscan monk and travelling companion of the conqueror of the Turks, János Hunyadi. József Damkó created a memorial to Capistranus that has adorned the square since 1922.

Many places on Castle Hill offer panoramic views of the Danube.

War Museum ▶ The northern side of Kapisztrán tér is occupied by the former Ferdinand Barracks, which is today the War Museum (Hadtörténeti Múzeum). However, the entrance to the museum is not here, but on Tóth Árpád sétány. Documents and diverse exhibits on the history of Hungary's wars from the 16th century onwards are shown here, with emphasis on developments since 1848. (Opening times: April–Sept Tue–Sun 10am–6pm, Oct–March Tue–Sun 10am–4pm; www.militaria.hu).

✶ **Országház utca** Országház utca (Parliament Lane) turns south from Kapisztrán tér and is the main street of Castle District. The northern section of the street is mostly characterized by Baroque buildings, while the southern section is mainly classical. Occasionally there are still Gothic and Renaissance details to be spotted, for example on house no. 10. The house at no. 2 was built as a city mansion in the second half of the 13th century. However, only a few individual fragments, such as the seating niches under the arched tracery in the entrance gate, recall its Gothic origins. The houses at nos. 18–22 date from the 15th century and have been remodelled several times. The Gothic quatrefoil moulding on the first floor of house no. 20 is beautiful. The nunnery of the Poor Clares at no. 28, founded in the Middle Ages, was redesigned by Franz Anton Hillebrandt, who supervised the building works at the Royal Palace in the 18th century. After that, the buildings housed the parliament and the Hungarian capital's highest law courts. From time to time, it is possible to attend high-quality musical performances in the Great Hall, which has been restored to its original design.

Cave system under the palace ▶ A cave system branching out in many directions that has given shelter and storage space to the population of Buda many times during war runs beneath the palace. Remains of old wells, various rooms and passageways, and a command post of the German Wehrmacht from the Second World War can be seen during a tour. Note that due to necessary stabilizing works, the underground spaces are occasionally closed to visitors, sometimes for long periods. (Entrance: corner of Dárda u. and Országház u.; normal opening times: Tue–Sun 10am–6pm).

Országház and **Fortuna utca** meet at the ►Matthias Church. Fortuna utca can be explored in a northerly direction from here. In the Middle Ages it was populated mainly by French craftsmen, who were working on the construction of the Royal Palace. Numerous buildings in the most lovely Baroque and late Rococo style give the street its character.

The **Museum for Trade and Gastronomy** shows its exhibits at Fortuna utca 4. The two sectors are presented in separate exhibitions. Among the notable displays in the gastronomy section are the interior of a Buda coffee house dating from 1870. The exhibition on trade and tourism conveys a good impression of advertising from posters of days gone by, as well as showing various curious exhibits. (Opening times: Wed–Fri 10am–5pm, Sat–Sun 10am–6pm).

Cemeteries

Kerepesi Cemetery (Kerepesi temetö)

Location: VIII, Fiumei út
Tram: 23, 24, 28, 37
Underground: M 2 (Keleti pu.)
City map: E/F 6/7

Resting place for famous people

Kerepesi Cemetery, one of the Hungarian capital's largest, has numerous impressive tomb monuments that make it well worth seeing. The leading figures of the country and city have been buried here from the mid-19th century onwards. Many great names from political and religious life found their final resting place in Kerepesi Cemetery: among others, János Arany, Mór Jókai (► Famous People), Alajos Hauszmann, Ödön Lechner, Ferenc Erkel, Loránd Eötvös, Tivadar Puskás and many more. Several highly positioned people who died abroad and whose remains have been returned to their homeland in recent decades also lie here; among others, Mihály Graf Károlyi, who was the president of the first Hungarian Republic and spent his last years in Paris. Today burials in this cemetery only occur in exceptional circumstances. The mausoleums for the politicians Lajos Kossuth (► Famous People), Lajos Batthyány and Ferenc Deák testify to the special honour accorded to them. The idea of creating a Pantheon to the Nation in this cemetery is raised every now and then, but has never been carried out. What was realized in 1958, however, was the monumental Pantheon to the Hungarian Workers' Movement (Munkásmozgalmi Pantheon).

New Municipal Cemetery (Új köztemetö)

Location: X. (Köbánya), Kozma út 8 **Underground:** M 3 (Köbánya-Kispest)

Here lies Imre Nagy

The new municipal cemetery is located far beyond the city centre in the district of Köbánya. At plot number 301, those executed after the 1956 uprising, among them their leader Imre Nagy (►Famous People), were buried in a mass grave. On 16 June 1989, the 31st anniversary of Imre Nagy's execution, the time had come to rehabilitate them. A state ceremony took place on Heroes' Square, as well as a ceremonial re-burial in newly created graves, an event of great significance for Hungarians which forced a renewed confrontation with their own history. On the wishes of his daughter, Imre Nagy, who was prime minister of a free Hungary for just a few days during the uprising, was re-interred at plot 301.

Schmidl family tomb

A memorial of quite a different kind awaits the visitor at the small **Jewish cemetery**, which adjoins the new municipal cemetery to the north (no connecting access). This is the unusual **mausoleum for the Schmidl family**, for which Ödön Lechner and Béla Lajta supplied the designs in 1902–03. Already characteristic for Hungarian art nouveau are the decorations on the façade, with their turquoise tiles; but the flower patterns taken from Hungarian folk art also point in that direction.

★★ Chain Bridge (Széchenyi lánchíd)

B 6

Bus: 4, 16, 105 **Tram:** 2

One of the emblems of the Hungarian capital, the Chain Bridge was Budapest's first permanent bridge across the Danube. Today it provides the shortest connection between Castle Hill and the shopping streets of Pest.

Building history

The bridge was designed by the English engineer William Tierney Clark and built between 1839 and 1849 under the supervision of the Scottish architect Adam Clark. Adam Clark also supplied the plans for the tunnel to Krisztinaváros (see below). The 375m/410yd-long and almost 16m/18yd-wide bridge is suspended from chains that are

fixed to massive pillars 48m/157ft in height. The stone lions lying on pedestals at the bridgeheads are the work of János Marschalkó. Whether or not the lions had tongues or not was long a matter for discussion in Budapest: their creator claimed – perhaps as a joke – that you had to stand directly opposite the animals in order to see their tongues. Along with all of Budapest's other bridges, the Chain Bridge was blown up by German troops in January 1945, but was already re-opened to traffic on 21 November 1949, exactly 100 years after its first inauguration.

! *Baedeker* TIP

Alternative steps

To save time or money when there are long queues at the Sikló, head for the Royal Steps that cover the few metres of elevation from the roundabout at Clark Ádám tér and to the Castle District.

On Clark **Ádám tér**, at the **Buda bridgehead**, stands the zero stone designed by Miklós Borsos in 1971 to mark the spot from which all distances from Budapest on outgoing Hungarian long-distance roads are measured.

At Clark Ádám tér, an entrance designed in classical style leads into the approximately 350m/380yd-long road tunnel that connects Buda with Krisztinaváros. The tunnel completed in 1857 was also the work of the bridge builder Adam Clark.

Sikló From the Buda bridgehead of the Széchenyi lánchíd it is possible to take the so-called Sikló cable car up to the Royal Palace. The nostalgic-looking cable car was built in 1870. It was returned to service after decades of neglect.

★ Danube Bend (Dunakanyar)

Excursion

Location: 20–60km/12–35mi north to north-west of Budapest
Buses: from Erzsébet tér

Access: Long distance route 11 and 12
Suburban train HÉV: from Batthyány tér

The Danube Bend is the name given to the roughly 60km/35mi stretch of the river which runs through particularly attractive scenery between Esztergom and Szentendre, where the Danube winds its way through the Visegrád mountains and turns in a southerly direction to Budapest.

Destination for river cruises The Danube Bend is one of the most popular excursion and leisure destinations in the region around the Hungarian capital. On the right bank, parts of the Bakony forest reach to the river and the Pilis Mountains (Pilis-hegység) rise to a height of 757m/2484ft. From the north, the up to 865m/2838ft-high Börzsöny Mountains (Börzsöny-hegység) push towards the river. The Danube takes a winding passage dictated by the rocky terrain, with a notable loop at Visegrád, and splits into two arms shortly before Vác, to embrace the island of Szentendre. The beautiful towns of Esztergom, Visegrád and Vác, as well as the artists' town of ►Szentendre. are especially appealing for visitors. Hiking enthusiasts and nature lovers are particularly drawn to the back country of the Danube Bend, to the Pilis Mountains and the Visegrád Hills to the south of the river, as well as to the less frequented Börzsöny Mountains or to the Cserhát hill country to the north and east of the Danube.

Esztergom

Location: approx. 60km/35mi north-west of Budapest

Esztergom (pop. 32,000), located on the right-hand terraces of the Danube, at the entrance to the Danube gorge through the central Hungarian highlands, is one of Hungary's oldest towns, with noteworthy buildings and historic monuments. The Magyars settled the area of Esztergom as early as the 9th century. During the Middle Ages, Esztergom rose to become one of the most important royal residences in the Hungarian empire alongside Székesfehérvár, and seat of the archbishop. King Béla III had the castle of Esztergom extended into a magnificent residence. Occupied during the Turkish wars, the town flourished once more in the 18th century. After the Second World War, several larger industrial companies were also settled here.

✶ **Cathedral**

Begun in 1822 by János Páckh and completed in 1856 by József Hild, the cathedral with its massive dimensions dominates the townscape of Esztergom. The eastern entrance is highlighted by an antique-style portal flanked by towers, and the crossing is crowned by a dome in the style of the Italian Renaissance. A cool classical sobriety reigns in the marble-clad interior. The most significant parts of the cathedral, which remain from the preceding building, are the 16th-century tomb chapel for Archbishop Tamás Bakócz and the cathedral treasury, with its unusually rich collection of sacred art,.

✶ **Royal Palace**

The remains of the palace built in the 10th and 11th centuries and extended in the 12th century – and therefore Hungary's oldest royal palace – can be found to the left of the cathedral. The János Vitéz Hall with its Renaissance frescoes, the room in which King Stephen was probably born, and the early Gothic castle chapel, which is a gem of religious architecture at the transition from Romanesque to Gothic, deserve special mention. At the southern and western side of the royal palace wall remains from the 14th and 15th century fortifications still survive.

Christian Museum In the former palace of the archbishop, in the Watertown district beneath the castle hill, the Christian Museum (Keresztény Múzeum) today presents its treasures. This provincial collection, famous far beyond the national borders, contains an extensive display of old Hungarian and early Italian Renaissance painting, as well as a high-quality collection of sculptures from the 14th to 18th centuries and historic crafts. The dual-towered Baroque church directly next to the museum was built for the Jesuit order between 1728 and 1738.

Széchenyi tér Then as now the former market square of Széchenyi tér, surrounded by lovingly restored houses from the 18th and 19th centuries, stands at the heart of the town's life. The town hall (Városháza) decorated by arcades and a Rococo façade on the south side is worth a look.

Vác

Location: 34km/21mi north of Budapest

Charming cathedral town Vác (pop. 35,000), on the left bank of the Danube Bend, has retained the charm of a pretty Baroque town despite industrial development on its periphery. Fortuitously located at a Danube crossing, Vác was the seat of a bishop from the 11th century onwards and, at the height of the Middle Ages, a regional trading centre protected by a royal castle. The town was severely ravaged during the Turkish wars and the Baroque town was built north of the medieval castle in the 18th century. The first Hungarian railway line, inaugurated in 1846, ran from Pest to Vác.

Historic centre The historic centre of Vác lies along the eastern bank of the Danube between Konstantin tér, which is dominated by the cathedral, and Március 15 tér (March 15 Square) to the north, which is lined by beautiful town houses.

✶ Cathedral ► Designed by the Viennese architect Isidore Canevale between 1763 and 1777, the cathedral with an antique-style columned portico in front of its west façade is as an early example of the classical style developed in France. The dome fresco of 1771 is the work of Franz Anton Maulbertsch. The two-storey bishop's palace, built between 1768 and 1775, is opposite the cathedral.

Piarist church ► The pre-eminent building on Szentháromság tér (Holy Trinity Square) is the former Piarist church of St Anne, dating from 1745. The area in front is adorned by a magnificent Baroque Holy Trinity column (1755), and opposite is one of the entrances to the thermal baths of Vác.

✶ Március 15 tér ► The triangular Március tér with its decorative fountains and sculptures was the heart of the historic town. With its surrounding Baroque and late Rococo houses, it forms an atmospheric ensemble. The former Dominican church on the south side has a beautiful Rococo interior.

A few streets north of Március tér, at the former edge of town, stands a classical triumphal arch, which was built to designs by Isidore Canevale in honour of a visit to Vác by Empress Maria Theresa in 1764.

◄ Triumphal arch

Visegrád

Location: 42km/26mi north of Budapest

Royal seat with palace

Visegrád (»high fortress«; pop. 2100) has an extremely picturesque site at the end of a loop in the Danube Bend and is a popular place for excursions because of the royal palace ruins and the high citadel with great views. The strategically important site above the Danube was already used to advantage by the Romans, who established a garrison here. Under King Béla IV, the lower castle was built on the banks of the Danube. It was connected to the mighty upper castle on the hill by a wall. Visegrád developed into a highly significant town politically and culturally under the regency of Charles I of Anjou, who moved his residence there in 1316. It experienced its final flowering in the second half of the 15th century, when King Matthias Corvinus I had the royal palace on the castle hill remodelled in the style of the Italian early Renaissance.

Cloister in the Royal Palace at Visegrád

The most impressive remnant of Visegrád's **lower castle** is the hexagonal, originally 31m/102ft-high Salomon torony dating from the 13th century. After successful renovation, it now houses a museum with valuable finds from the former royal palace, including the red marble Hercules fountain. The water bastion (Vízibástya) on the banks of the Danube was part of the lower castle and served to guard the waterway and the water supply to the palace. This Romanesque building was reconstructed in 1937.

✶ Royal palace

The site of the royal palace above Fö utca (entrance at house no. 27), which was built in the first half of the 14th century and magnificently remodelled in the style of the Italian early Renaissance by King Matthias, were buried by earth slips over the course of centuries, and have been excavated and gradually exposed only since 1934. So far, the northern part of the palace, which was the royal residence, has been uncovered. The heart of the grounds, which extend over several terraces and once included numerous magnificent buildings, a court garden, baths, and around 350 sumptuous rooms, is the late Gothic court of honour lined by arcaded walks.

Citadel (upper castle) A serpentine road signposted from the centre of town leads ruins of the upper castle at a height of 315m/1000ft. The core of the castle is surrounded by several circular walls with gates and draw bridges; the best preserved tower gate is the eastern one, an interesting example of Hungarian castle architecture.

Elizabeth Bridge (Erzsébet-híd)

B/C 7

Bus: 5, 7, 7A, 8, 112

Extending from Rákóczi or Kossuth Lajos utca, the modern Elizabeth Bridge crosses the Danube.

The present bridge replaces a predecessor constructed from 1898 to 1903, which for many years was the largest arched bridge in the world. It was destroyed in the Second World War. The suspension bridge was built to designs by Pál Sávoly between 1961 and 1964, and is 378m/413yd long and almost 30m/33yd wide. Its rather sombre, modern design forms an attractive contrast to the Chain Bridge with its massive bridge posts. The bridge received its name from the Austrian Empress and Hungarian Queen Elizabeth (Sisi), who promoted the Compromise between Austria and Hungary. A memorial to the monarch, who is deeply honoured by Hungarians and was assassinated in 1898, by György Zala is today located north of the Buda bridgehead, in the middle of a small green space.

★ Ethnographic Museum (Néprajzi Múzeum)

B/C 5

Location: Kossuth Lajos tér 12
Underground: M 2 (Kossuth tér)
Bus: 2
Tram: 2

A visit to the Ethnographic Museum is recommended not only for its collections but also for its architecture. This is exactly the right place to find out about Hungarian culture.

It is housed in the former building of the supreme court at ►Kossuth Lajos tér, which was completed in 1896, just in time for the millennium jubilee. The designs were drawn up by the much-employed architect Alajos Hauszmann, who united elements of Renaissance, Bar-

The magnificent entrance hall of the Ethnographic Museum

oque and classical style for this monumental building. The sculptural decorations on the façade are focused on the former function of the building as a palace of justice: above the six high columns carrying the tympanum the »Goddess of Justice« drives a three-horse chariot, a work in bronze by Károly Senyei.

The interior is also not short of pomp. The museum rooms are grouped around an extensive hall, whose broad dual staircases leading up two storeys, elaborate marble cladding and gold-leaf stucco details are worthy of the building's original purpose. This is also recalled by the allegorical representation of Law and Justice on the ceiling fresco by Károly Lotz. The room above the entrance hall, which is used for lectures and concerts, is also worth viewing.

Opening hours:
March–Oct
Tue–Sun
10am–6pm,
Nov–Feb
Tue–Sun
10am–5pm

Exhibition on Hungarian national culture

The extensive collection on Hungarian national culture and art is shown on the first floor. The theme-based exhibition has explanations in Hungarian and English. In the first room, the various national groups of the Pannonian basin are introduced by means of their folk costumes. The next room is dedicated to institutions that shaped life in the country, such as the church and the village community. Common crafts and trades are presented in the following rooms, and there are also two rooms dedicated to Hungarian building skills and domestic culture. The following room exhibits products from local art and craft work. The typical Hungarian farmhouse is the topic of a further exhibit. The exhibition ends with a representation of the different stages of life, such as birth and death, and the customs and festivals associated with them, which provide a vivid picture of rural life in Hungary.

★ Ferenciek tere (Franciscan Square)

C 7

Location: V district
Bus: 5, 7, 7A, 8, 15, 112, 173
Underground: M 3 (Ferenciek tere)

Ferenciek tere, on the southern edge of central Pest, is one the squares of Budapest with the heaviest traffic, yet it is still one of the most interesting squares, a place of pulsating city life.

★ **Párisi udvar**

The department stores around Ferenciek tere represent the most diverse styles of late historicism. On the north-western side of the square, at the beginning of the Pest pedestrian zone starting with Kigyó utca, Párisi udvar displays its somewhat faded but fantastically designed art nouveau shopping arcade, with shops and cafés that hold a particular nostalgic attraction.

! *Baedeker* TIP

Going up!

Párisi udvar was originally built as an apartment block in 1911. The stairwells, which have old-fashioned elevators with cast iron gates, are worth exploring. This is also an opportunity to get a little closer to the interesting roof construction of the shopping arcade.

★ **Clothilde Palaces**

On its western side, the square is framed by the two mirror-image Clothilde Palaces which open up a view of the Elizabeth Bridge ► Elizabeth Bridge. These buildings were constructed as apartment blocks in 1902 by Kálmán Giergl and Floris Korb, by order of the Habsburg Duchess Clothilde. Their magnificent, though in the meantime blackened, façades with their curved gables and turrets were inspired by Spanish Baroque architecture.

Franciscan church

To the north-west, Ferenciek tere opens onto a small square dominated by the Franciscan church (Ferenciek temploma) and the attached house of the Franciscan order next door. After Turkish rule, during which it was turned into a mosque, the Franciscan church was demolished and replaced by a new Baroque building in the mid-

18th century. The historicist spire of the choir was designed by Ferenc Wieser in 1858.

Figures of St Peter of Alcantara, St Francis and St Anthony, as well as the coat of arms of the Franciscan order (above the portal) form the sculptural decoration of the main façade towards Frenciek tere. A bronze relief on the north-western exterior wall (on Kossuth Lajos utca) recalls Baron Wesselényi, who saved many people from drowning during the catastrophic floods of 1838. ◄ Exterior

A magnificent high altar has survived from the original interior of the church. The richly embellished side altars, as well as the wooden pulpit with its 12 apostles, were brought into the church in the 19th century. The walls are decorated by paintings by Károly Lotz (1895) and V. Tardos-Krenner, (1927). ◄ Interior

★★ Fishermen's Bastion (Halászbástya)

A/B 6

Location: Szentháromsag tér **Bus:** 16

Hardly any other building in Budapest is visited, admired and photographed by tourists from all over the world as much as the Fishermen's Bastion that rises behind the Matthias Church on the eastern edge of Castle Hill.

The bastion is one of the emblems of the Hungarian capital and a significant architectural monument whose creation – like so many of Budapest's memorials – was closely associated with the jubilee celebrations in 1896. The name of the structure originates in the former purpose of this place: in the Middle Ages there was a defence post here for the Budapest guild of fishermen who used to hold their market on Castle Hill. The Budapest architect Frigyes Schulek (1841–1919), who had given the Matthias Church its present-day neo-Gothic appearance, seemed the best architect for the Fishermen's Bastion, which was built between 1895 and 1902. For the mighty bastion he chose Romanesque style which he effectively mixed with designs inspired by other historic building eras. The picturesque ensemble of the old-

Wonderful views of the Danube can be had from the viewing platform of the Fishermen's Bastion

style fortifications of the Fishermen's Bastion and the Gothic ►Matthias Church are typical of the romanticized picture of the Middle Ages that emerged during the course of the nationalist movement in the 19th century, to which architects such as Frigyes Schulek also paid tribute. The Fishermen's Bastion viewing platform commands a breathtaking panorama of the left bank of the Danube with Parliament and the Pest side of the city.

Equestrian statue of Stephen

In 1906, Alajos Stróbl, one of the most popular sculptors of his day, created the bronze equestrian statue of the holy monarch Stephen (Szent István), who went down in history as the first Christian ruler of the Hungarians, for the southern courtyard of the two at the Fishermen's Bastion. The plinth, meanwhile, with its four lions and the reliefs around its sides showing scenes from the life of Stephen, was also designed by Frigyes Schulek.

Double stairway

From the bastion, a magnificent double stairway leads down Castle Hill towards Watertown (►Víziváros), past a bronze sculpture of St George. At the foot of the staircase stands a bronze memorial to János Hunyadi by István Tóth, dating from 1905.

Fövám tér (Customs Square)

C 7

Tram: 47, 49
Bus: 15
Trolley bus: 83

The main attraction at lively Fövám tér (Customs Square) is the market hall. Here locals buy their meat, fish and vegetables, and tourists buy their salami, bright red paprika necklaces and wine.

Today the square at the Pest bridgehead of Freedom Bridge is once more called Fövám tér (Customs Square). Up until a few years ago, it was named after the Bulgarian campaigner for the workers' movement Georgij Dimitroff. The two-storey main customs house in neo-Renaissance style, which stands side-on to the square, was built onto Fövám tér between 1871 and 1874, from designs made by Miklós Ybl, the architect of the Budapest opera house. The building has been used by the (Közgazdaság Tudományi Egyetem) University for Business Sciences since 1951, and the magnificent gala courtyard of the 170m/185yd-long building has been remodelled into an auditorium.
Behind the university, when approached from the Danube, stands the **central market hall** (Központi vásárcsarnok), built by Samuel Pecz in 1896. Of the five market halls that were opened in Budapest at the end of the 19th century, this was the largest. Next to the West Railway Station (►Great Ring), it is a further example of an iron and

glass construction in Budapest. The combination of a contemporary construction with traditional architectural forms is typical for these buildings at the transition to the modern age. In the case of the market hall, with its elevated centre joined to low aisle-type extensions, the architect has recalled the form of medieval churches.
The locals appreciate the market hall most for the wealth of provisions on offer, from fresh fruit and vegetables, to spices, meat and sausages, as well as fish and baked goods. Even craftwork, textiles and basketwork are available here. (Opening times: Mon 6am–5pm, Tue–Fri 6am–6pm, Sat 6am–2pm).

Always lively: the Central Market Hall

Freedom Bridge

The steel Freedom Bridge (Szabadság-híd) was opened to traffic in 1896 and connects Fövam tér with Gellért tér on the Buda side of the Danube. This 331m/362yd-long and 20m/22yd-wide metal construction was the first Danube bridge to be rebuilt after its destruction at the end of the Second World War, and was already re-opened by 1946.

★ Franz Liszt Academy of Music

D 6

Location: Liszt Ferenc tér 8
Tram: 4, 6
Underground: M1 (Oktogon)
Bus: 4

The Academy of Music has a delightful foyer, while concerts in the large hall with its superb acoustics provide a veritable treat for the ears.

World class academy of music

This musical educational facility named after Franz Liszt (► Famous People), the founder of Budapest's first music school and initiator of a higher college of music, is today an academy that is known far beyond Hungary's borders. After Franz Liszt, famous music personalities such as Béla Bartók (► Famous People), Zoltán Kodály (► Famous People), Ernö Dohnányi and Leo Weiner taught here. Furthermore, the academy owns the most important collection of Hungarian music literature.
Built between 1904 and 1907, the building of the Franz Liszt Academy, an imposing mansion on Liszt Ferenc tér, is rightly considered a **masterpiece of art nouveau** in Budapest. The plans were drawn up by the two architects Flóris Korb and Kálmán Giergl, who had al-

ready collaborated on the Clothilde Palaces (► Ferenciek tere). The seated bronze figure of Franz Liszt by Alajos Stróbl looks down from the main entrance; in the foyer the composers Béla Bartók and Frederic Chopin are honoured with a bust and a statue.

✶ **Interior** It is not absolutely necessary to attend a concert to view the foyer, though considering the superb acoustics in the large hall, this pleasure is highly recommended. During lesson hours, it is also possible to reach the foyer through the side entrance on Király utca. Not only the richly ornamented walls and columns are worth a look, but also the *Fountain of Youth* fresco by the art nouveau painter Aladár Körösfö-Kriesch.

Large hall ► The large hall is on the ground flour. With its two galleries it can hold an audience of up to 1200 and has unusually good acoustics. Attractive reliefs by the artists Groh and Telcs decorate the corners

Small hall ► of the hall. The small hall on the first floor can hold an audience of around 400 and is less grand. The wall painting by J. Zichy that decorates the foyer symbolically represents the individual phases in the development of Hungarian music.

✶✶ Gellért Bath (Gellért fürdö)

C 8

Location: XI district, Kelenhegyi út 2–4 **Tram:** 18, 19, 47, 49
Bus: 1, 7, 7A, 86, 173

The famous medicinal spa and hotel is one of the most beautiful of its kind in Budapest and an important art nouveau monument in the Hungarian capital.

A spa that already existed here in the 13th century used the thermal waters of Gellért Hill for healing treatments. According to a report by the chronicler Evliya úelebi from Istanbul, the Turks turned the spa into a luxurious bath house, but the spa on Gellért Hill also enjoyed great popularity under the Habsburg rulers. After that building was demolished around the end of the 19th century, the present building, which has been restored to its former splendour, was created between 1911 and 1918 to designs in late Secessionist style by Ármin Hegedüs, Artúr Sebestyén and Izidor Stark that united the hotel and thermal baths under one roof. The opulently designed entrance to the thermal bath lies on the narrow Kelenhegy út, while the hotel and café face onto Szent Gellért tér. The spa installations, such as the thermal bath with sliding

! *Baedeker* TIP

Night bathing to music

On Fridays and Saturdays in July and August, from 8pm to midnight, the wave pool of the Gellért Bath has night bathing with music.

Wellness à la Art nouveau: the part of Gellért Bath that is reserved for men

roof, the jacuzzi and saunas, as well as the exterior facilities with the wave pool, have all been modernized.

★ Gellért Hill (Gellért-hegy; witches' citadel)

B/C 7/8

Location: I and XI district **Tram:** 19
Bus: 27

Gellért Hill (235m/771ft) is probably the most notable physical feature of the Hungarian capital and offers fine views. This eastern flank of this chunk of dolomite drops steeply down towards the Danube. At its peak stands the Liberty Statue built in 1947: the 14m/46ft-high figure with a palm frond is visible from far and wide.

Viewpoint with healing springs

The western side of the hill, on the other hand, consists of stepped terraces that were once vineyards. Several medicinal thermal springs rise along its geological fault line and feed the ►Gellért Bath, the Rudas Bath and the Raitzen Bath. The hill is named after Bishop Gellért, who served during the time of King Stephen I (around 974–1038). There are various legends regarding his death: one of them says that the martyr was rolled down the hill in a barrel; another says that he was harnessed to a wagon, stoned, and his heart pierced by a lance. In earlier times, another legend held that Gellért Hill was a witches' citadel (► Baedeker Special, p.178). The Turks kept a small fortification on Gellért Hill, and the Habsburg troops occupied the excellent observation post during the liberation wars in 1848–49. Since the end of the 19th century a well-to-do villa district has developed on the slopes of Gellért Hill, which is considered one of the city's best residential areas.

★ Gellért Memorial On the north-eastern slope of Gellért Hill, above the bridgehead for the Elizabeth Bridge, stands the monumental bronze sculpture of the bishop and martyr St Gellért . It was created by Gyula Jankovits in 1902 and is surrounded by a semi-circular colonnade. An artificial waterfall burbles beneath the memorial. The best view of the memorial is from the Elizabeth Bridge, which leads directly towards the pointed cliff that gives the saint's statue its dramatic site. In order to see the saint from close up, it is necessary to climb up the steps from the bridgehead. It takes about 20 minutes to continue from the memorial to the summit of the hill and its citadel (see below), an enjoyable walk with wonderful views of the city.

Citadella The Citadella, built at the highest point of Gellért Hill between 1850 and 1854 is still in good condition. The fortification was militarily unnecessary at that time and its intended function was probably to remind the population of Buda and Pest, who had risen up against Habsburg rule in 1848, of Austrian hegemony and to warn against further liberation attempts.

Part of the fortress, which is over 200m/220yd long and up to 60m/70yd wide, is today open to tourists. A large firework display is held here every year on the Hungarian national holiday of 20 August. (Opening times: mid March–mid Oct daily 8am–10pm, mid Oct to mid March, daily 9am–4pm).

Baedeker TIP

View of Buda and Pest

There is a fantastic view of the Royal Palace, the Danube and the Pest bank – especially worthwhile when illuminated at night – from the viewing platform on the access road to Gellért Hill and the Citadella.

Liberation Memorial The Liberation Memorial, also known as Liberty Statue, was erected on the south-eastern tip of Gellért Hill in 1947 to honour the Soviet soldiers who fell during the fight against fascism during the Second World War, and despite a revised view of history, has emerged as one of Budapest's emblems. It is made up of a colossal 14m/46ft-high female figure standing on a limestone pedestal and holding a palm frond in her raised arms. The two heroic male figures at the feet of the triumphant Goddess of Victory embody progress and destruction. Originally, there was also a flag-carrying Soviet soldier between them, who can today be viewed with the other monumental statues of the Soviet era at the ►Sculpture Park.

Jubilee Park On the southern slope of Gellért Hill, the Jubilee Park has attractive promenades and fine statues, among them also the work *Budapest* by István Kiss. With its generously proportioned children's playground and green spaces, this park attracts many visitors on nice days.

He was rolled in a barrel down this hill and into the Danube: the martyr Saint Gellért→

HUNGARY'S SEETHING CAULDRON

Budapest has a witches' citadel: Gellért Hill, from which hot springs bubble, is considered the medieval cradle of Hungarian witchcraft. Even today, this city in the twilight between east and west, between dream and reality, is partial to the supernatural. The profession of witch is officially recognized here.

The Hungarian capital. a city bursting with vitality, has always also had a darker side: next to smiles and jollity, it was synonymous with destructive obsessions; next to limitless exuberant love, dark passions too always flourished here: a contradictory character that is the essence of this metropolis in the middle of Europe.
No wonder that in this pressurized atmosphere things are not always as they should be: today's Budapest has long been regarded as the cradle of Hungarian witchcraft. Witches are said to have once had their homes and the site of their dances on Gellért Hill, which is why among the more timid souls in the city it was considered dubious or even suspicious to spend time up there after sunset.

Witch by Profession

Budapest may have seen and experienced countless changes throughout its history, but its partiality for magic and witches is far too closely connected with Budapest's identity for it to have been consigned to the rubbish dump of intellectual history during eras more focused on reason, such as the Enlightenment, objective socialism or post-modernism. A few twists of its fate may have seemed like magic, as far as the city was concerned. Even today, in Hungary the

profession of witch is an officially recognized status, whose practitioners are naturally obliged to pay taxes and national insurance; and there are more than a few of them: the Hungarian association of witches can point to around 11,000 members after all. Budapest continues to be the centre of all spiritual activity – Hungary's seething cauldron, so to speak.

The Luckless Monk

Gellért Hill's secret heritage, however, is only likely to become apparent on closer inspection. At 235 meters/771 feet high, the first impression is primarily the beautiful view of the Buda and Pest quarters, of the Danube and the Elizabeth Bridge that can be enjoyed from its peak. The best view, however, is the privilege of the lady with the palm frond, who was erected as a monument to freedom in 1947 on the occasion of liberation from the Nazis. Gellért Hill is also associated with other aspects of the city's history. It owes its name to the Benedictine monk Gellért, who preached the Christian faith as first bishop among the Magyars, and died a martyr's death for his beliefs in 1046.

The mountain is guarded by the Citadella, which Austria built after defeating the Hungarian campaign for independence in 1848–49, for the purpose of better controlling the unruly city. Yet the bare facts alone do not always tell the whole story. Those who visit Gellért Hill after dusk, in the half light, just before the mountain and the spa hotels are illuminated in the evening glare of lights, can – with a little imagination – transport themselves back to those times when witchcraft was still efficacious up here. In the opinion of local aficionados, by the way, this continues to be the case. Modern witches of both genders are extremely popular, as the people of Budapest enjoy thumbing their nose at fate as much as they ever did, by procuring advance information on their destiny for themselves.

Helpful Magic

Thus black and white magic continue to flourish here, more than in almost any other place in Europe. Reading cards and pendulum-swinging are two of the standard services provided by contemporary Budapest witches. But the best among them also have other arts in their repertoire that go far beyond the offerings of common fairground fortune-telling. Among these, for example, is the so-called love bandage, which uses a complicated ritual that includes the burning of photos, the production of wax figurines and the murmuring of magical incantations, either to achieve liberation from the torture of love or to bind the object of desire to the fortune seeker – whichever is requested.

Mysterious Magic

The reason that the mythical origin of all Budapest witchcraft is to be found on Gellért Hill is probably the fact that it is a special place in more ways than one. Warm mineral water bubbles up from several springs, which must have always seemed mysterious and magical to people. Thanks to this water there are medicinal spas at the foot of the mountain. The thermal baths of Rudas fürdö were used for healing purposes as early as the Middle Ages, and the grounds of today's Gellért Baths also already housed a first spa in the 13th century. Who would have been capable of establishing with total conviction where healing ended and magic began when the ground steamed and bubbled there? Consequently it was an ideal breeding ground for myths … for historical reports on the activities of witches are rather rare. Instead the tradition of medieval magic on Gellért Hill flourishes, and supernatural occurrences and magical formulas that have endured since the Middle Ages are still cherished and passed on by the initiated.

Gellért Hill *Map*

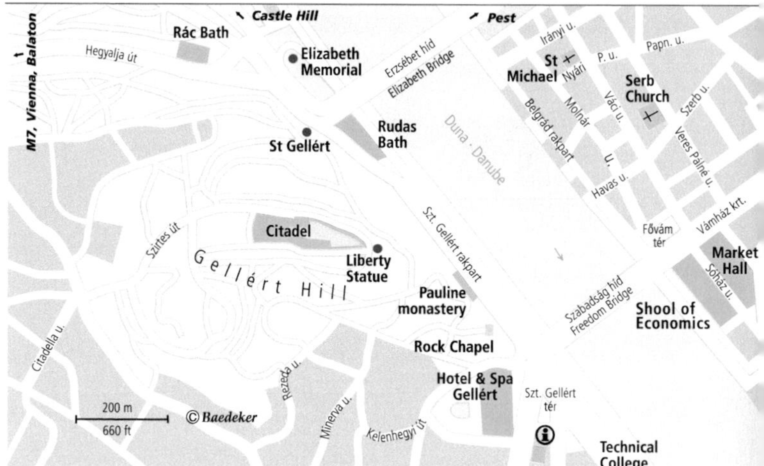

Rudas Bath

The old Rudas Bath (Rudas fürdö) lies at the foot of Gellért Hill, close to the Buda bridgehead of the ► Elizabeth Bridge (Döbrentei tér 9). The thermal springs here were already in use during the Middle Ages and the first bath house was built at that period. The Turks extended the facilities in the 16th century and the typical dome construction with the octagonal central room survives from that time.
In addition to the steam bath, it is possible to enjoy the medicinal waters of the Juventus and Hungária springs in a drinking hall. While textile-free bathing in the Turkish bath was the preserve of men until 2006, there is now a visiting day reserved for women (every Tuesday 6am–8pm; further opening times on ► p.70 and atwww.budapestspas.hu).

Cave chapel

At the main entrance to the Géllert Cave lies the cave or cliff chapel, based on the grotto at Lourdes and founded by the Pauline order in 1931. The Pauline order was active in Hungary from the 14th century onwards, but was dissolved by Joseph II in 1786, and only readmitted in 1931. The grotto was blocked off after the Communists dissolved the order once more at the beginning of the 1950s, but it has been accessible again since 1992. The chapel is almost always open, except during mass.

Pauline monastery

The Pauline monastery nearby in historicist style dates from 1932 and can only be viewed from outside (Szent Gellért rakpart 1/a). It was home to students of the Budapest ballet institute from the dissolution of the order by the Communists until 1989. After that, the building was returned to the Pauline order.

Gödöllö

Excursion

Location: 20km/12mi east of Budapest **Access:** Car or train

The attraction of a trip to Gödöllö is its palace in which Empress Elizabeth liked to stay. Extensive restoration work has restored the building to its former glory.

Grassalkovich Palace

Opening hours: April–Oct daily 10am–6pm, Nov–March Tue–Sun 10am–5pm

★ An extensive park surrounds the Baroque palace in the middle of town, which Prince Antal Grassalkovich built in close proximity to his estates between 1744 and 1748. The building plans for the princely residence were drawn up by the famous architect Andreas Mayerhoffer, and the palace was redesigned by the renowned Hungarian architect Miklós Ybl in the 19th century. Hungary gave the palace – Europe's largest Baroque palace after Versailles – to its ruling couple after the Austro-Hungarian Compromise of 1867. Empress Elizabeth (»Sisi«) loved to spend time here.

Magnificent halls, salons and princely quarters, including Sisi's dressing room, are today part of the **palace museum**, which offers an interesting insight into the luxurious life of the nobility of the 18th and 19th centuries. A memorial exhibition covers the life and death of the empress so deeply cherished in Hungary.

The **Baroque theatre** in the south wing, which still contains unique original stage sets, can be viewed during performances and tours (www.kiralyikastely.hu).

★ Great Synagogue (Dohány utcai zsinagóga)

C 6

Location: VII, Dohány u. 2 **Underground:** M 1, M 2, M 3
Trolley bus: 74 **Bus:** 7, 7A, 78

The Great Synagogue on Dohány utca (Tobacco Lane), also known as Tobacco Synagogue, is one of the most significant and historically important monuments in Budapest.

Opening hours: May–Oct Mon–Thu 10am–5pm, Fri 10am–3pm, Sun 10am–2pm; Nov–April Mon–Fri 10am–3pm, Sun 10am–1pm

The greatly increased Jewish community inaugurated its new synagogue in 1859 at the border between the old city of Pest and the newer district of Elizabeth Town (VII district), which was soon to become a ghetto. It was constructed in the Moorish-Byzantine style of romantic historicism to plans by the architect Ludwig Förster. Two polygonal towers over 30m/100ft high dominate the façade.

The interior of the synagogue, which can hold around 3000 people, was designed by Hungarian artists and craftsmen, including the famous architect Frigyes Feszl. Delicate columns of cast iron form the filigree supporting structure for the broad triple-aisled room. The two side aisles have galleries for the women. The magnificent organ has been played in the past by such renowned musicians as Franz (Ferenc) Liszt (► Famous People) and Camille Saint-Saëns. The rabbis who have served here include such outstanding characters as Majer Kayserling, Samuel Kohn and Simon Hevesi. **A cemetery** for the martyrs of the Budapest Ghetto can be found in the garden of the Great Synagogue. Several thousand Jewish victims of fascism are buried here in two mass graves.In front of the martyrs' cemetery stands the smaller **Heroes' Synagogue**, also built in oriental style, which was erected in the 1930s for the Hungarian Jewish soldiers who fell in the First World War.

Inside the Great Synagogue

Jewish Museum

The Jewish Museum has been built on the spot where Theodor Herzl's (► Famous People) birthplace stood (Országos Zsidó Vallási és Történeti Gyüjtemény), next to the Great Synagogue, on the corner of Dohány utca and Wesselényi utca. It houses one of the most extensive collections of central European Jewish sacred art, including

Great Synagogue Plan

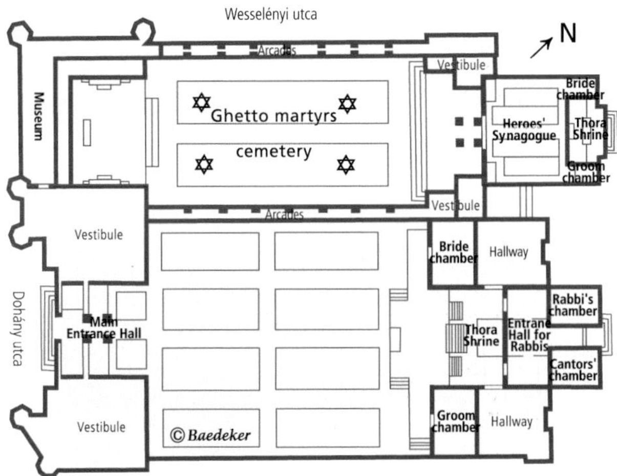

Thora decoration in the Jewish Museum

A memorable documentation of the Hungarian Jews' fate is shown at the very impressive Holocaust Memorial on Páva utca, in the IX district, opened in 2004.

SURVIVAL: JEWISH BUDAPEST

The Jewish community has been integral to Budapest for hundreds of years and, especially towards the end of the 19th century, it contributed towards the cultural and economic renaissance of the city. Despite Nazi efforts to eradicate it completely, Jewish culture and lifestyle has endured to this day in the district of Erzsébetvaros (Elizabeth Town) – named after the Habsburg empress and Hungarian queen – which is also where the Jewish ghetto was located during the Second World War.

The horrific scale of the holocaust is revealed in numbers that tell of the efficiency of the National Socialists' machinery of extermination: over 500,000 of 820,000 Hungarian Jews were murdered in Auschwitz. About 200,000 of those lived in Budapest at the beginning of the war. For even at the end of the 19th century, Budapest held a virtually magnetic appeal for Jews from rural Hungary because it had more liberal laws on buying property and admission to the professions, as well as a cosmopolitan atmosphere. The new arrivals quickly got used to the big-city lifestyle and, just as in other European cities, the Jews made a considerable contribution to the development of their homeland. Even at the beginning of the 20th century, the climate was still relatively free of resentment: Jews worked as craftsmen and merchants and ran restaurants, cafés and cultural institutions.

Life in the Ghetto

And, just as all over the rest of Europe, they could not believe what was happening around them. But in November 1944, the Nazis created a ghetto behind a fence of planks in Elizabeth Town, a predominantly Jewish district since the middle of the 19th century. 2600 buildings there were designated as »star buildings« and assigned as homes to Jews from all around the city. More than 65,000 people lived here when the ghetto was liberated by the Red Army on 18 January 1945. Thousands of Budapest Jews owe their survival to the Swedish diplomat Raoul Wallenberg. He issued a protective pass to every family that could demonstrate a connection to Sweden – even if it was by copying an address from the Swedish telephone book available at the main post office. Wallenberg himself, who had arrived in Budapest with two backpacks, a sleeping-bag, a coat and a revolver on

9 July 1944, was arrested by the Soviets in 1945, and his fate has never been ascertained.

Long History

Jewish culture in Budapest can look back on a long history: the Jews were officially granted freedom of religious expression by King Béla IV, in the 11th century; from the 13th century, they were entrusted to work as treasurers in the financial affairs of the monarchy. At that time the mint, at the heart of the developing Jewish quarter, was also housed in Buda Castle. At the end of the 18th century, the Jewish community moved to Pest, where the large synagogue on today's Dohány utca was built between 1854 and 1859.

Jewish Culture Today

Today around 80,000 Jews live in Budapest, many of them in Elizabeth Town, the city's densely populated VII district. During the era of socialism, little was done to maintain the housing from bourgeois days. In fact, the generously proportioned apartments were divided up and redivided, at first inhabited by two families and later by even more. Yet this quarter with its boxed-in back yards, side yards and inner courtyards continues to develop its very own atmosphere, as before. Kosher restaurants and butchers, events such as the Jewish cultural festival, and the synagogues, confirm a lively culture lovingly maintained, and the Jewish Museum recalls the golden age.

Near the Great Synagogue, which has always been the religious centre of the liberal Budapest Jews, Jewish clergy are trained in central Europe's only rabbinical seminary. The synagogue itself, completed in 1859, was restored just a few years ago. The American actor Tony Curtis, son of a Jewish Hungarian immigrant, contributed the largest portion of the necessary money. The bath-house of the Jewish orthodox community – which has around 3000 members today – and a synagogue built in 1912 are located on Kazincy Street. Jewish restaurants all around Klauzál Square, once the main square of the ghetto, and on the surrounding streets and lanes, make the culinary aspect of Jewish culture most tangible with their kosher specialties, such as »gefilte fis«, or »sólet«, a bean stew with goose meat; with »pászka«, a bread of unleavened dough, and with sweet almond bread for dessert.

many valuable items, such as old Torah and Talmud scripts, Chanukkah candlesticks, as well as other items used during celebrations and also in daily life. The Holocaust is recalled in a separate room.

Orthodox Synagogue

Budapest's orthodox Jews built their main synagogue on Rumbach Sebestyén utca (no. 11–13) between 1870 and 1872, in close proximity to the Great Synagogue, to designs by the great Viennese art nouveau architect Otto Wagner. Stylistically, the Orthodox Synagogue is very similar to the Great Synagogue.

! *Baedeker* TIP

Holocaust memorial

In the small garden north-east of Heroes' Synagogue, at the back of the Great Synagogue, a memorial by the artist Imre Varga to the victims of the Hungarian holocaust was inaugurated in 1992: a weeping willow, whose leaves – small metal plates – are each engraved with the name of a Jewish victim of fascism.

The **Jewish ghetto** was located at Wesselényi utca. A relatively high percentage of Budapest's Jews were saved from the abuses of fascist thugs, not least because the Swedish embassy and its legate Raoul Wallenberg bought dozens of houses in Budapest, which it considered its sovereign territory. The Budapest ghetto was the only one of its kind liberated (by Soviet troops) in time to prevent the planned deportation of its inhabitants. (► Baedeker Special p.184).

Klauzál tér ►

Lively trade has sprung up in this quarter once more. Especially around Klauzál tér, it is now possible to buy kosher food, sample excellent wine and enjoy other kosher specialties.

Holocaust Museum

(Holokauszt Emlékközpont)

D 8

Location: IX, Páva utca 39
Tram: 4, 6
Underground: M 3 (Ferenc körút)

Opening hours:
Tue–Sun 10am–6pm

Since 2004 Budapest has possessed eastern Europe's first Holocaust Museum. It is comprised of modern, mostly underground, exhibition rooms by the Hungarian architect István Mányi, and the wonderfully restored synagogue designed by Leopold Baumhorn (originally completed in 1924), as well as a black memorial wall in the courtyard on which gradually the names of the over 50,000 Hungarian Holocaust victims are being engraved. Recently a glass tower was added to the courtyard. It houses the staircase that leads to the exhibition rooms. The tower is called the Tower of Lost Communities. The names of 1,441 communities are engraved in the glass; these no longer exist because all of the members were deported during the Holocaust.

Heroes' Square: where the great names of the past meet those with aspirations

★★ Hösök tere (Heroes' Square)

E4

Underground: M 1 (Hösök tere)
Trolley bus: 75, 79
Bus: 4, 20, 30, 105

Spacious Heroes' Square on the western edge of the ►Városliget woods forms the imposing finale for ►Andrássy út, which leads directly to this square from the city centre. Skateboarders do their turns under the stern gaze of the Hungarian national heroes while traffic buzzes all around.

Stage for history

The occasion for creating a monumental memorial for the heroes of Hungarian history was the celebration of the 1896 millennium jubilee. The architect Albert Schickedanz and the sculptor György Zala were entrusted with the design of the square. Schickedanz also designed the two monumental buildings flanking the square: the ►Museum of Fine Arts and the Palace of Art. Heroes' Square was only completed in 1927, three decades after building began.
Over the past hundred years, Hösök tere has again and again been a stage for decisive moments in Hungarian history. During the 1918–19 revolution, the sculpture of Emperor Franz Joseph was smashed as a symbol for the break with the Habsburgs, the entire square draped with red cloth, and the statues of Árpád replaced with a sculpture of Marx and a monument to workers and farmers.

Hösök tere was also repeatedly the stage for political demonstrations after 1945, as well as in 1989, when Imre Nagy (► Famous People) and his companions were posthumously rehabilitated in a solemn ceremony of state.

★ **Millennium Memorial** The Millennium Memorial is the dominant monument on the square. (Millenniumi emlékmü) Visible from afar, the 36m/118ft-high column crowned by a bronze figure of the Archangel Gabriel – a work by György Zala – rises between the two semi-circular colonnades. The bronze equestrian group at the base of the monument represents the Magyar chieftain Árpád and the six other leaders who are credited with conquering the land in 896. Hungarian kings from the Árpád dynasty to the Anjou dynasty were placed in the left colonnade; on the right, statues honour Hungary's revolutionary heroes. Sculptures by György Zala crown the corner pillars of the colonnades. The figures cast in bronze embody work and wealth, war and peace (the chariot to the left of the column is war, the one to the right is peace), and also science and fame. On the square in front of the millennium column there is a memorial stone for the national heroes who have fought for Hungary's freedom and independence.

Palace of Art (Mücsarnok) The Palace of Art to the right of the Millennium Memorial is also part of the construction activities for the 1896 jubilee. The magnificent building completed in 1895 was built as an art exhibition hall in neo-classical style to plans by Albert Schickedanz. Before then, the building at Andrássy út 69 served that purpose, but no longer offered enough exhibition space by the beginning of the 1890s. Today the works of contemporary Hungarian artists, including works by famous craftsmen, designers and photographers, are presented in this large exhibition hall. (Opening times: Tue–Sun 10am–6pm).

★ Inner City Parish Church

(Belvárosi plébániatemplom)

C 7

Location: Március 15 tér / Szabadsajtó út **Tram:** 2

Bus: 2, 7, 8, 15, 112

The inner city parish church is the oldest religious building in the Pest quarter of the city. It stands on the remains of the Roman Castrum Contra Aquincum, at the Pest bridgehead of the ► Elizabeth Bridge.

A small church, in which Bishop Gellért was interred in 1046, existed here in the 11th century. The building received a semi-circular choir in the 12th century, when the church was already under the patronage of the royal family. A major extension in the French Gothic style took place under King Sigismund, and Pest's main church received its side chapels in the second half of the 15th century. Under Turkish rule the inner city parish church was used as a mosque. Relics of a Turkish mihrab (prayer niche) still survive on the south-eastern wall of the choir today.

The church was badly damaged during a fire in 1723, and received its present-day appearance during the Baroque reconstruction undertaken by Georg Paur, who began with the erection of the south tower in 1726 and completed the works with the northern tower in 1739–40. Jószef Hild undertook a restoration of the church in classical style during the years 1805–08. However, this was altered four decades later by Imre Steindl, who remodelled it in Gothic style. After the church was badly damaged during the Second World War, rebuilding began in 1948; but with the reconstruction of the ►Elizabeth Bridge, from 1961 onwards, an urban planning problem

Municipal Parish Church Plan

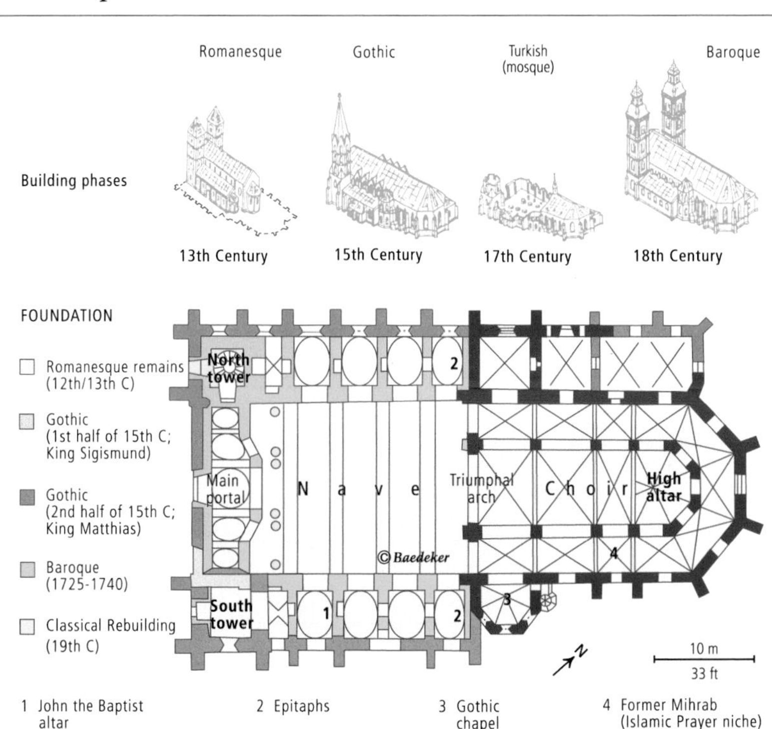

1 John the Baptist altar
2 Epitaphs
3 Gothic chapel
4 Former Mihrab (Islamic Prayer niche)

emerged at the Pest side of the bridgehead. The inner city parish church was simply in the way, a problem that was solved by leaving a truly breathtakingly narrow space between the bridge and the south-eastern side of the church.

Exterior Two building styles, Gothic and Baroque, characterize the church: the nave and the double-tower façade have survived in the Baroque style, whereas the choir, which is almost as long as the nave, retains its Gothic appearance. There is a beautiful Holy Trinity statue by Anton Hörger over the main portal on the west. Hörger, a sculptor from Buda, also created the figure of St Florian behind the choir, which was erected to honour the patron saint after the great fire of 1723.

Interior The interior is that of a vaulted hall church without aisles but with four chapels on each side, which were created by dividing the medieval aisles. Adjoining to the east is the wonderful Gothic ambulatory choir, which is clearly separated from the nave by its narrow supports. Also of note are the two Renaissance funerary monuments of red and light yellow marble in the northern chapels. The pulpit of 1808 is the work of the Pest master carpenter Philipp Ungnad. Fragments of 15th-century Gothic frescoes can be admired in the spaces between the pointed arches in the polygonal southern chapel. The present high altar is the work of Károly Antal and Pál Molnár and dates from 1948.

Károlyi Palace

C 7

Location: VI district, Károlyi Mihály utca 16

Underground: M 3 (Ferenciek tere)
Bus: 15, 15A

Károlyi Palace, a mansion with a colourful history, today houses a literature museum.

History The building named after its last owner, the Hungarian politician and first president of the republic Mihály Károlyi (1875–1955), was built as a single-storey townhouse at the end of the 17th century. An 18th-century Baroque façade had to give way to renovation in the new classical style in 1832–34. In 1848–49 the Austrian general Julius Haynau lived in Károlyi Palace during Hungary's battle for independence, which he was supposed to suppress. Hungary's first prime minister, Count Lajos Batthyány, was arrested here in 1849. There is a memorial room in honour of Mihály Károlyi. The literature muse-

Petőfi Museum ► um carries the name of Hungary's most famous poet from the revolutionary era, Sándor Petőfi (► Famous People). It contains exhibits from Hungarian literature and collections of texts by the country's outstanding poets and writers. Manuscripts, books and magazines, an audio archive and works by various artists make a visit to the museum worthwhile. Changing exhibitions complement the main presentation. (Opening times: Tue–Sun 10am–6pm).

Kiskörút (Little Ring)

C 6/7

Location: V district
Bus: 1, 9
Tram: 47, 49

The Little Ring, between the ► Chain Bridge and the Freedom Bridge (► Fövám tér), encompasses the old city centre of Pest, which is today referred to as Budapest city centre. This ring road traces the old city walls of Pest.

The individual sections have their own names: József Attila utca, Bajcsy-Zsilinszky út, Deák Ferenc tér, Károly körút, Múzeum körút, Kálvin tér and Vámház körút. Erzsébet tér also counts as part of the Little Ring.

Erzsébet tér (Elizabeth Square)

Underground: M 1, M 2, M 3 (Deák tér)
Bus: 4, 16, 105

Former cemetery

Erzsébet tér was once a cemetery. Today, the Danubius Fountain, designed by Miklós Ybl and originally erected on Kálvin tér, stands in the middle of the green space of Erzsébet tér. The fountain figures by Leó Feszler were replaced by copies made by Deszö Györi in 1959, after severe damage during the Second World War. They symbolize the Danube and its great tributaries, the Drava, Tisza and Sava. A marble memorial by György Kiss in honour of Mrs Veres (1815–1895), who dedicated herself to the provision of education for women, was erected on the eastern side of the square in 1906. On the north-western side of the square the bronze shepherd by J. Horvay has been playing his pipes since 1929.

Flowers for the weekend

Deák Ferenc tér

Underground: M 1, M 2, M 3 (Deák tér)

Ferenc Deák Square (Deák Ferenc tér), which adjoins Erzsébet tér in the south-east, is one of the most important traffic junctions in the city centre. The three underground lines meet here. Right by the entrance to the underground stations the exclusive Porsche showrooms catch the eye.

! *Baedeker* TIP

The early days of the Underground

The Underground Museum (Földalatti Vasúti Múzeum) is beneath Deák Ferenc tér in a tunnel dug in 1896 for Europe's first electric underground railway. The exhibited documents, models and information boards on the history of mass transport in Budapest are of limited interest, but the carriages from the earliest metro complete with wooden benches are worth a visit. (Opening times: Tue–Sun 10am–5pm).

The **Lutheran church** on the south side of the square is a monument of a special kind (Evangélikus templom). The building of this church was begun ten years after Emperor Joseph II's religious toleration edict in 1781, which permitted membership of the Protestant churches and the building of Protestant places of worship. It was completed by Mihály Pollack in 1809. The church received its classical entrance portal crowned by a pediment during the renovation by József Hild in 1856. The altar is notable for its copy of Raphael's *Transfiguration.*

Protestant National Museum

Mihály Pollack also designed the building adjacent to the church, a parish office and Protestant secondary school, which today houses the small Protestant National Museum (Evangélikus Országos Múzeum). Diverse liturgical objects and many important documents of the Hungarian Protestant Church can be viewed in this museum. The absolute highlight of the exhibition is the will written by Martin Luther in 1542. (Opening times: Tue–Sun 10am–6pm).

Károly körút (Charles Ring)

Madách houses

Károly körút has developed into an important shopping street in recent years. From Deák tér the generously proportioned, symmetrical complex of multi-storey brick buildings that embrace the Imre Madách tér is already noticeable. This complex, built in 1937, known as the Madách houses, is one of the few examples of Expressionist brick architecture in Budapest and shows similarities to the high-rise buildings that emerged in other European cities during the 1920s and 1930s. The Madách houses are home to the Madách Theatre; opposite is the exhibition hall of the city council (no. 4). The Madach Theatre was renovated and now houses three separate theatres. These have a very up-to-date programme. The largest theatre shows world-class musical productions. The smaller ones have a wide range in their repertoire.

Múzeum körút (Museum Ring)

Two leading Hungarian educational and cultural institutions can be found on Museum Ring. Imre Steindl, builder of the parliament, and Antal Weber designed the buildings of the natural science faculty of the Eötvös Loránd University in neo-Renaissance style. The design for the Hungarian ► National Museum is by Mihály Pollack. The house at no. 7, completed by Miklós Ybl in 1852, is also noteworthy. Fragments of the Pest city wall were found in the courtyards of houses no. 17 and 21.

Major neo-Renaissance buildings

Kálvin tér (Calvin Square)

Underground: M 3

Kálvin tér lies at the southern edge of the Pest city centre. Remains of the former Kecskemét Gate of old Pest's fortifications were found here during building works and incorporated into the new Hotel Korona building. An outstanding example of the old cityscape, partly destroyed during the Second World War, is the former tavern »The Two Lions« at no. 8, dating from 1818.

Street entertainer

This church in strict classical style was erected between 1816 and 1859 to designs by Josef Hofrichter and with the assistance of József Hild, who created the façade. Its has a noteworthy portal, whose four columns carry a tympanum. In the interior note the fine coffered ceiling and the organ by Hild. On the left wall are the tomb of Countess Zichy designed by Frigyes Feszl, and a figure of the deceased originating from the workshop of the sculptor Raymond Gayard (1854). The church treasury contains valuable gold items from the 17th, 18th and 19th centuries.

The dominant building on **Szabó E. tér**, which adjoins to the east, is the apartment block built to designs by Arthur Meining in 1887. Today it houses the municipal Ervin Szabó Library, named after the Hungarian sociologist Ervin Szabó (1877–1918).

Vámház körút (Vámház Ring)

Vámház körút has developed into a very busy shopping street in recent years, not least because of the ever-lively central market hall in close proximity at ►Fövám tér. One of the most beautiful buildings on this section of the ring road is the house at no. 12, built in the classical style. There is a pretty sculpture of a dancer in its courtyard.

✶ Kossuth Lajos tér (Lajos Kossuth Square)

B 5

Location: V district
Tram: 2, 2A
Underground: M 2 (Kossuth Lajos tér)

The large Kossuth Lajos tér, framed by monumental showpieces, is one of the most impressive squares of the Hungarian capital.

Magnificent centre

On its western flank stands the ►Parliament building, on its eastern flank the former Palace of Justice which today houses the ►Ethnographic Museum, as well as the Agricultural Ministry (Földmüvelésügyi Minisztérium), built in the neo-classical style in 1885. The southern side of Kossuth Lajos tér is taken up by the modern building of the Hungarian Chamber of Commerce, which was completed in 1972.

Memorials

A memorial recalling the Battle of Independence in 1848 has stood on the northern side of the green square since 1952. **Lajos Kossuth** (►Famous People), who went down in history as the man who proclaimed Hungarian independence, stands at the highest point of the memorial. The figures on the lower pedestals represent the Hungarian people taking up Kossuth's call to resistance against Austria. There were already uprisings against Habsburg rule 150 years earlier. They are remembered on the opposite, narrow side of the square, with an equestrian statue of Prince **Ferenc Rákóczi II**, created by János Pásztor in 1935. He is honoured as the most important leader of the fight for independence in the early 18th century. On the small green space at the entrance to Vecsey utca stands a small bridge as a memorial to Imre Nagy (►Famous People), whose reforming policies cost him his life in 1956.

Honvéd utca, Ministries

The roads north and east of Kossuth Lajos tér are characterized by imposing buildings, whose façades reflect the stylistic variety of late historicism. Several of these are seats of ministries, including the buildings at Honvéd utca 13–15, in which the Ministry for International Economic Relations resides, and those at Honvéd utca 26–30, which contain the Ministry of Defence. The continuation of Honvéd utca has lovely Art nouveau townhouses.

Március 15 tér (15 March Square)

C 7

Location: V district
Tram: 2, 2A
Bus: 2, 7, 7A, 8, 15, 112, 173, (Contra Aquincum)

The square at the Pest bridgehead of the ►Elizabeth Bridge recalls 15 March 1848, when civil war broke out.

The Romans left their mark here

The dominant building on Március tér is the ►inner city municipal church with its sweeping Baroque façade facing the Danube. Long before the building of the church the Romans had a camp here, Castrum Contra Aquincum, so called because it was located on the opposite side from the ►Aquincum garrison, on the unsecured side of the Danube at that time. Contra Aquincum therefore formed a forward defence post intended to protect the Danube crossing. The remains of this fortification, which were exposed and conserved during several excavation campaigns, along with historical documentation can be seen in the lower area of the square. The legionaries' fountain was created by the artist Tar in 1970.

Baedeker TIP

The little princess

Level with the ►Vigado on the Danube Corso, a bronze princess with her back to the Danube by László Marton has watched the crowds go by on the promenade since 1990.

Petőfi tér

The square that adjoins Március 15 tér to the north-east is named after the Hungarian poet Sándor Petőfi (► Famous People), and serves as stage for annual patriotic festivities on 15 March. A bronze memorial made by Adolf Huszár in 1882 commemorates Petőfi with some pathos in the middle of the square.

◄ Greek Orthodox Church

On the eastern side of Petőfi tér stands the Greek Orthodox Church (Görögkeleti görög templom), which was built to designs by József Jung in 1790 and remodelled by Miklós Ybl in the 19th century. The interior is memorable for an iconostasis by Miklós Jankovich and a painting by Anton Kochmeister. (Opening times: Mon–Thu noon–4pm).

✶ **Danube Corso**

The promenade along the Pest bank of the Danube, which begins between Március 15 tér and the ►Elizabeth Bridge and leads to the ► Chain Bridge, is called the Danube Corso (Dunakorzó). Particularly when it is illuminated in the evening, there are wonderful views of the ►Fishermen's Bastion, the ►Matthias Church, the ►Royal Palace, the Gellért Memorial, the Citadella and the Liberation Memorial on ►Gellért Hill from here. All in all, the Corso is a very busy place with much to do and see. Many of the top-class hotels in Budapest are located here; excursion boats stop on their trips up and down the river and quieter streets run into Pest.

Margaret Island (Margit-sziget)

B/C 2–4

Tram: 4, 6
Bus: 26, 26A
Micro bus: During the summer daily, 10am–6pm

With its baths and gardens, Margaret Island, almost 2.5km/1.5mi long and up to 0.5km/550yd wide, is Budapest's top leisure and recreational centre close to the city.

Popular recreational park Many visitors are drawn to the thermal springs, the spa and exercise pools, the restaurants, sports pitches and playgrounds, as well as well-kept gardens and promenades, not to mention a few historically important urban architectural remains.

By car the island is accessible only at the northern end, on a ramp that branches off the Árpád Bridge. Vehicles are only allowed as far as the spa hotel car parks. In the south, Margaret Island can be reached on foot or via public transport across Margaret Bridge (Margit híd), from whose central pier there is access to the island.

History The Romans used the thermal springs at the northern end of the Danube island. Premonstratensians, Dominicans and Franciscans built their monasteries here in the 12th and 13th centuries. At the end of the 18th century, the Habsburg Archduke Johann, who lived as palatine in Budapest, had the island made into gardens. Between 1868 and 1870, a spa building (Margit fürdö) was constructed to plans by Miklós Ybl. It was destroyed during the Second World War. The Grand Hotel (Margitszigeti Nagyszálló), also designed by Ybl, opened its doors in 1873. A spa centre was created on the island with the thermal spa hotel added in 1978. A branch of this hotel is also the thermal spa hotel Helia on the Pest side, and the thermal spa hotel Aquincum on the Buda bank.

Island names During the time of Arpád rule, the island was a popular hunting ground known as Rabbit Island (Nyulak szigete). The Danube island received its present name in the 14th century, in memory of the canonized Princess Margaret (1252–1271), a daughter of the Hungarian King Béla IV. She became a nun in the Dominican nunnery in accordance with a vow made by her father.

Unification Memorial The petal-shaped metal work by István Kiss was inaugurated in 1972, on the occasion of the centenary of the unification of Óbuda, Buda and Pest. The insides of the petals record various episodes from the Danube capital's recent history. A colourful spectacle on summer evenings is to be seen next to the Unification Memorial, when the water jets of the large fountain are illuminated by coloured lights.

Water spectacle ►

Margaret Island Map

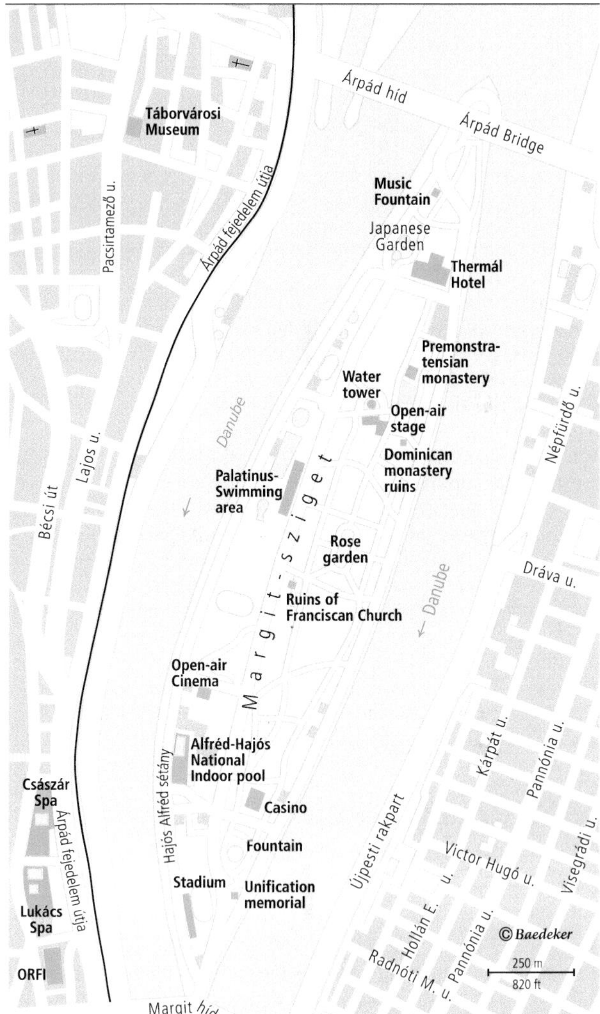

Ruins of the Franciscan Church

Only a few little fragments survive from the 13th–14th-century church of the Franciscan monastery, including a section of its western side, and parts of the north wall, the apse, and the tower.

Palatinus lido

Fed by thermal waters, the facilities of the Palatinus lido (Palatinus strandfürdö), extend across an area of over 7ha/17 acres, and include a wave pool, diverse swimming pools, medicinal baths and children's pools which can take up to 20,000 visitors. Opposite the lido there is a pretty rose garden.

Ruins of the Dominican nunnery The remains of a Dominican nunnery that became derelict during the Turkish era were discovered on Margaret Island after the catastrophic floods of 1838. The nunnery church was erected in the 13th century, rebuilt in the 14th and extended in the 15th century.

Water tower The 52m/170ft-high water tower with viewing platform was built in 1911 and has been carefully restored. Next to the tower, an open-air theatre holds 3500 spectators.

Premonstratensian monastery Several foundations still survive of the Premonstratensian monastery built in the 12th century. The monastery church was rebuilt in Romanesque style in 1930–31. A bell cast in the 15th century hangs in the tower, which is one of the oldest in Hungary.

Grand Hotel Margitsziget In its day, the Grand Hotel Margitsziget was the top hotel of the recently united capital. Built in 1873, it has been repeatedly renovated and remains a popular high-class hotel, not least because of its unique location in the middle of a park on Margaret Island, yet it is close to the city. It gained its present appearance after being taken over by an international hotel chain. An underground passage connects it with the facilities of the Thermal Hotel Margitsziget.

Thermal Hotel Margitsziget The modern Thermal Hotel Margitsziget, now famous well beyond Hungary's borders, was completed in 1978. It was designed by G. Kéry and has state-of-the-art spa facilities. An artificial stone garden (Sziklakert) laid out for the hotel is much admired for its rare flora.

★★ Matthias Church (Mátyás-templom)

A 6

Location: Szentháromság tér **Bus:** 16, 16A
Internet: www.matyas-templom.hu

The Matthias Church stands directly in front of the Fishermen's Bastion. Its painted interior today attracts admiring visitors from all over the world.

Top sight Buda's Church of the Blessed Virgin is one of the Hungarian capital's top sights and has its origin in a sacred building which was erected between 1255 and 1269, during the time of King Béla IV. It has been remodelled numerous times since then. In the second half of the 14th century, the basilica was converted into a hall church, the aisles extended to the east and given polygonal endings, and a magnificent

Gothic portal with a representation of the Virgin Mary's death in the tympanum erected on the southern façade. Charles Robert of Anjou was crowned King of Hungary in the Church of the Blessed Virgin in 1309. Side chapels, an oratory for the royal family and a new south tower were added under King Matthias, after whom the church is now named. The church fell victim to a fire in 1526 and fifteen years later, when the Turks occupied the city, it was turned into a mosque. After the expulsion of the Turks by the Austrians, the Jesuits took over the Matthias Church and renovated it in the Baroque style.

Frigyes Schulek gave the Matthias Church its present form between 1874 and 1896. The Baroque architecture fell victim to his puritanical intention to restore the building's Gothic appearance. The church suffered heavy damage at the end of the Second World War and was painstakingly rebuilt during the post-war years.

Exterior

The western façade facing Szentháromság tér, with its portal and wonderful rose window, is largely the result of Schulek's remodelling. Schulek had a low building with pointed roof and patterned roof tiles built around the lower section of the northern Béla tower, originally dating from the 13th century; whereas the southern, 80m/260ft-high Matthias Tower remains square at its base and then becomes octagonal from the second floor.

★ ◄ Portal of the Virgin Mary

The most important survival from the Gothic church is the portal of the Virgin Mary on the south side, today protected by Schulek's porch. The wonderful relief in the gable illustrating the Virgin Mary's death dates from the 14th century. The entrance is flanked on either side by statues of the canonized kings Stephen and Ladislaus.

Matthias Church Plan

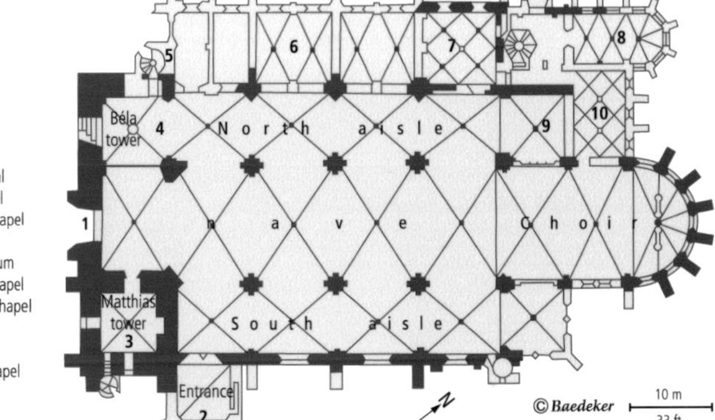

1 Main portal
2 St Mary portal
3 Loreto Chapel
4 Baptismal Chapel
5 Entrance for church museum
6 Emmerich Chapel
7 Holy Trinity Chapel
8 St Stephen's Chapel
9 Ladislaus Chapel
10 Sacristy

MATTHIAS CHURCH

★★ The Matthias Church with its colourful roof tiles is a conspicuous landmark of the city. However, its atmosphere and true splendour can only be experienced by visiting the inside of the church: every square inch of the enormous nave is covered with frescoes and painted decoration. The church glows in the rich colours of the dim light that filters through the stained-glass windows.

Opening times:
Mon–Fri 9am–5pm, Sat 9am–1pm, Sun 1–5pm
Services: 7am, 8.30am and 6pm
Museum:Sun–Fri 9am–5pm

① **Béla Tower**
King Béla IV founded the church. The tower, which still incorporates some original Gothic parts, was named after him.

② **Matthias Tower**
The tall and slender tower is adorned by the raven coat of arms of King Matthias.

③ **Main entrance**
The tympanum of the main entrance in the west of the church holds a 19th-century Madonna and child between two angels by Kajos Lontai.

④ **Baroque Madonna**
According to legend, this figure was hidden within the wall of the church during the siege of Budapest by the Turks. When the church was destroyed in 1686, the Madonna reappeared miraculously: an omen of defeat for the Turks.

⑤ **St Mary's Door**
St Mary's Door, with a representation of the Assumption of the Virgin, is a wonderful work of Gothic sculpture.

⑥ **Royal tomb**
Here lie the mortal remains of King Béla III and his queen, Anne de Chatillon.

⑦ **Pulpit**
The richly decorated pulpit bears images of the four doctors of the church and the four evangelists.

⑧ **Windows**
The wonderful stained-glass windows on the south side of the church date from the 19th century.

Emperor Franz Joseph I of Austria and his bride Elizabeth (here as portrayed by Romy Schneider and Karl-Heinz Böhm in the movie »Sissi«) – better as Sisi – were crowned King and Queen of Hungary in the Matthias Church in 1867. Franz Liszt composed his famous Coronation Mass for the event.

All interior wall surfaces are magnificently painted.

Main altar: At the heart of the magnificent choir stands the neo-Gothic main altar.

Coronation mosaic: Emperor Franz Joseph I and his bride Elizabeth ask for divine blessing.

Glazed tiles: Visible from afar, they decorate the church roof.
1
2
3
4
5
6
7
8

Interior The interior of the Matthias Church is decorated with geometric patterns and plant ornamentation that recalls the decoration of a mosque. Bertalan Székely and Károly Lotz designed the frescoes as well as the stained glass in the choir, done in the 1890s. The neo-Gothic main altar and the pews are by Schulek.

DON'T MISS

- St Mary's Door
- Baroque Madonna
- Tomb of king Béla and Anne de Châtillon

In the **Loreto Chapel** in the Matthias Tower there are two important items from the Baroque era: the red marble Madonna and the ebony carved Madonna on the altar panel. The columns of the **baptismal chapel** in the Béla tower have retained their medieval capitals. The north choir is a chapel dedicated to St Ladislaus; the frescoes by Károly Lotz show scenes from the saint's life. Behind railings in the Holy Trinity Chapel in the north aisle are the sarcophaguses of King Béla III and his wife, which were originally in the cathedral at Székesfehérvár. They were moved to the Matthias Church in 1848. An altar painting by Mihály Zichy from 1894 adorns the chapel dedicated to St Emmerich.

Church Museum The crypt, the royal oratory with its flags that were raised on the occasion of the coronation of King Charles IV and Queen Zita on 30 December 1916, the sacristy and the side galleries all serve as the Church Museum today. Relics, vestments and other sacred art are shown here, as well as copies of the royal crown and orb which are kept in ►Parliament.

★★ Museum of Fine Arts

(Szépmüvészeti Múzeum)

E 4

Location: XIV, Hösök tere
Trolley bus: 75, 79
Underground: M1 (Hösök tere)
Bus: 4, 20, 30

Next to the National Gallery on Castle Hill (►Royal Palace), the Museum of Fine Arts is the most important and extensive art collection in the Hungarian capital and one of the great European galleries with works of old masters.

Opening hours: Tue–Sun 10am–5.30pm; www.szepmuveszeti.hu

This large collection of Italian, Spanish and Dutch painting enjoys international renown. The presentation of the collection in a »classical« 19th-century museum building is interesting, with long corridors for the large-scale paintings, cabinet rooms for the smaller formats and intimate subjects, as well as individual rooms, such as the Renaissance hall, where the architectural setting and the exhibits complement each other.

History of the collection

The history of the collection begins in the year 1870, when the Hungarian state purchased a collection of paintings, drawings and prints from Count Miklós Esterházy. The National Museum – as it was called then – originally found a home in the building of the Hungarian Academy of Sciences (► Roosevelt tér). Through a systematic buying policy, as well as the incorporation of various private collections and gifts, including a row of painted panels from the estate of János László Pyrker, Archbishop of Eger, and paintings from Archbishop Arnold Ipolyi's collection, the museum collection expanded rapidly. Soon sculptures were also bought, in addition to paintings and graphics. The departments created most recently are the antiquity collection (1908) and the Egyptian collection (1934). The plan for an imposing new museum building grew out of the preparations for the millennium celebrations of 1896. The monumental building, designed by Albert Schickendanz and Fülop Herzog, was finally opened to the public in 1906. Numerous quotes from Greek antiquity and the Italian Renaissance embellish the façade and the interior. The entrance side is dominated by the mighty portal, whose Corinthian pillars carry a tympanum relief of the *Battle of the Centaurs*, a copy of the sculptures from the pediment of the Temple of Zeus in Olympia.

Renaissance hall in the Museum of Fine Art

Art from antiquity, the print collection and 19th-century paintings and sculptures can be seen on the **ground floor** of the Museum of Fine Arts. The painting galleries for all significant European schools from the 13th to the 18th century can be found on the first floor. The basement is reserved for the Egyptian department and 20th-century art, as well as changing exhibitions.

The entrance to the antiquities department lies at the right-hand side of the ticket hall. Objects from the first, second and third millennia BC are shown here, including gold and bronze works, and also terracotta. The art of the fourth and fifth millennia BC includes the bronze Grimani jar (mid-5th century BC), vases, and an Attic tomb relief. Among the items from the first millennium BC are Etruscan, Roman and Greek objects; a lovely marble dancing figure (mid-3rd century BC), as well as a Tyche statue are of particular interest here. A beautiful example of sculpture from late antiquity is the relief on the Attic marble sarcophagus from the 3rd century AD. The two-storey hall exactly opposite the main entrance is home to Italian Baroque painting, including the works of such famous names as Guido Reni and Andrea Vaccaro. In the axis of the Baroque room lies the impressive Renaissance room, which recalls an Italian palazzo with its surrounding galleries. It provides a suitable setting for sculptures and frescoes of the 14th to 16th centuries by Girolamo Romanino, Giulio Campi and other Italian Renaissance artists.

Baroque room, Renaissance room ►

Graphics collection ►

The exhibition room for the graphics collection, which contains about 10,000 drawings and around 100,000 prints, is reached from the Renaissance hall. All important schools and epochs of European art are represented in this collection. Periodic exhibitions are mounted from the extensive collection to illuminate individual aspects, or highlight schools or outstanding artists and their circle. Studies by Leonardo da Vinci, Raphael, Tintoretto and Veronese are part of this collection, as well as drawings by Dürer, Cranach, Rembrandt, Manet, Cézanne, Gainsborough and numerous other renowned artists.

19th century ►

A tour of the ground floor ends in the department for 19th-century paintings and sculptures, which is housed in the wing to the left of the main entrance. The three rooms with Ionic columns and a heavy coffered ceiling are architecturally impressive. In the domain of sculpture, French masters like Meunier, Rombaux, Despiau, Rodin, and Maillol take centre stage. In painting, German-speaking artists such as Achenbach, Waldmüller, von Stuck, von Uhde, Piloty, Böcklin, Leibl, Menzel and others are represented by individual works, but the development of French painting – from the Romantic period to Realism and Impressionism – can also be followed in works by Delacroix, Courbet, Daubigny, Corot, Manet, Monet, Pissarro, Renoir, Toulouse-Lautrec, Cézanne and others.

✓ DON'T MISS

- Maso di Banco: *Coronation of the Virgin*
- Raphael: *Esterházy Madonna*
- Titian: *Doge Marcantonio Trevisani*
- Rembrandt: *The Old Rabbi*
- El Greco: *Repentant Mary Magdalene*
- Goya: *The Water Carrier*
- Dürer: *Portrait of a Young Man*
- Leonardo da Vinci: equestrian statue of the French King François I

First floor ★

Italian painting ►

The sequence of rooms devoted to old masters on the first floor begins with Tuscan panel painting from the 13th to 15th centuries, including Maso di Banco's *Coronation of the Virgin*. The collection is particularly rich in the art of the quattrocento (15th century) and the cinquecento (16th century). With the so-called Esterházy Ma-

Museum of Fine Arts Plan

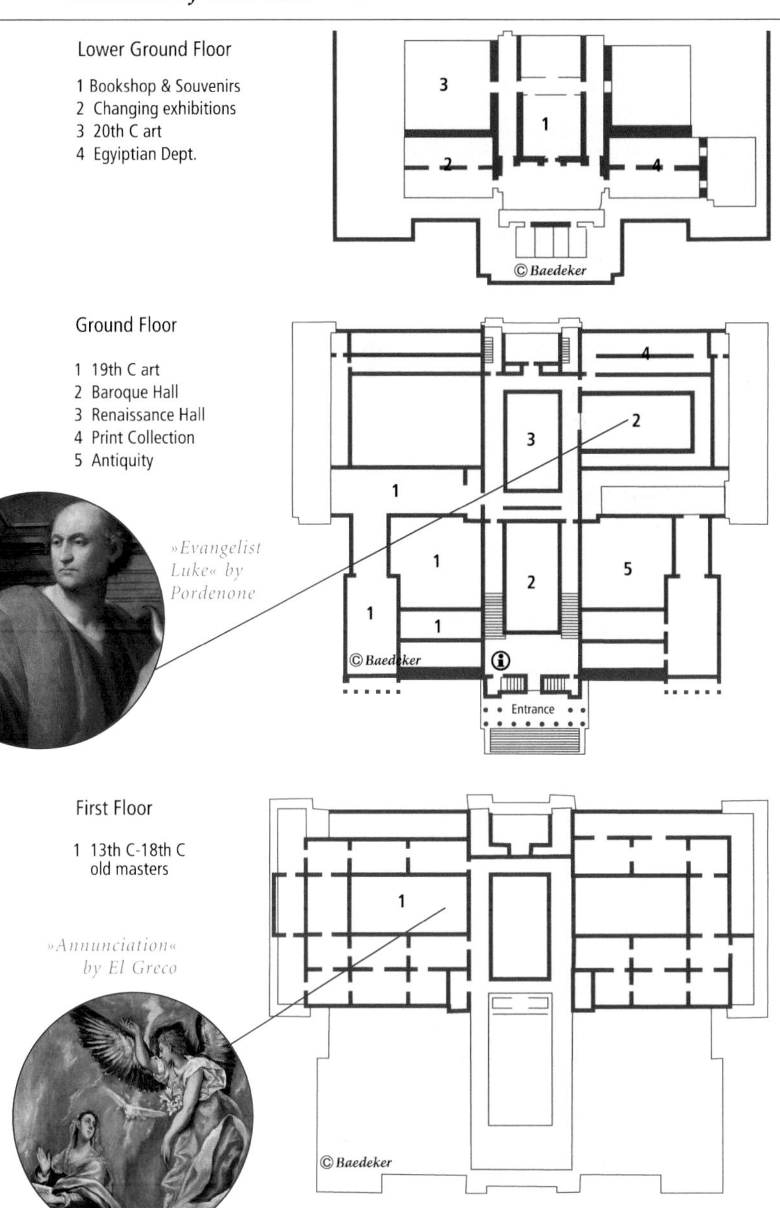

»Evangelist Luke« by Pordenone

»Annunciation« by El Greco

donna by Raphael, named after its former owners, the Esterházy family, the gallery owns an outstanding work of the Italian Renaissance. By the same artist, the collection also contains a youthful portrait of the humanist Pietro Bembo (around 1504). Art of the 15th and 16th centuries from central Italy is represented by works from the school of Giovanni Santi from Urbino, as well as by Domenico and Rodolfo Ghirlandaio, while northern Italian painting from the 14th to 16th centuries is well covered by works of Gentile Bellini of Venice, and Michele Pannonio, an artist of Hungarian origin, among others. The cinquecento is illustrated by the works of numerous renowned artists, among them Giorgione, Sebastiano del Piombo, Lorenzo Lotto, Filippino Lippi, Correggio, Jacopo Bassano, Jacopo Tintoretto and Veronese. Lombard painting, which was lastingly defined by Leonardo da Vinci – himself only represented by drawings in the graphics collection – can be discovered through many works of lesser-known masters. There is the portrait of the Doge Marcantonio Trevisani (after 1553) by Titian. Of the representatives of Italian Baroque painting, special mention should be made of Bernardo Bellotto, Bernardo Strozzi, Giovanni Battista Tiepolo and Canaletto.

! *Baedeker* TIP

Orientation aid

It is not so easy to locate the most significant works right away in the Old Masters Gallery, which is crammed with paintings, but help is at hand: the English-language audio guide available at the cash desk leads straight to the collection's highlights.

★ Dutch painting ►

Beyond the halls and several cabinet rooms for Italian painting there is the equally high-calibre Netherlands department. An outstanding work of early Dutch painting is *John the Baptist's Sermon* (1566) by Pieter Brueghel the Elder, but Hans Memling, Petrus Christus and Gerard David and others are also represented.

The three Rembrandt paintings are indisputably the highlights among the art of the golden age (17th century), especially *The Old Rabbi* of 1642 and *The Angel appears to St Joseph*, as well as portraits by Frans Hals. Dutch landscape painting is represented, among others, by Jan van Goyen, as well as by Salomon and Jacob van Ruisdael; but plenty of space is devoted to genre painting and still-lifes.

Flemish painting, spread across two rooms, includes paintings by Peter Paul Rubens, Anthony van Dyck and Jacob Jordaens alongside works of less well-known masters.

The department of **Spanish painting** is also of high quality. Spanish and Portuguese masters from the 15th and 16th century lead on to works by El Greco (*Repentant Mary Magdalene*, before 1580), the outstanding artist of Mannerism in Spain. Most of the famous names of Spanish Baroque painting are present, among others Francisco de Zurbarán, Jusepe de Ribera and Murillo. The museum possesses five works by Francisco di Goya, including *The Water Carrier*, *The Grinder* (both before 1812), and the *Portrait of Señora Bermúdez* (around

1785). One work by Diego Velázquez hangs in the exhibition: the stylistically early work, *Farmers' Meal.*

Highlights of 15th- and 16th-century **German painting** are Hans Holbein's *Death of the Virgin* (around 1490), Albrecht Dürer's *Portrait of a Young Man*, as well as Lucas Cranach's *The Angel appears to St Joachim* (1518). Hans Baldung Grien and Albrecht Altdorfer are also represented. The artistic trends and associations of the Baroque epoch are introduced by way of a small, but representative selection of Austrian and German artists: Franz Anton Maulbertsch, Jan Kupetzky, Angelika Kaufmann and others.

One room each is dedicated to 18th-century **English painting**, with works by Gainsborough, Hogarth and Reynolds, and 17th- and 18th-century **French painting**, including canvases by Chardin, Lorrain and Poussin.

The museum's **sculpture collection** encompasses predominantly Italian artists. The exhibits are spread among the relevant departments of painting. The highlight of the collection is the equestrian statue of French King Francois I by Leonardo da Vinci. Several Baroque sculptures are also remarkable, among others those by Georg Raphael Donner and Johann Christoph Mader.

Annunciation by El Greco

Basement

◄ Egyptian department

The Egyptian department housed in the right wing of the basement houses monuments from the Old, Middle and New Kingdoms, as well as from antiquity. The especially outstanding pieces are the tombs from the various epochs, a diorite pharaoh's head, a limestone male head, as well as animal statues and other small figures of bronze that show the high standard of casting techniques in ancient Egypt. The stone relief from a Ptolemaic temple is also remarkable.

20th century ► The department in the left wing offers a cross section through the artistic trends of the 20th century. Works by Oskar Kokoschka, Hans Arp, Marc Chagall, György Kepes, Pablo Picasso and Victor Vasarély attract many admirers.

Nagykörút (Great Ring)

B 4–D 8

Tram: 4, 6 **Bus:** 12, 12 A

The Great Ring Road (Nagykörút), arcs around Pest city centre in a semi-circle over three miles long from the eastern bridgehead of the Margaret Bridge to the eastern bridgehead of Petöfi Bridge. The West Railway Station designed by the Parisian firm Eiffel is an outstanding building here.

Drained Danube arm With the exception of Szent István körút, the individual sections of the Great Ring are named after members of the Habsburg imperial house: Teréz körút (Theresa), Erzsébet körút (Elizabeth), József körút (Joseph), Ferenc körút (Franz). Opened to traffic in 1896, the Great Ring follows a drained arm of the Danube. In 1867 there were still plans to make it navigable, but these were then abandoned. Numerous significant buildings from the fin-de-siècle era line the Nagykörút.

Szent István körút

Northern section Szent István körút (St Stephen's Ring) is the northernmost section of the Great Ring. It begins at Jászai Mari tér, which is named after Mari Jászai (1850–1926), who was one of the greatest European actresses of her day. The highlight of this section of the ring is the Comedy Theatre (Vigszínház; no. 14), built to plans by Fellner & Helmer from Vienna in the 1890s and rebuilt after severe war damage.

★ West Railway Station and Nyugati tér

Underground: M 3 (Nyugati pu.)

Eiffel built here Extended at great cost after 1978, Nyugati tér (West Square) also acts as forecourt to the West Railway Station (Nyugati pályaudvar), a protected monument which, next to the market hall on ►Fövám tér, is the most important and perhaps most beautiful example of cast-iron architecture in the Hungarian capital. The first trains in Hungary departed from the site of the West Railway Station as early as 1846. It is a terminus comprising two brick side-buildings with brick curtain walls and a glass-roofed hall above the railway tracks at the centre. The platform hall is supported by filigree cast-iron supports, like the ones developed for the Crystal Palace in London. The designs for what at the time was a highly modern construction were produced by the Eiffel firm in Paris. It is well worth taking a look into the interior of the platform hall: everything appears to be as in the old days. Being at the end of the line, the Nyugati pályaudvar is only significant for local rail transport.

Café New York

This world-famous coffee house (Erzsébet körút no. 9–11) was simply the most fashionable place to meet in the first three decades of the 20th century and, as such, it was famous well beyond Hungary. It was re-opened after extensive renovation work in 2006. It is located on the ground floor of a magnificent neo-Renaissance palace that was built for the »New York« insurance company between 1891 and 1893, and today houses a luxury hotel.

Teréz körút and Erzsébet körút

Madách Theatre

From the West Railway Station, Teréz körút (Theresa Ring) leads to Erzsébet körút (Elizabeth Ring). Several noteworthy buildings stand along Erzsébet körút, which crosses ►Andrássy út at the Oktogon: the Madách Theatre opened in 1961, (Madách Színház; no. 29) and evolved out of a tavern built in the 19th century. The wall mosaics by Eszter Mattioni are an attractive feature of this much-frequented venue.

József körút and Ferenc körút

Rabbinical seminary

Eastern Europe's only rabbinical seminary can be found at József körút 27. Attached to a Jewish secondary school, it owns one of the most extensive libraries in the world for oriental studies.

The last section of the Great Ring runs right through district IX, formerly known as Francistown (Ferencváros). Like the district, the street was named after the Austrian Emperor Franz I. Like so many other south-eastern districts, Ferencváros is characterized by industrial settlements and workshops.

Petöfi Bridge

The Petöfi Bridge is the southernmost road connection across the Danube in central Budapest. On the other side of the Danube lies the Lágymányos district, which was built on former marshy terrain.

Millennium District and Palace of Arts

National Theatre

South of the Great Ring, in the Millennium District, a large cultural centre has been created with the new, architecturally interesting **Na-**

tional Theatre (Nemezeti Szinház) and the Palace of Arts, opened in 2005.

Ludwig Museum

Opening hours: Tue–Sun 10am–6pm; Internet www.ludwig museum.hu

In addition to the **national concert hall** with its superb acoustics and 1700 seats, the Palace of Arts also houses the **Ludwig Museum for Modern Art** (Ludwig Múzeum Budapest – Kortárs Müvészeti Múzeum). Until 2004, it was still housed in the Royal Palace. Today Hungarian and international contemporary art are given equal prominence here. On display are works by Sándor Molnár, Imre Bukta, Mikláos Erdély, Tibor Vilt, Valéria Sass and Tibor Csernus, as well as paintings and sculptures by Pablo Picasso, Andy Warhol, Roy Lichtenstein, Robert Rauschenberg, Jaspar Johns, Rudolf Hausner, David Hockney, Jörg Immendorf, Gerhard Richter and others, representing extremely diverse trends in international art.
The museum, founded in 1989 with 70 contemporary works of art donated by the German collectors Irene and Peter Ludwig, is the most significant collection of international contemporary art in all of Hungary. The collection was increased in 1991 by 91 works on permanent loan, and has also been expanded step by step with works by Hungarian artists.

Nagytétény Palace

Excursion

Location: XXII district, Kastélypark u. 9 – 11
Tram: 41

Railway station: Nagytétény
Bus: 3, 13, 103, 113

The main sight at Nagytétény is the Baroque palace, in which a department of the ►Arts and Crafts Museum is now housed.

Nagytétény Palace (Nagytétényi Kastélymúzeum) is located in the Hungarian capital's rural southern district of the same name, on the Buda side of the Danube, where a Roman garrison existed from the 2nd to 5th centuries. Nagytétény is probably named after the Magyar leader Tétény, and had importance as a wine-growing area in the Middle Ages. It was granted a charter to hold markets in the 15th century. The settlement was extensively destroyed during the Turkish wars, after which numerous families came to re-settle Nagytétény from south-western Germany. Their houses characterize the townscape to this day.

! *Baedeker* TIP

Beware of sharks!
The Tropicarium/Óceanárium at Nagytétényi út 37–45 contains everything that swims in the world's waters: sharks, rays, alligators, iguanas, snakes, but also indigenous fish. (Opening times: daily 10am–8pm; www.tropicarium.hu).

This country residence was built in the 18th century, using building remains from the 15th century. The palace was badly damaged in the Second World War, but was painstakingly restored a few years ago and has now been made accessible as a museum.

Opening hours:
Tue–Sun
10am–6pm

Palace Museum

In addition to the superbly worked 15th–19th-century furniture, predominantly originating in Hungary and Germany, the collection is noteworthy for its oven tiles, or rather its domestic ovens. There are valuable paintings, carpets, faïence and clocks from the 18th to 19th centuries in several rooms. Interesting exhibits from the Roman period are shown in the palace stables.

★ National Museum (Nemzeti Múzeum)

D 7

Location: VIII district, Múzeum körút 14–16
Underground: M 3 (Kálvin tér)
Tram: 47, 49
Bus: 9
Internet: http://origo.hnm.hu

With its eight conspicuous columns and huge open-air steps, the National Museum is one of the city's most impressive buildings. The history of the country is comprehensively featured here, from the Stone Age to the present.

Opening hours:
Tue–Sun 10am–6pm

In the 19th-century history of Budapest, the Széchenyi family appears again and again; so too with the Hungarian National Museum (Magyar Nemzeti Múzeum), which owes its foundation to Count Ferenc Széchenyi's commitment. Although the institution was already established in 1802, and Mihály Pollack was hired to design the building, the classical-style museum was not inaugurated until 1847.

! *Baedeker* TIP

Looking for an old Baedeker?

There are a number of well stocked second-hand bookshops opposite the National Museum, on Múzeum körút, that sell books in other languages than Hungarian. With a bit of luck, it is possible to pick up a small rarity, for example an old Baedeker from the 19th or 20th century.

A memorial completed by Alajos Stróbl in 1893, to the famous Hungarian poet János Arany (1817–1882), stands in front of the museum. Further busts and memorials of famous people can be found in the park-like museum garden.

Ground floor

The exhibition on the ground floor encompasses the pre-history of Hungary from the Stone Age, the Roman era and the early Middle Ages. The finds from Vértesszölös and Sümeg are noteworthy in the

Hungarian National Museum Plan

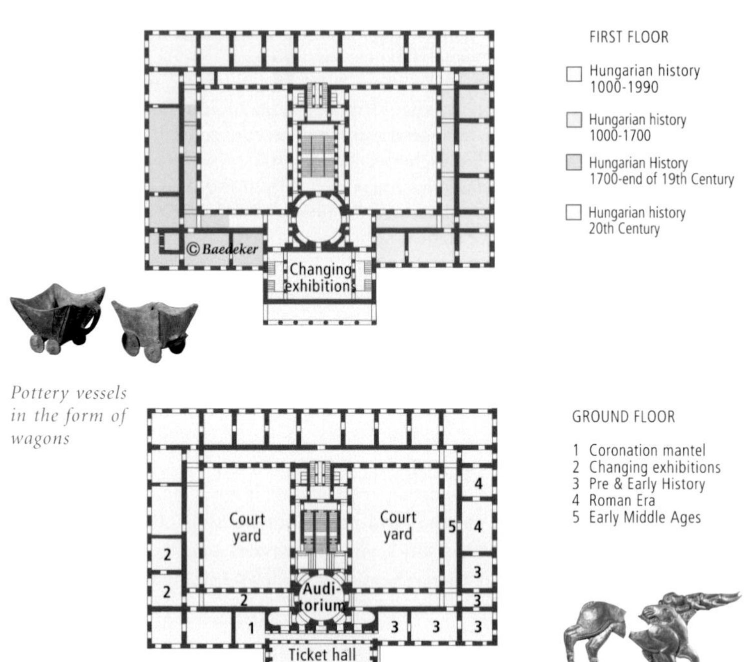

Pottery vessels in the form of wagons

Scythian stag

department for pre-history. The highlight of the Bronze Age collection is the chariot from Pécel. From the migration era there is Hunnish jewellery, a Carolingian sword, as well as utensils from Slavic tribes. Until 2000, the Hungarian monarchy's royal insignia could be viewed in a hall in the left wing, but is now exhibited at ► Parliament. Only the coronation mantel remains in the National Museum. It was gifted to the Székesfehérvár basilica by St Stephen in 1031 and only served as part of the ruling insignia from the end of the 12th century onwards. The coronation mantel is of gold-embroidered Byzantine silk with pearl decorations.

First floor The first floor is reached via a magnificent stairway painted with a series of allegorical frescoes by Károly Lotz und Mór Than. The first room is a domed hall, which is dedicated to changing exhibitions, as is the large hall behind it. Hungarian history from the time its state

was founded – or rather from St Stephen I's coronation as Hungarian king in AD 1000 – to the expulsion of the Turks in the late 17th century, is highlighted in the rooms of the south wing.
Hungarian history from Rákóczi's battles for independence at the beginning of the 18th century to the collapse of the socialist system in 1990 is vividly presented in the north wing. The individual independence battles of Hungarian history are accorded special prominence. The exhibits include Hungarian and Turkish weapons, souvenirs from the independence battles of Prince Ferenc Rákóczi, and Baroque art. Furthermore, documents and exhibits cover the 18th-century farmers' revolts, the Hungarian Jacobin movement and the revolution of 1848–49.

Lower ground floor

The lapidarium with exhibits from the Middle Ages and early antiquity is housed on the lower ground floor and contains the museum's tombstone collection, as well as fragments of medieval architecture. The Roman lapidarium on the lowest basement floor presents important Roman fragments from the Hungarian region, among them a floor mosaic from the 3rd century BC found in Baláca by Veszprém.

Népliget (public park)

F/G 8/9

Location: X district **Underground:** M3 (Népliget)

At 112ha/277 acres Népliget is the Hungarian capital's largest park. It was laid out to the south-east of the city centre in the 1860s. The planetarium is worth a visit in bad weather.

The Népliget received a make-over according to the latest ideas in garden design on the occasion of the centenary jubilee celebrating the unification of Óbuda, Buda and Pest. Diverse monuments, water features, flowerbeds, meadows and mature trees make a stroll enjoyable, especially during the warmer times of year. The central bus station is also at the park, where coaches leave for and arrive from all over Europe. From time to time the park is also used for car and motorbike races. The park is also a meeting place for the local gay scene, especially after dark.

Planetarium

In the south-west part of the Népliget, the laser theatre of the planetarium transports visitors into a world of visual effects (every evening except Sun). Tickets can be had from the planetarium desk, from Music Mix Ticket Service (Váci u. 33), from the Central Ticket Office (Andrássy út 18), as well as at various hotel receptions. Programme information: www.lasertheater.hu (Hungarian only) or tel. 263-08 71.

Óbuda (»old oven«)

A–C 1–3

Location: III district
Suburban train HÉV: Batthyány tér–Szentendre
Bus: 6, 18, 37, 42, 106
Tram: 1

Until its amalgamation with Buda and Pest in 1873, Óbuda was a sleepy little town and, in spite of large-scale urban renewal and modernization, it has managed to retain something of its former atmosphere.

According to tradition, the old settlement where evidence of settlement from prehistoric times has been discovered and where the Romans founded their garrison ►Aquincum shortly after the birth of Christ, was Attila the Hun's residence in the 5th century. The town experienced a significant upturn under the Árpáds and, during the Middle Ages, the Hungarian queens had a palace here. The town, which had been overshadowed by the developing royal city of Buda, was completely obliterated during the Turkish era,. In 1659 it came into the ownership of the Counts Zichy, who settled farmers from Austria and Moravia here to work their lands after the expulsion of the Turks, and in this way the town revived.

The figures with umbrellas were made by Imre Varga.

✶ Fö tér and around

city map: B 1

Fö tér is the old main square of Óbuda, just a few steps north-east of Flórián tér. Today it is surrounded by depressing high-rise residential blocks that provide an unattractive background for the pretty square lined by one- to three-storey houses. On the northern side of Fö tér stands the former neo-Baroque town hall of Óbuda. Opposite is the once-famous Sipos Halászkert fish restaurant.

At Fö tér no. 4 an 18th-century building holds the **Kun folk art collection**, which was gathered together over decades by a husband and wife.

The **Imre Varga Museum** is not far from the figures with umbrellas. It is in one of the low single-storey dwellings on Laktanya utca (no. 7), which leads off the square in a northerly direction. The museum contains numerous models of the master's great works, busts of famous people and copies of several other works. The small attractive garden of the house, with portrait sculptures of renowned Hungarian contemporaries, is also worth seeing. (Opening times: Tue–Sun 10am–6pm).

Former silk-weaving workshop

The oval building a few blocks north of Fö tér, at no. 44 on Harrer Pál utca, was built as a silk-weaving workshop by József Tallherr in 1785. Today it is a historic industrial monument and recalls the textile production in Óbuda that was promoted by Emperor Joseph II.

✶ Zichy Palace (Zichy-kastély)

City map: B 1/2

Two museums in one

An unpretentious Baroque palace, built in the mid-18th century by Henrik János Jäger for Count Nikolaus Zichy, stands between Fö tér and Szentlelék tér adjoining to its south. It was restored after heavy damage during the Second World War and now serves as a cultural centre. Two interesting museums are ranged around the large courtyard of this building complex: the Lajos Kassák Museum and the Vasarély Museum.

◄ Lajos Kassák Museum

The courtyard with the main palace building is reached via an entrance through the west wing of the palace, which faces towards Fö tér. A small museum dedicated to Lajos Kassák, the versatile proponent of Hungarian avant-garde, has been installed on the first floor of this beautifully renovated Baroque building. The life work of this writer, publicist and artist is shown in a three-room permanent exhibition that betrays great attention to detail and commitment to the artist. Temporary exhibitions enrich an interesting show. Kassák (1887–1967), who lived in Óbuda from 1954, promoted the Hungarian avant-garde movement as publisher of the magazine *MA* (Today), which appeared from 1916 to 1925 and combined the most diverse contemporary trends, from Dadaism and Constructivism to Expressionism and Futurism. (Opening times: mid-March–Oct Tue–Sun 10am–6pm, Nov–mid-March Tue–Sun 10am–5pm).

Opera performance at Zichy Palace

Vasarély Museum ► The entrance to the Vasarély Museum, which is located in one of the wings of Zichy Palace, is on Szentlelék tér. Victor Vasarély (1908–1997), who originally came from Pécs in southern Hungary and made his home in France, is considered the most important representative of Op Art. The richly endowed show gives a representative view of the artist's work. (Opening times: mid March–Oct Tue–Sun 10am–6pm, Nov–mid March Tue–Sun 10am–5pm).

Óbuda parish church To the south of Zichy Palace, separated from it by the wide carriageway that extends from Árpád Bridge, the old parish church (Szent Péter és Pál plébániatemplom) stands on Lajos utca, Buda's former main street. It was commissioned by the Zichys between 1744 and 1749 and designed by Johann Georg Paur.

Former Óbuda synagogue There was a synagogue for the resident Jewish community in Óbuda in the 18th century. When that community grew larger, András Landherr designed a larger house of worship, which was built at Lajos utca no. 161, to the south of the Óbuda parish church, between 1820 and 1825. The classical building is no longer used as a synagogue and nothing survives of its interior.

Roman Remains in Óbuda

Roman military bath Fürdö Museum On Flórián tér, today an important traffic junction at which the road leading from the Árpád Bridge crosses Szentendrei utca, in the 1st century AD there was a Roman garrison, around which a civilian settlement later developed (► Aquincum). On the northern side of the square, underneath an access road for the Árpád Bridge, a number of remains can still be seen, including the partly reconstructed ruins of a bath with underfloor heating, as well as hot and cold pools and surviving parts of a centurion's house. The bath was presumably in use from the 1st to the 4th century AD. The little Fürdö Museum provides a vivid description of Roman bathing culture. (Opening times: May–Sept Tue–Sun 10am–6pm, 2nd half of April and Oct Tue–Sun 10am–5pm).

Concrete housing with a view of antiquity

The medieval remains of the queens' residence and Óbuda's 18th-century Reformed Church can be seen at the southern edge of the square, near Cálvin köz.

The remains of the Roman garrison were found during excavations in 1950, to the south of Flórian tér, on Pacsirtamezö utca. In addition to the surviving walls of the former south gate and other buildings dating from the 2nd to 4th centuries AD, tools, containers, burial gifts and sarcophaguses came to light. A beautiful fresco from the 3rd century, which shows a hunting scene, was also revealed.

Mosaic in the Villa of Hercules

Amphitheatre

Follow the broad Pacsirtamezö utca even further south to the remains of an amphitheatre built in the 2nd century AD on the corner of Nagyszombat utca. The ruins were exposed in 1940. The elliptical arena, 131m/143yd long and 107m/117yd wide, once held around 15,000 spectators, who could follow Roman contests here.

Cella trichora

On the corner of Raktár utca/Hunor utca, north-west of Flórián tér, is a historically interesting survival: the ruin of what has become known as the »cella trichora«, an early Christian tomb.

✶ **Hercules Villa**

Even further north of Flórián tér, at Meggyfa utca nos. 19–21, the remains of a Roman villa4, probably from the 3rd century, were exposed. The mosaics show scenes from the legends of Hercules and Dionysus. (Opening times: May–Sept Tue–Sun 10am–6pm, 2nd half of April and Oct Tue–Sun 10am–5pm).

Kleinzeller Museum (Kiscelli Múzeum)

Location: Kiscelli út 108 **city map:** A 2
Bus: 60, 165 **tram:** 17

Opening hours: April–Oct Tue–Sun 10am–6pm, Nov–March Tue–Sun 10am–4pm

The quarter of Óbuda where the Counts of Zichy initially built a chapel, to which a monastery was added in the 1740s, is called Kleinzell or Kiscell. A copy of the pietà from the Austrian pilgrimage site Mariazell was brought to the chapel, which is how it got its name of Kleinzell (small chapel). At the beginning of the 20th century the building, formerly part of the Trinitarian monastery dissolved in 1783, came into the possession of an Austrian art and antiques lover, who also brought here the Baroque portal originally made in 1799 for the seat of the Jesuit order in Vienna. His art collection has been incorporated into the newly founded branch of Budapest's Historical Museum (► Royal Palace) which has been installed in the rooms of the former Trinitarian monastery.

An exhibition gives a good insight into the economic and cultural life of the three Danube towns of Óbuda, Buda and Pest from the end of the Turkish occupation onwards.

★★ Parliament (Országház)

B 5

Location: V district, Kossuth Lajos tér
Tram: 2
Underground: M 2 (Kossuth tér)
Trolley bus: 70, 78

The most imposing structure on the Pest side of the Danube bank is the giant neo-Gothic parliamentary complex. It is considered an outstanding achievement of Budapest architecture and is one of the landmarks of the Hungarian capital.

The building of a parliament in Budapest as a place where the legislative assembly, or rather the Hungarian estates, could meet was already agreed after the Compromise of 1867 with Austria, but was only realized with considerable delay. Until 1847 the legislative assembly had its permanent seat in Pressburg, today's Bratislava, and was then moved to Pest, where it met in various buildings until the new parliament was completed. After a 20-year period of construction, the huge complex was inaugurated in 1904. The neo-Gothic façade conceals a highly modern iron construction, which gives the complicated room designs the necessary stability.

Exterior The focus of the building is the 96m/315ft-high dome over the central section. It is a synthesis of a neo-Gothic buttress system and a Renaissance dome. To left and right long symmetrical wings enclose no less than ten courtyards. The building is also remarkable for its total of 691 rooms. The south wing houses the parliamentary chamber for the House of Representatives, the northern one the congress hall, formerly seat of the upper house. Both halls protrude from the roofline with their corner turrets and are therefore also recognizable from the outside. 88 statues from the workshops of a range of Hungarian sculptors decorate the façades of Parliamentar: on the Danube side are Hungarian tribal leaders and kings, on the eastern entrance side, facing Kossuth tér, eastern Hungarian army leaders and princes from the independence battles of the 17th and 18th century.

Interior On the eastern side, at Kossuth Lajos tér, steps lead to the tripartite main portal flanked by two bronze lions. The monumental nature of the exterior is also continued inside. The extensive entrance hall and stairwell is decorated with ceiling frescoes by Károly Lotz and sculptures by György Kiss. The bust of the architect Imre Steindl by Alajos Stróbl stands in a niche.

Parliament Plan

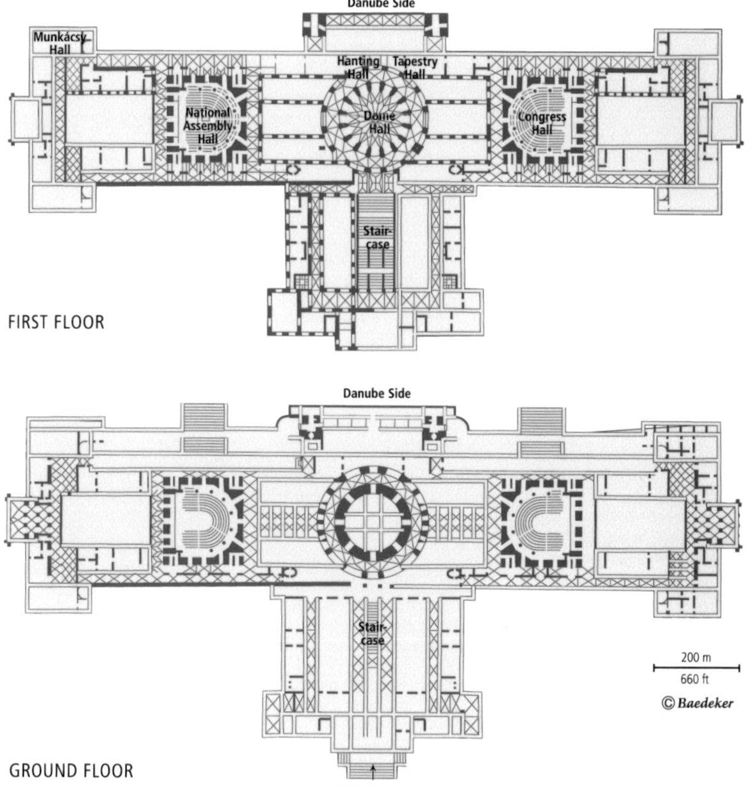

The magnificent 27m/89ft-high domed hall, sixteen-sided and borne by 16 pillars with portraits of outstanding Hungarian leaders, is on the first floor. Paintings by Aldar Körösföi-Kriesch hang in the hunting hall (Vadászterem), and behind that, in the tapestry hall (Gobelinterem), a truly colossal wall tapestry shows a gathering of the Magyar princes who founded the country. The large assembly chamber is especially impressive, with frescoes by the renowned artist Károly Lotz, and the large-format painting *Conquest*, with which the history painter Mihály Munkácsy made his name.The beautiful stained glass windows are by Miksa Róth, one of the leading glass painters of his time. The decorative grates over the heating vents cover up an ingenious system that also cools the building by means of huge blocks of ice in the summer.

PARLIAMENT

★★ **Parliament is the largest building in Hungary: with a length of 286m/880ft it surpasses the British parliament buildings by 6m/20ft, and has a height of almost 100m/328ft. Close to 700 magnificent rooms within its walls were designed and decorated by the leading artists of the country in the 19th century. Similarities with the Palace of Westminster are no coincidence: the British parliamentary system was a model for the Hungarian state.**

Visits only as part of a guided tour:
English-language tours daily 10am, noon, 1pm, 2pm and 6pm from Gate X

① **Parliamentary Chamber**
A splendid room surrounded by galleries

② **Congress Hall**
Heart of the north wing

③ **Munkácsy Room**
The painting of the *Conquest of Hungary* is a work of the Hungarian artist Mihaly Munkácsy (1844–1900).

④ **Domed Hall**
This columned hall is at the centre of the Parliament building.

⑤ **Royal insignia**
The royal insignia, with the exception of the coronation mantle, are kept in the Domed Hall.

⑥ **Main entrance**
Two stone lions guard the main entrance.

⑦ **Dome**
The columns of the Domed Hall meet at a height of 96m/315ft to form the great golden star.

⑧ **Statues**
88 statues adorn the façade of the building.

Ante-chambers
Not only the main halls of Parliament have magnificent and sumptuous interiors.

St Stephen's Crown
The Hungarian coronation insignia, including the richly decorated crown, sceptre, imperial orb and sword, are displayed in Parliament at present. Only the coronation mantle can be admired in the National Museum

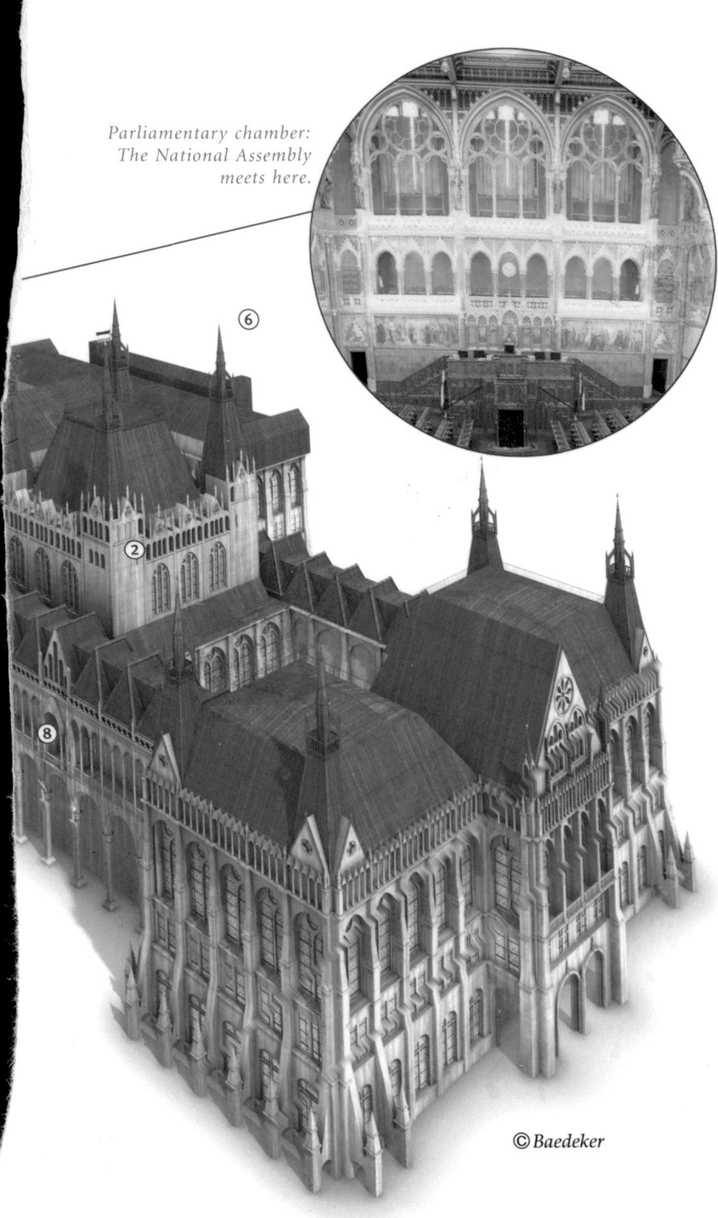
Parliamentary chamber: The National Assembly meets here.
6
2
8
© Baedeker

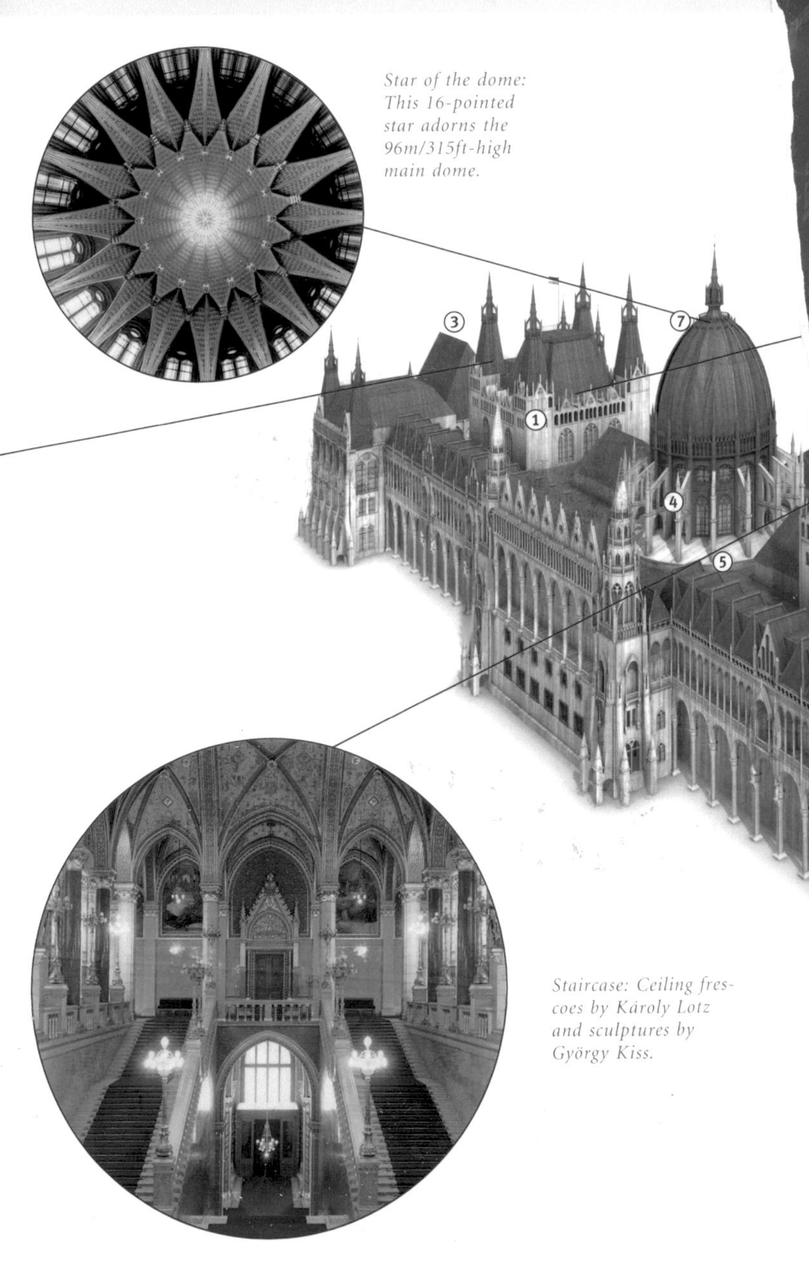

Star of the dome: This 16-pointed star adorns the 96m/315ft-high main dome.

Staircase: Ceiling frescoes by Károly Lotz and sculptures by György Kiss.

The parliamentary library (Országgyülési Könyvtár), with its rich collection of legal, state and historic literature, can be reached via the southern gate on the Danube side of the parliament.

★ Coronation insignia

The coronation insignia, which were taken out of the country by Hungarian fascists in 1945, have been kept in Parliament since 1 January 2000, after an extensive political debate. American occupation troops found these valuable items in Austria and took them to the USA, where they were carefully held at Fort Knox until their repatriation to Hungary in 1978. St Stephen's crown, decorated with precious stones and pearls, is adorned by representations of saints and the characteristic crooked cross above the crossing point of the two headbands. Next to the crown lie the sceptre, orb and sword. The coronation mantel is exhibited at the ►National Museum. It remains undecided whether or not the coronation insignia will remain in Parliament long-term; a return to the National Museum or presentation in the ►Royal Palace are being considered.

★ Post Savings Bank Building

C 5/6

Location: V district, Hold utca 4 **Bus:** 5, 15

National architectural heritage: the former Post Savings Bank building is considered a jewel of Hungarian art nouveau.

Representative of the Hungarian national style

One block east of ► Szabadság tér, behind the National Bank on the narrow Hold utca, stands the former Post Savings Bank building. Together with the ►Arts and Crafts Museum it is considered the most representative example of the Hungarian national style in Budapest, an architectural style that evolved as a Hungarian variation of European art nouveau and developed its own characteristics. (►Baedeker Special, p.40).

The pioneer and most important proponent of the national style was Ödön Lechner, who also produced the designs for the Post Savings Bank building, which opened in 1901. Characteristic of art nouveau as a whole are the broad spatial treatment of the façade and the continuous flowing form details, such as can be seen on the small gable ornamentation and the divisions of the window. The Hungarian element is particularly apparent in the roof zone, with its colourful glazed tiles – from the Zsolnay factory in Pécs, of course – and the folk art flower motifs on the battlement-style gables. Lechner brilliantly carried the Secessionist style through into the interior, whose ironwork balustrades and etched windowpanes have survived a major reconstruction. His use of natural light and the latest technology (lifts) also made it an amenable workplace.

★ Rákóczi út (Rákóczi Street)

C 7–E 6

Location: Border between VII and VIII districts
Bus: 7, 7A, 78
Underground: M 2 (Astoria, Blaha L. tér, Keleti pu.)

Rákóczi út is one of the Hungarian capital's liveliest shopping streets. It is lined by several large department stores and a wide selection of small but exclusive shops and major cultural facilities.

Pulsating shopping street

This traffic artery named after the leader of the independence movement of the early 18th century, Prince Rákóczi, is a continuation of Kossuth Lajos and leads to the East Railway Station. Rákóczi út was already an important transport route in the Middle Ages, when it led to the eastern Pest city gate (Hatvan Gate), which stood at the present-day junction of Rákóczi út and the Little Ring. After the construction of the East Railway Station in 1884, many high-rise office and department stores were built here. This is also where the College for Theatre and Film Arts (Színmüvészeti Föiskola) and the adjoining Odry Theatre (Odry színház) are based.

Roosevelt tér (Roosevelt Square)

B 6

Location: V district
Tram: 2, 2A

The greatest eye-catcher on the double square on the Pest side of the ► Chain Bridge is Gresham Palace. Thanks to its impressive lighting, it even manages to outshine the neighbouring Academy of Sciences, especially at night.

The square is named after the former US President Franklin D. Roosevelt, who is honoured for his efforts to free Hungary during the Second World War. Markets were still held on the square at the beginning of the 19th century, and there was also a landing quay for Danube freighters until the building of the Chain Bridge.

Two men who had a decisive influence on Hungary's political and economic development in the 19th century are commemorated on the square: a statue of Count István Széchenyi by József J. Engel (1880) looks down on the northern section of the square; on the narrow southern side of the square, Ferenc Deák is immortalized by a sculpture by Adolf Huszár (1882).

Built in 1907 to designs by Zsigmond Quittner and the brothers László und József Vágó for the English insurance company Gresham, Gresham Palace is one of the defining examples of architecture in the Secessionist style in Budapest. Until a buyer with the necessary fi-

Newly renovated Palais Gresham

nancial resources was found, the impressive building was left to go to ruin but, after many years of meticulous renovation, the elegant Four Seasons Hotel opened its doors in Gresham Palace in 2003.

The northern side of Roosevelt tér is dominated by the monumental neo-Renaissance building of the Hungarian **Academy of Sciences** (Tudományos Akadémia), whose foundation goes back to an initiative by István Széchenyi in 1825. This centre of Hungary's highest-ranking scientific establishment was completed to plans by the Berlin architect Friedrich August Stüler. The design for the building took as its model the palace architecture of the Italian High Renaissance, the era when scientific research was born. The statues of famous scientists that decorate the façade also indicate the building's purpose. A bronze relief from 1893 showing the foundation of the academy by Count Széchenyi in 1825 is especially noteworthy. Frescoes by Károly Lotz adonr the hall of the academy. Today numerous research institutes are affiliated to the academy. Its internationally renowned scientific library possesses an important collection of oriental literature.

Eötvös Square The small Eötvös tér adjoins Roosevelt tér to the south, with a memorial by Adolf Huszár created in honour of József Eötvös. The southern side of the square is taken up by the two five-star hotels Sofitel Atrium and Intercontinental, both built in the early 1980s. Though built by Hungarian architects, their international architectural style does not really fit Budapest's historic building framework. Nevertheless, the roofed courtyard of the Sofitel Atrium is worth seeing for a model of Hungary's first airplane suspended high up.

Rose Hill (Rosado)

A 3/4

Location: II district, west of Margit híd

Rose Hill (Rosado) has long been part of the Hungarian capital's most favoured neighbourhoods. Exclusive villas, some with overgrown gardens, boulevards and pedestrian paths stretch all the way to the cool Hüvösvölgy valley.

★ **Tomb of Gül Baba** On the property of an old villa at Mecset utca 14 stands the tomb (türbe) of Gül Baba (Turkish: Father of Roses), built between 1543 and 1548 and surrounded by gardens. He lived in Buda as a Turkish dervish and died during a ceremony in 1541 at the Matthias Church when it was a mosque. The modest octagonal domed structure in which his sarcophagus is kept is today a museum commemorating Gül Baba. (Opening times: May–-Sept Tue–Sun 10am–6pm, Oct Tue–Sun 10am–4pm).

Village-like atmosphere Gül Baba utca

Before the great Hungarian composer Béla Bartók (► Famous People) emigrated to the USA in protest against the emergence of fascism in Hungary, he lived in a villa on Rose Hill, at Csalán út 29, which has been open to the public for some time as a **Béla Bartók Memorial** (Bartók Béla Emlékház). Several items of his furniture and musical instruments have been left in their original places. Occasionally chamber concerts are also held here. The memorial in the garden was created by the Hungarian sculptor Imre Varga. (Opening times: Tue–Sun 10am– 5pm).

★★ Royal Palace (Budavári Palota)

B 6/7

Location: South side of Castle Hill
Bus: 5, 16, 78
Cable car: Clark Ádám tér–Szent György tér

The Hungarian kings built their residence high above the Danube. Today the Royal Palace is among the most popular destinations in the capital, not least because of the magnificent view.

History of the Royal Palace

The construction of the first castle was closely linked to the Mongol invasions of the years 1241–42. King Béla IV had numerous fortifications built in the country in the 13th century as protection from further attacks and to control the Danube, and fortified Buda with a royal castle of which, however, nothing remains. A small palace was built in its place under King Charles Robert of Anjou in the 14th century, on top of which King Louis of Anjou built himself a magnificent palace after the royal residence had moved from Visegrád to Buda. A few fragments, for example the so-called Stephen's Tower, a Gothic residential tower, and the lower section of a palace chapel have survived from this period. His successor Sigismund had the res-

ROYAL PALACE

★★ **The former residence of Hungarian monarchs occupies the whole southern tip of Castle Hill. The palace originated in the 13th century, when King Béla built a castle here. Since then additions and alterations have been made in almost every style and under every dynasty. After far-reaching destruction in the Second World War, the palace was restored to its 19th-century appearance. Most of the former palace buildings are now open to the public and now house important cultural institutions.**

① National Gallery
Three wings of the Royal Palace are devoted to the National Gallery and its extensive collection of Hungarian art from the high Middle Ages until modern times.►p.230
The Royal Palace was a ruin when the German forces withdrew in 1945? It was completely burnt out, and the royal furnishings and many works of art perished in the flames. When the palace was reconstructed, restoration work concentrated on its architectural form. The interiors are plain, designed to present exhibitions. There are no longer any sumptuous royal apartments.

② Historical Museum
Exhibition on the history of Budapest and remains of the medieval palace ►p.234

Turul: According to one legend, the Hungarian people are descended from this mythical bird.

③ Széchenyi National Library
The largest and most important library in Hungary ►p.234

④ Lion Gate
The Lion Gate gives access to the rear courtyard of the palace.

⑤ Matthias Fountain
Alajos Strobl made the fountain in 1904. It tells the story of King Matthias Corvinus and the peasant girl Ilonka.

⑥ Gallery
The oldest part of the palace

⑦ Dome
Constructed in the classical style following the destruction of the original Baroque dome in the Second World War

©Ba

Lion Gate:
sculpted the
in the inne

idence massively extended to the north with the New Palace, which does not survive. The living quarters were equipped with heating systems and the fortifications were improved all around. Under King Matthias Corvinus, who is remembered as a promoter of the Renaissance and humanism, the royal palace was extended magnificently in the style of the early Renaissance. The Turks did not destroy the royal palace during their 150-year rule, but nor did they do anything towards its maintenance. Sigismund's so-called New Palace served as an armoury and was totally destroyed by an explosion in 1578, while the other royal buildings fell victim to the sieges and battles of 1686. After victory over the Turks by the Holy Alliance, the damaged fortifications were initially restored and renewed, but it was only in the 18th century that the Habsburg kings undertook the building of a new palace. A new residence was built north of Stephen's Tower under Charles III in 1719, to plans by the Italian architect Fortunato Prati. Maria Theresa finally ordered the further extension of the rather humble palace, which was completed in 1770. From then on, the palace was a symmetrical three-part building, comprised of a south wing (the original palace and today's E wing), a higher central wing (today's D wing), and a northern wing (today's C wing). The planning was placed in the hands of Jean Nicolas Jadot, who was active as an architect at the court of Vienna. The Baroque architect Franz Anton Hillebrandt supervised the construction. For almost a hundred years no further building works were undertaken on the palace, in which the representatives of the Habsburg emperors (palatines) had lived since 1790. Only in 1867, after the Austro-Hungarian Compromise, were renewed plans made for an extension, which was this time entrusted to the Hungarian architect **Miklós Ybl** and, after him, to **Alajos Hauszmann**. Ybl built a massive wing (F) on the western side of Castle Hill, which was completed in 1891. Hauszmann completed the imposing construction with a central domed building (62m/203ft) facing the Danube, as well as the adjoining two wings (A and B), which were matched stylistically to the existing sections. Reconstruction of the palace, as well as the excavation and preservation of the medieval remains was begun in 1950.

What to See in the Royal Palace

Szent György tér

From the ►Castle District or coming up by **cable car** from Watertown (►Viziváros), the first place reached is the Szent György tér, the northern forecourt of the Royal Palace, which becomes Disz tér to the north (►Castle District).

Staircase ►

The forecourt of the Royal Palace facing the Danube, which is also where the main entrance to the Hungarian National Gallery is located, can be reached via a neo-Baroque double staircase »guarded« by the eagle named Turul, the emblem of the Arpáds.

Royal Palace Plan

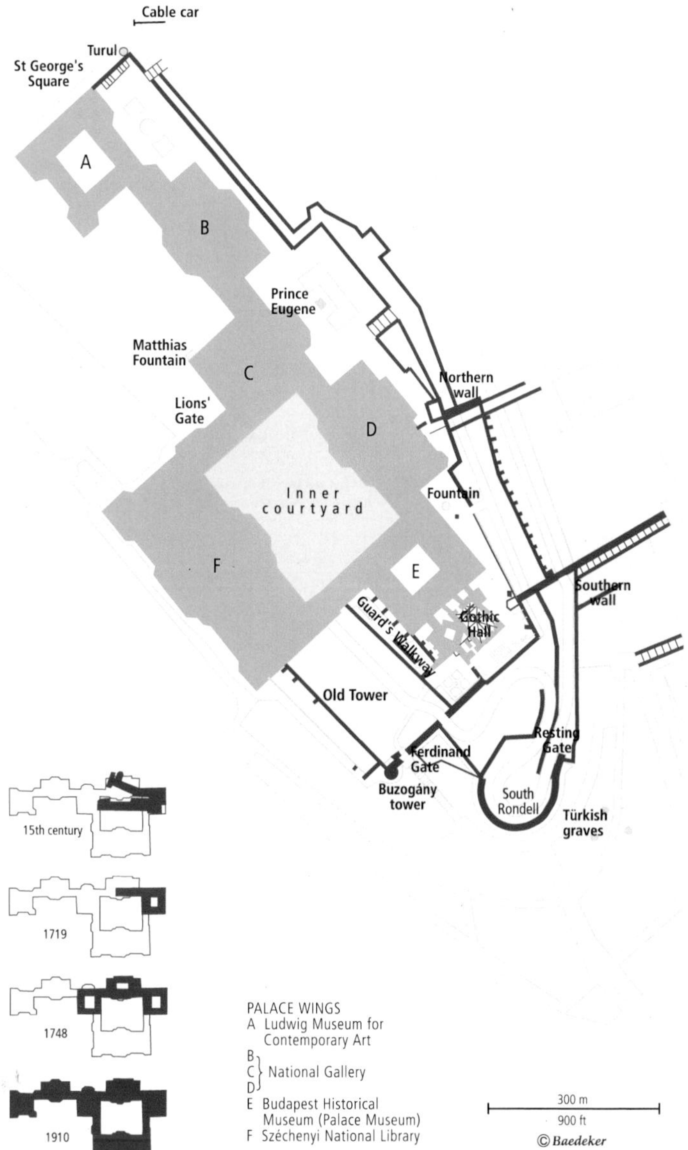

PALACE WINGS
A Ludwig Museum for Contemporary Art
B, C, D National Gallery
E Budapest Historical Museum (Palace Museum)
F Széchenyi National Library

Equestrian statue of Prince Eugene The bronze memorial for the conqueror of the Turks, Prince Eugene of Savoy, was built in the tradition of Baroque equestrian statues by József Róna in 1900, and was placed in front of the domed building of the Royal Palace.

✶ Matthias Fountain Near the equestrian statue, an opening leads to the western forecourt of the Royal Palace, on whose south side (the northern wall of C wing) a monumental fountain encased by Corinthian columns, designed by Alajos Stróbl in the style of a Roman Baroque fountain (1904), catches the eye. The wall behind it is like a stage set for the raised bronze figure of the youthful King Matthias, who is styled as a hunter. Below the king, to the left, is the mournful seated figure of a girl, which originates in a folk legend that grew up around the ruler and is intended to express his popularity among the people. According to this legend, the farm girl Ilona fell in love with Matthias when the king went hunting incognito. When the girl later realized that the unknown youth was her king, she fell into deep sorrow for the rest of her life.

The centre of the forecourt is decorated with a sculpture called the *Horse Guardian*, created by Gyögy Vastagh in 1898, and originally intended for a different place in the palace grounds.

Lion's Gate The inner prestige courtyard of the palace grounds is reached through the Lion's Gate, a work of the Hungarian sculptor János Fadrusz (1904). Here the entrances to the **Széchenyi National Library** (see below) and the **Budapest History Museum** (see below) can be found, as well as an entrance to the **National Gallery** (see below), whose main entrance is on the Danube side. The two aggressive-looking stone lions at the gate entrance guard access to the inner courtyard, where two further roaring stone sentinels await.

✶✶ National Gallery

Location: Wings B, C, & D

Opening hours: Mid March–Oct Tue–Sun 10am–6pm, otherwise, Tue–Sun 10am–4pm; internet: www.mng.hu

The Hungarian National Gallery (Magyar Nemzeti Galéria), which was founded in 1957 from various municipal and private collections, along with stored departments from the ► Museum of Fine Arts, is housed in the three main wings of the palace over four floors. Until its move to the rooms of the Royal Palace in 1975, the works used to be viewed in the former Palace of Justice on Kossuth tér, which today exhibits the treasures of the ► Ethnographic Museum. The National Gallery's holdings encompass Hungarian art from the early Middle Ages to the present, as well as a collection of medals. The development and characteristics of Hungarian painting, sculpture and graphics are extremely well documented by the works gathered here.

The rooms with medieval pictures and 19th-century paintings and sculpture on the first floor are especially interesting (B wing).

Changing exhibitions ► On the occasion of major cultural events, special exhibitions are mounted on diverse subjects in several rooms of the National Gallery.

Hungarian National Gallery Plan

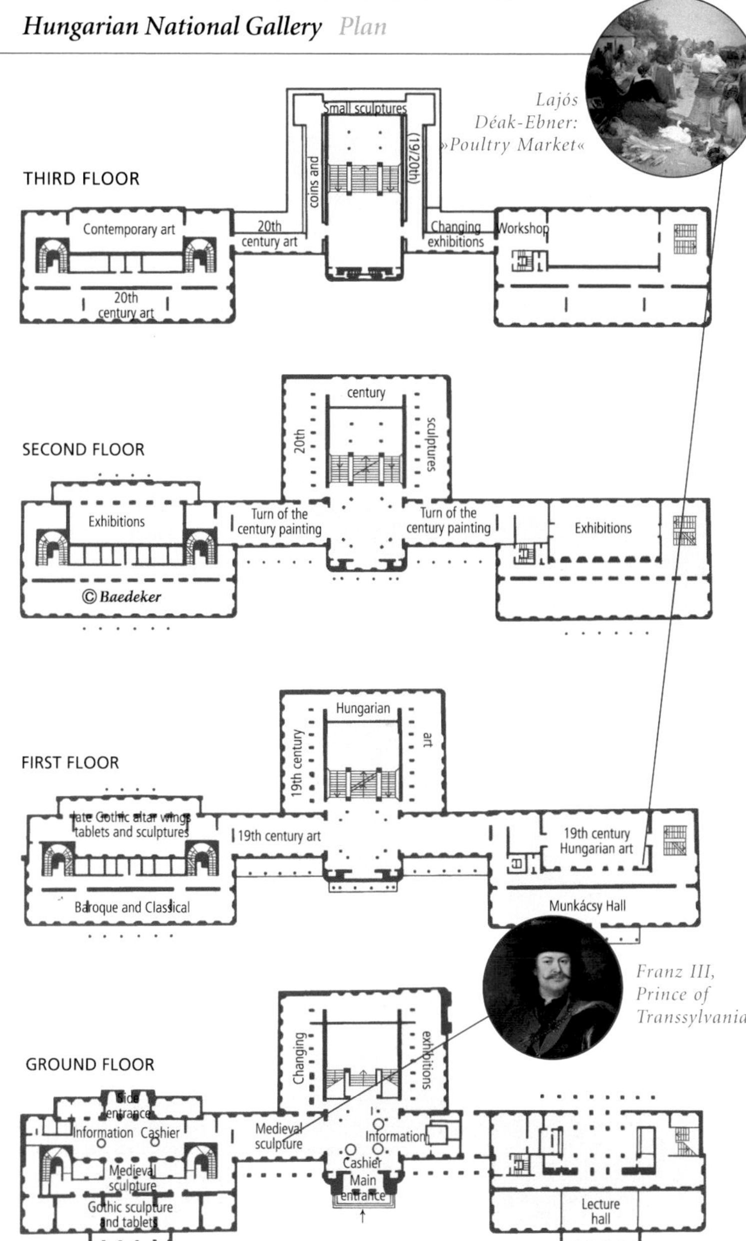

Lajós Déak-Ebner: »Poultry Market«

Franz III, Prince of Transsylvania

Ground floor In the hallway of D wing, on the ground floor, medieval stone carvings are displayed, especially architectural fragments from the country's most notable Romanesque and Gothic churches, as well as wooden sculptures and paintings from the 14th and 15th centuries. The so-called »soft style«, which was common throughout Europe around 1400, is impressively illustrated by the wooden sculpture of St Dorothea from Barka, and by the Toporc Madonna; the altarpieces from Jánosrét, which were made in the final third of the 15th century are also worth seeing.

First floor The first floor houses three sections: late medieval altarpieces and sculptures from the 15th and 16th centuries, painting and sculpture of the late Renaissance and Baroque, and painting and sculpture from the 19th century. The staircase leads first to a long room with 19th-century paintings and sculptures. These works mostly illustrate significant events in Hungarian history.

Late Gothic altar wings from the 15th and 16th centuries are gathered in the Great Throne Room and several smaller rooms around it. The ***Visitation of the Virgin*** is of particular interest. It was part of an altar in Selmecbánya and was signed by a master M.S. and dated 1506. The work stands at the transitional point between late Gothic and the modern age: while the rendering of the folds in the clothes of the two women, ornamental and without depth, is still faithful to medieval way of thought, the representation of the landscape already heralds the arrival of a new era that looks beyond medieval conceptions of form.

Farm Girl by Mihály Munkácsy

A relatively high standard is also maintained in the section for Baroque painting and sculpture from the 17th and 18th century, which can be found in the room facing the Danube. If, next to the few Hungarian artists such as **Jakáb Bogdány** or **Ádám Mányoki**, the names in the collection are almost exclusively German, Austrian and Bohemian – among others, **Joseph Heintz the Elder**, **Johann Kupetzky**, **August Querfurt**, **Franz Anton Maulbertsch** and **Franz Sigrist** – then the exhibition is simply a reflection of the fact that artistic life in 17th- and 18th-century Hungary was dominated by foreign painters, who were brought into the country by their noble patrons. Almost all genres are represented by the works exhibited: still lifes, as well as landscapes, royal portraits, allegories and biblical themes.

- Gothic altar painting St Anne
- »Picnic in May«: The Hungarian painter Pál Szinyei Merse was inspired by the two »Déjeuner sur l'herbe« paintings of his French colleagues Edouard Manet and Claude Monet.

The art of the 19th century housed in B wing is entirely Hungarian once more. A stroll through the many rooms amply illustrates that this era of Hungarian painting has been unjustly neglected abroad. The first room after the staircase is, just as in D Wing on the opposite side, dedicated to historical painting, mostly in large format. Important representatives of this genre are **Bertalan Székely**, **Gyula Benczur** and **Viktor Madarász**.
The most significant and popular representative of his era, **Mihály Munkácsy**, is given an entire room, where the painter's famous village and tavern scenes (among others, including *The Condemned Man's Last Day, 1870) can be found. In the second half of the century,* **László Paál**, whose landscape pictures are scattered around the Munkácsy exhibition, pioneered Hungarian open-air painting, along with **Pál Szinyei Merse**. The small sculptures in the Munkácsy room are by **György Zala**.
The most significant sculptors at the turn of the 20th century were **György Zala, Alajos Stróbl** and **János Fadrusz**, whose works in Budapest are not only encountered at the National Gallery.

2nd and 3rd floor

The development of Hungarian art into the 20th century is represented on the second floor with works by **Simon Hollósy**, **János Thoma**, **József Réti**, as well as by pieces from members of the **Nagybányai artists' colony** (among others, Károly Ferenczy and József Rippl-Rónai). On the third floor there is a collection of Hungarian painting and sculpture from the era between 1918 and 1945, including work by **Béla Czóbel**, **József Egry** and **István Szönyi**. Leading artists of recent decades, such as **Endre Domanovszky**, **Vladimir Szabó**, **Marianne Gábor**, **Endre Balint** and **Béla Kondor** are also represented. One of the few internationally famous painters from Hungary was an outsider in his own land, who never found recognition during his lifetime. **Tivadar Csontváry** (1853–1919), famous for his expressive naïve pictures, is represented through several paintings in the exhibition. One of his major works hangs in the National Gallery's main stairwell: *The Ruins of Taormina Theatre (1905).*

◄ Tivadar Csontváry

Coins, small sculptures, prints

Exhibits from the numismatic collection and collection of small sculptures are spread throughout the exhibition rooms of the different epochs. The National Gallery also owns an extensive graphics collection, part of which is shown in the museum.

Ludwig Museum for Contemporary Art

Location
A wing

The Ludwig Museum for Contemporary Art was housed in the northernmost wing of the Royal Palace (A) until 2005, but its collection is now to be found in the **Palace of Arts** in the Millennium Quarter south of the ►Great Ring.

Széchenyi National Library

Location
F wing

The Széchenyi National Library (Nemzeti Széchenyi Könyvtár) has been housed in F wing of the Royal Palace since 1985. This institution, founded by Count Ferenc Széchenyi in 1802, is Hungary's largest and most important library. Around six million books, manuscripts and a whole range of writings are stored here, including more than 625,000 manuscripts and around 183,000 maps. Prize pieces of the collection are the »Budapest Notes«, which are among the oldest medieval song scores, as well as some of the codices from King Matthias Corvinus' library. This manuscript collection of originally around 2000 volumes was already famous far beyond Hungary's borders during the Renaissance ruler's lifetime (opening times: Mon 1–6pm, Tue–Sat 10am–6pm).

✶ Historical Museum

Location
E wing

The Budapest Historical Museum (Budapesti Történeti Múzeum) in the south-eastern wing of the Royal Palace (E wing) introduces the history of the Hungarian capital from pre-history to modern times. Visitors can see not only remains of the medieval royal palace, but also precious works of art and other items found during excavations. The exhibition on the upper floors of the museum provides vivid information on the development of Budapest, or rather its municipal districts of Óbuda, Buda and Pest, which were independent until 1873. The historical survey ranges from the Stone Age and the Roman era, when a garrison and civil settlement was built in Óbuda, right up to the end of the Second World War and the post-war years. Archaeological finds, tools and craftwork, as well as artistic metal and ceramic items, textiles, photos, domestic goods and other objects convey a lively and all-encompassing picture of life in the Hungarian metropolis.

Medieval castle chapel

The **medieval remains of the royal castle** are especially worth seeing., A model of the medieval royal residence in the entrance hall of the lower ground floor helps to give an idea of the overall design

The gallery of the castle

of the former castle. In the partly reconstructed rooms of the medieval castle that follow, woodcarvings, painted oven tiles, kitchen utensils and weapons from the 14th and 15th century royal palace are shown. In the Renaissance hall, which was not part of the medieval castle, there is, among other paintings, a portrait of King Matthias Corvinus and Beatrice of Aragon – his second wife – under whose reign Italian Renaissance artists came to the royal court at Buda. The so-called Gothic Hall, with its two aisles and low-reaching cross-rib vaulting, is very beautiful. The cool dim passages and vaults of the southern part of the medieval castle section, as well as the dark chapel and the royal cellar in the northern section are also very interesting to explore. (Opening hours: March–mid-May daily except Tue 10am–6pm; mid-May–mid-Sep, daily 10am–6pm; mid-Sep–Oct, daily except Tue 10am–6pm; Nov–Feb daily except Tue 10am–4pm).

Remains of the Medieval Fortifications

To the south, below wings E and F of the Royal Palace, several sections of the medieval fortifications of the castle, mostly built in the first half of the 15th century, have been reconstructed and can be seen from the terrace of the Historical Museum. The square **tower** (Buzogány torony) next to **Ferdinand's Gate** is especially imposing. In front of it is the southern rondel, above which is the **murder gallery**, which completes the fortification above, along with the tower gate with portcullis and drawbridge, which was named **»gate of rest«**. Outside of the castle walls there are still several tombs from the time of the Turks.

★ St Stephen's Basilica (Szent István-bazilika)

C 6

Location: V district, Szent István tér **Underground:** M 1 (Arany János utca)

The Basilica of St Stephen, built in the neo-Renaissance style, is one of the most impressive religious buildings in the Hungarian capital. Marble and stucco adorn the interior, and one of Europe's largest bells hangs in the tower. A visit to the basilica treasury is also worthwhile.

Imposing church

The monumental size of the basilica is underlined by its 96m/315ft-tall central dome and two west towers in height 80m/262ft. In 1845

St Stephen's Basilica Plan

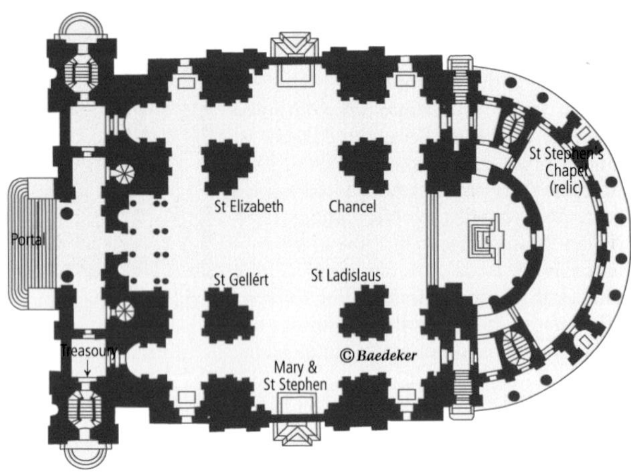

the design of the church was entrusted to József Hild, who had already made a name for himself as the architect of the cathedrals in Eger and Esztergom. He was still largely a devotee of the classical style, and the ground plan of the building in the shape of a Greek cross and the central dome survive from his plan. After Hild's death in 1867, Miklós Ybl brought new ideas that eventually gave the church its monumental neo-Renaissance style. St Stephen's was completed by József Kauser after the death of Ybl in 1905.

Sculptural decoration One of the special features of the St Stephen's Basilica is Leó Feszler's sculptural decoration on the façade. The twelve apostles embellish the choir apse, while the four evangelists stand in niches on the drum of the dome. Portraits of the church fathers are set into the two tower façades and Patrona Hungariae surrounded by saints occupies the tympanum above the narthex. A new nine-ton bell, one of the largest in Europe, has rung from the basilica since 1989. It was donated as an expression of thanks to the Hungarian people for their participation in the political events that led up to the reunification of Germany.

Interior The marble and gold-leaf stuccoed interior is predominantly the work of Ybl, who recruited Hungary's leading contemporary artists for the various tasks. A sculpture on the first right-hand pier of the dome representing Bishop Gellért and St Emmerich was made by Alajos Stróbl; on the second right-hand pier is the holy King Ladislaus, a work by János Fadrusz. St Elizabeth by Károly Senyei stands on the second pier on the left. The dome mosaics representing biblical scenes were produced in the Salviati workshop in Venice to designs by Károly Lotz. A sculpture of St Stephen by Alajos Stróbl in Carrara marble under the magnificent semi-circular canopy over the high altar is a further reference to the patron saint of the basilica. The bronze reliefs by E. Mayer on the apse wall show scenes from St Stephen's life. Of the paintings in the side altars, special mention should be made of the second altar to the right of the main entrance, which originates from the workshop of Gyula Benczúr: it shows St Stephen offering the crown to the Virgin, the Patronia Hungariae – a popular subject in Hungarian Catholic iconography.

! *Baedeker* TIP

Domes and constructions

There is a wonderful view across Budapest from the platform around the basilica dome. Even the ascent of the dome is interesting. Visitors who are daunted by the steps can complete two thirds of the ascent by elevator, after which iron steps lead to the space between the inner and outer part of the dome. Here it is hard to escape the question of why such dome constructions don't regularly collapse – as this one actually did in 1868. (Dome access: April–May daily 10am–4.30pm, June–Aug 9.30am–6pm, Sept –Oct 10am–5.30pm).

St Stephen's »Holy Right«, the bones of his right hand, are kept in a shrine in St Stephen's Chapel. Every year on 20 August, the national holiday in honour of the canonized king, the relic is carried through the city in procession.

Treasury

The treasury of St Stephen's Basilica holds magnificent vestments and extremely valuable liturgical objects from various Hungarian, Austrian and German workshops. (Opening times: April–Sept daily 9am–5pm, Oct–March daily 10am–4pm).

★ Sculpture Park (Szoborpark)

Excursion

A »museum« of a special kind is located in the XXII district: all monuments banned from the city streets and squares after the end of socialism have been gathered in the sculpture park.

Location and access

The Szoborpark lies far beyond Budapest's centre in Budafok (XXII - district), on the corner of Balatoni út (national route 7) and Szabadkai utca. This museum-like ensemble is quickly reached by car. By public transport there are two options: a direct bus from Deák Ferenc tér (March–Oct, daily 11am and 3pm; July–Aug, additional buses at 10am and 4pm; Nov–Feb, daily 11am); or bus no. 14 or 114 from Kosztalányi tér, south-west of the Hotel Gellért, to bus stop Jókai Mór utca, then change to blue bus no. 50. The sculpture park is directly opposite the terminal bus stop for no. 50, at the entrance of Szabadkai utca into Balatoni út.

Heroic relics in the Sculpture Park

Sculpture cemetery

After the political turnaround, over 40 pro-Soviet or rather pro-communist monuments found a new home in the sculpture park (Szoborpark) opened in 1994. The double portrait of the »fathers of communism«, Marx and Engels, welcomes visitors at the entrance to the sculpture cemetery. Until the change of regimes, this work created in 1971 by the sculptor György Segesdy adorned Jászai Mari tér in Pest. Some visitors familiar with Budapest in earlier days might recall the flag-carrying Russian soldier who used to stand in front of the Freedom Monument on Gellért Hill, but who also had to give way to the historic changes. The public is now exposed to him only in the context of a visit to the sculpture park. (Opening times: daily 10am to dusk; information on the internet: www.szoborpark.hu).

★ State Opera House (Állami Operaház)

C 6

Location: VI district, Andrássy út 22
Trolley bus: 70, 78
Tours: daily 3pm and 4pm
Underground: M 1 (Opera)
Bus: 4

The State Opera House is one of the most beautiful opera houses in the world. A tour provides an impression of its splendour, but it is even better to experience a performance here.

Huge and magnificent building
photo on p.240 ▶

The State Opera House was built in neo-Renaissance style between 1875 and 1884 to designs by Miklós Ybl on the newly created ►Andrássy út, which was also laid out on the basis of plans supplied by Ybl. As one end of the opera house borders the magnificent boulevard, it is necessary to step into the adjoining side streets in order to get an idea of the vast dimensions of the building. The entrances lie behind a covered drive-in for carriages, which is constructed along the first floor as a balustraded loggia. In the niches on both sides of the vehicle access, sculptures by Alajos Stróbl commemorate the composer Franz (Ferenc Liszt), as well as Ferenc Erkel, the first director of the opera house. The balustrade above is crowned by sculptures of famous composers by Gyula Donáth, György Kiss and Alajos Stróbl.

Ticket sales in the foyer of the opera house, Mon–Fri from 11am, Sat and Sun 11am–1pm; on the internet at www.opera.hu

✶ **Interior**

The heart of the opera house is the magnificent foyer with its double marble staircase at the centre. Ybl engaged the most renowned Hungarian artists of his day for the painting and sculptural decoration. The ceiling frescoes, which partly create the illusion of a coffered ceiling, are by Bertalan Székely, the wall paintings with scenes from Greek mythology by Mór Than. Alajos Stróbl completed the bust of the architect Miklós Ybl. The three-storey auditorium, designed as a loggia theatre, has exceptionally good acoustics. The ceiling and wall frescoes there were painted by Károly Lotz und Mór Than.

★ Szabadság tér (Freedom Square)

C 5/6

Location: V district
Bus: 15
Underground: M 2 (Kossuth tér)

Szabadság tér, one of the city's most beautiful squares, enchants visitors with its variety of magnificent buildings in several different architectural styles.

Panoply of architectural styles

Freedom Square was laid out in the late 19th century after the decommissioning of a military barracks there. The commanding building on the square is the former stock exchange on the west side, built between 1902 and 1905, a magnificent edifice at the transition between historicism and art nouveau which is now home to the Hungarian State Television (MTV). Opposite stands the National Bank (Magyar Nemzeti Bank), designed by the Ignác Alpár which by now takes up an entire block with its offices, including the former ► Post Savings Bank building by Ödön Lechner behind it to the east. A few steps left of the National Bank, the corner building housing the American Consulate is also worth a glance.

Office blocks, obelisk

To the north, a semi-circle of office blocks designed in a unified style at the end of the 19th century and the beginning of the 20th century closes off the square. The obelisk with a relief by the artist Károly Antal at the centre of the semi-circle has a special status, as it is apparently the only Soviet memorial that was allowed to remain in the

city after Hungary's political turnaround. Some of those memorials are today on view at the ►Sculpture Park.

★ Szentendre

Excursion

Location: 20km/13mi north east of Budapest

Access: HÉV Budapest – Szentendre; during the summer boats depart from Budapest's Vigadó tér

The charming Danube town of Szentendre, with its crooked lanes and bumpy cobblestones, has attracted artists since the beginning of the 20th century. Today visitors come from all over the world to visit the little galleries and museums, marzipan and souvenir shops.

The small town on the hilly right-hand bank of the Danube is one of the most popular destinations for a short excursion from the capital – especially during the warmer times of year, when it is possible to arrive by boat. Consequently this »Hungarian Montmartre« gets very crowded in during the high season.

Town of the Hungarian Serbs

The origins of this settlement go back to the 4th century BC, when Celts settled here. The Romans built a garrison on the shores of the Bükkös stream in the first century AD, and called it Ulcisia Castra (Wolf Castle). It was first mentioned in documents in the 12th century, and Serbs came to Szentendre in several waves from the 14th century onwards, bringing their culture, Orthodox religion, customs and building traditions to Hungary. Szentendre experienced an economic upturn in the 18th century, when the town became the religious and cultural centre of the Hungarian Serbs and seat of the Greek Orthodox church. The tourist development of the town began in the early 20th century.

Baedeker TIP

Hungarian culinary specialties

For a pleasant atmosphere, good meals and an interesting décor, try the tiny Aranysárkány restaurant (The Golden Dragon) on Alkotmány ut 1/A, tel. 020/30 14 79.

What to See in Szentendre

★ Fö tér

The main square of Szentendre, which has long been protected by a preservation order, is the triangular Fö tér, surrounded by pretty merchant houses of the Baroque and Rococo style. A merchant's cross donated after a catastrophic plague epidemic has stood in the

← *Highlight of a visit to Budapest: a performance in the Opera House*

Szentendre Map

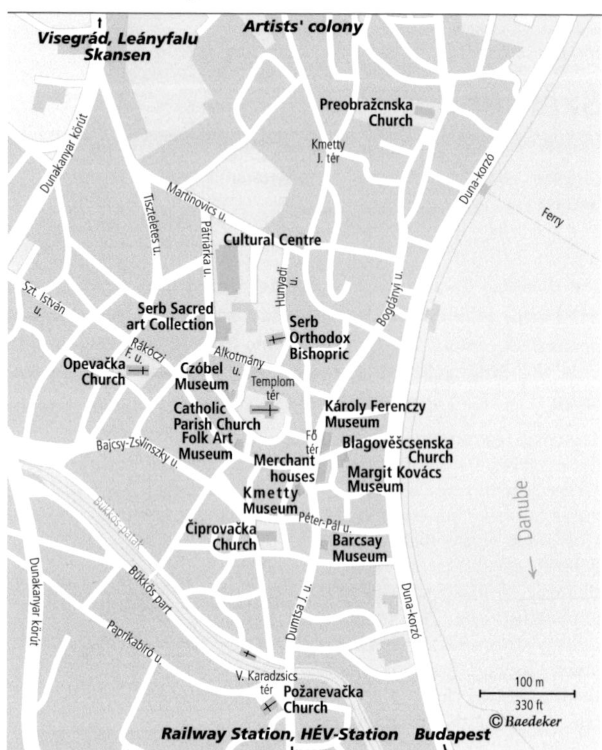

middle of the square since 1763: a richly embellished cast-iron cross on a pediment decorated with icons. The beautiful Serbian Orthodox **Blagoveštanska church**, stands on the Danube side of the square, which was built to designs by Andreas Mayerhoffer in the middle of the 18th century. The iconostasis created in 1790 for the church interior is the work of a Serbian artist. The **Károly Ferenczy Museum**, housed in the Rococo building dating from 1797 to the left of the Blagoveštanska church (Fö tér 6), preserves the artistic heritage of the Ferenczy family, as well as numerous local history exhibits. (Opening times:Tue–Sun 10am–4pm).

Kmetty Museum

On the opposite side of the square, the Kmetty Museum housed in the Baroque house at no. 21 invites visitors to discover the work of the Cubist painter János Kmetty (1889–1975). A noteworthy feature here is the so-called Dalmatian shop window, a wooden frame that was turned down during shop opening times and used as a counter. (Opening times:Tue–Sun 9am–5pm).

✶ **Görög utca, Margit Kovács Museum**

The work of Hungary's most famous female sculptor and ceramic artist Margit Kovács (1902–1977), who combined folk art motifs with modern elements, can be viewed in the Baroque building on picturesque Görög utca. (Opening times: April–Oct Tue–Sun 9am–6pm, Nov–March Tue–Sun 10am–4pm).

Folk Art Museum

Return to Fö tér for a small stroll down Rákóczi utca, where the historic building of the Folk Art Museum still gives an impression of traditional building techniques. The two rooms exhibiting folk culture and art curiosities can be visited quickly before continuing the climb up the castle hill.

Mobile knife-grinder

The walled **Templom tér** on the top of castle hill was the centre of the medieval settlement. Today it makes for a wonderful viewpoint, with many market stalls selling folklore souvenirs. The Catholic parish church goes back to the 13th century. The present church is predominantly 18th-century, but the tower window and the sundial still survive from the 14th and 15th century. Opposite the church, the art of the Hungarian painter Béla Czóbel, who died in 1976, can be seen in a small museum.

The most elegant of Szentendre's total of seven Baroque churches is the **Serbian Orthodox cathedral** on Alkotmány utca, which was consecrated in 1764 and is known as the Belgrade Church. Inside the church the painted and gold-leaf iconostasis carved out of lime wood is worth seeing. Diagonally across, the collection of Serbian sacred art housed in the former bishop's palace displays art and religious objects.

✶ **Hungarian Open-Air Museum**

Opening hours: April–Oct Tue–Sun 9am–5pm

An excursion to the open-air museum approx. 3km/2m north-west of Szentendre is highly recommended. A visit to this exhibition of Hungarian folk architecture and domestic culture and lifestyle, also called Skanzen after the famous open-air museum in Stockholm, is a journey into Hungary's rural past, introducing the lives of different social groups and classes of country people between the late 18th century and the early 20th century. On view are characteristic settlement groups with buildings typical of regions from western Transdanubia, from the Upper Tisza area, the small plain and the great plain, as well as from the Balaton uplands. In addition to the domestic homes furnished in historically precise detail, a whole range of different agricultural and craft installations, mills, animal sheds, barns, a smithy, a weaving workshop, as well as village churches and cemeteries give insight into the daily life of the rural population. On the hill above this settlement group stands the Greek Orthodox church built in log-house style from the small village of Mándok, which represents the basic type of an Orthodox church in the northern and eastern Carpathian mountains. (www.skanzen.hu).

Tabán

B 7

Location: I district
Tram: 18, 19
Bus: 5, 7, 78, 86

Green areas and arterial roads characterize Tabán today and visitors go to the Semmelweis Museum or take the steps up towards the castle.

The Tabán district lies between Castle Hill and ►Gellért Hill. In the 18th century, Serb refugees settled here in Tabán, and the old district was one of the most appealing quarters of Budapest until the historic houses were demolished in the 1930s. Relics of the former district have survived on Szarvas tér, where the Golden Stag tavern and the parish church can be found.

The Golden Stag tavern

The Golden Stag tavern (Arany Szarvas) at the bottom of the steps leading to the magnificent Royal Palace (Szarvas tér 1) specializes in game dishes. It was built in Rococo style in the 19th century and has a golden stag (Arany Szarvas) above the entrance.

Tabán parish church

The Tabán parish church (Tabáni plébánia-templom) dedicated to St Catherine of Alexandria was built between 1728 and 1740 and replaced a medieval church that was known as the Mustafa Mosque during Turkish rule. The treasures of the Baroque church include a copy of the carved Tabán Christ underneath the gallery. The 12th-century original can be seen in the Budapest Historical Museum (► Royal Palace).

Rác Bath

Rác Bath, which was built and expanded under Turkish rule, lies just a little south of the Tabán parish church, on Hadnagy utca. The medicinal springs used here were already known in the 15th century.

Semmelweis Museum

The birthplace of the famous Hungarian doctor Ignác Semmelweis (► Famous People) stands at Apród utca 1–3, at the south-eastern base of Castle Hill. Today the Baroque building with Rococo façade houses a museum of the history of medicine (Semmelweis Orvostörténeti Múzeum; opening times: Tue–Sun 10.30am–6pm).

Ybl Miklós tér

The elongated square on the banks of the Danube underneath the Royal Palace carries the name of the famous architect Miklós Ybl (1814–1891), who significantly contributed to the appearance of Budapest with his buildings in the second half of the 19th century, including the great ► St Stephen's Basilica. The memorial to him on the square dates from 1896 and is the work of sculptor E. Mayer. Several buildings designed by Ybl are ranged around the square.

★ ◄ Royal Steps

The broad and magnificent Royal Steps that lead up from the banks of the Danube to the Royal Palace, built between 1875 and 1882, are one of the most impressive legacies of this architect, who carried out many commissions.

★ Town Hall (Városháza)

C 6/7

Location: V district, Városház utca 9 – 11
Tram: 47, 49
Underground: M 1, M 2, M 3 (Deák tér)

The mighty 190m/210yd-long Baroque building in the heart of Pest, which has been used as a town hall since 1894, was originally built as a hospital for invalids returning from the Turkish wars.

Hospital for war invalids

The Viennese architect Anton Erhard Martinelli supplied the designs for the building complex, which takes up an entire block. It was commissioned by Emperor Charles VI and built between 1716 and 1728, and accommodated up to 2000 people. At the time of its construction the building stood at the north-eastern edge of Pest. Above the gates of the main body of the building there are two beautiful reliefs: one commemorates Charles VI as its patron, representing him as King Charles III of Hungary, the other shows Prince Eugene of Savoy, who emerged as a hero of the Turkish Wars.

Pest district authority

A building complex with three courtyards erected in the 19th century, which now houses the district authority for Pest, adjoins the town hall at Városház utca 7.

★ **Art nouveau houses**

To the west of the town hall lies **Szervita tér** (Servita Square). Two remarkable art nouveau houses stand on the west side of the square: on the former bank building Török at no. 3, built in 1906 by Ármin Hegedüs and Henrik Böhm, the sweeping gable with its shining gold mosaic stands out. The female figure in the centre of the picture embodies Patrona Hungariae. By contrast, the façade with its large areas of glass on the department store at no. 5 is considerably more sober. It was built to designs by Béla Lajta in 1912.

★ University Church (Egyetemi templom)

C 7

Location: V district, Papnövelde utca 5 – 7

Bus: 15

A Turkish mosque once stood on the site of today's University Church, which is considered the most beautiful Baroque church in the city.

Budapest's finest Baroque church

The University Church would hardly be discovered on a casual stroll, as it lies in southern Pest on Egyetem tér, facing a narrow side street that barely allows its imposing exterior to make an impression. It was built for the Pauline order on top of a Turkish mosque between 1725 and 1742. The architect was an Austrian, Andreas Mayerhoffer. The two massive towers were only completed in 1771. The main façade of the church is topped by a pediment with representations of the hermits Paul and Anthony, as well as with the emblem of the Pauline order: a palm between two lions and a raven. A Madonna on a globe can be seen under the pediment.

★ Interior

The interior is aisle-less with pilasters and enclosed side chapels. The vaulted ceiling was embellished with a fresco containing scenes from the life of the Virgin by Johann Bergl in 1776; here the architecture of the church is continued in the painting after the example of Italian Baroque art. The choir stalls and the sculptures on the main altar – the hermit saints Paul and Anthony – were carved by József Hebenstreit in 1746. At the centre of the altar there is a copy of the Black Madonna from Czestochowa in Poland, which was probably made in 1720. The pulpit, stalls and doors, as well as the sacristy cupboards with inlaid decoration, which contain valuable monstrances, cups and vestments, all originate from different workshops of the Pauline order of monks.

✓ DON'T MISS

- Ceiling frescoes
- Black Madonna
- Pulpit

Former Pauline monastery

The 18th-century former Pauline monastery adjoins the church and was designed by Matthias Drenker. There is a ceiling fresco, painted by Pietro Rivetti in 1803, in the library, which also holds some medieval manuscripts. Since 1805 it has been used by the theological faculty of Hungary's first university (which was transferred to Pest in 1784), as the Pauline order was dissolved by Joseph II in 1786.

The library building completed in 1775 stands a little further towards the city centre, at Ferenciek tere no. 10. The university library collection possesses numerous medieval codices amongst other treasures. Its interior has wonderfully decorated book cases with a continuous gallery and two spiral staircases. The ceiling fresco was painted by Pietro Rivetti in 1803.

★ **University library**

★ Váci utca

C 6/7

Location: V district
Bus: 2, 15
Underground: M 1 (Vörösmarty tér), M 2, 3 (Deák tér), M 3 (Ferenciek tere)

The Hungarian publicist György Dalos once aptly described Váci utca as »a mixture of flea market and respectable shopping street«. Here, in the busy pedestrian zone of Pest city centre, the capital's most elegant shops can be found, as well as the chic boutiques of international fashion houses, shoe and leatherware shops, new and antiquarian bookshops – among others Libri for foreign-language books – antique shops, jewellery and craft shops, espresso bars, wine bars and the offices of leading airline companies, but also cheap book stalls and street artists, all of which combines to give the street its characteristic flavour. The much less frequented section of Váci utca to the south of Szabadsajtó út is comparatively humble, quiet and much less hectic – more charming, in fact, than the overdone, highly commercialized northern part.

The underground walkway that connects the northern section of Váci utca with the southern one is decorated with interesting historic **photographs** by the Hungarian artist György Klösz of Budapest street scenes from the late 19th century and early 20th century.

A former hotel where the eleven-year-old Franz Liszt gave his first concert in Pest in 1823, is now home to the **Pest Theatre** (Pesti Színház; no. 9). The foyer with its beautifully crafted dark mosaics is very elegant.

The **New Town Hall** (Új Városháza; no. 62–64) was built in the neo-

CUKRÁSZDAS IN BUDAPEST

For non-Hungarians this word is almost a tongue-twister: cukrászda. What would be called a patisserie or a salon de thé in French has a special tradition in Budapest, a tradition that is at least as old as, if not older than, that of the Viennese coffee house.

Café Gerbeaud on Vörösmarty tér is a good place to begin. It has existed since 1858 and remains the most beautiful and stylish coffee house on the square to this day. There are many reasons for the popularity of Gerbeaud: for some it is the interior of the building, which has not changed significantly since the 19th century; for others it is the overwhelming choice of cakes and gateaux, a mixture of Swiss inventiveness and Austrian variety – even if the high tourist demand has resulted in an enormous decline in quality. For others still it is the coffee, which is of an excellent standard here, always served, just as it should be, with a small glass of water.

Elegance in the Castle District Ruszwurm coffee house on Castle Hill is also steeped in tradition. It is much more intimate than Gerbeaud on Vörösmarty tér and its pastries and cakes are at least as good. Part of the furniture still dates from the founding era of the café in the 1820s. It makes an ideal place to recover from a sightseeing tour of the Castle District. Those who cannot find a table in Ruszwurm should try Café Korona on Disz tér.

Artists' Rendezvous

On the magnificent Adrássy ut, on the way to Heroes' Square, there are no less than two beautiful old coffee houses, Lukács (at no. 70), and Müvesz (at no. 29) opposite the State Opera House. Müvesz, with its numerous mirrors and sculptures in the style of the late 19th century, used to be one of the most popular meeting places for artists, and was therefore given the name »artists' café«. Today its clientele is colourfully mixed, but no less interesting.

The old gentlemen in the Astoria on Kossuth Lajos út look back on an eventful life and continue to meet at their regular coffee house, as ever.

Danube View

Café Gellért was and is very sophisticated and elegant, and is part of the long-established hotel and thermal bath of the same name. In the summer, the wonderful terrace with a view of the Danube and the Pest riverbank is the ideal place to enjoy a cup of coffee. The character of the establishment is best described as modestly elegant, which goes for the interior, as well as the service and the clientele. That the menu is excellent goes without saying.

Literary Café

The formerly legendary literary Café New York at no. 9–11 on Erzsébet körút demands a category of its own. In culinary terms it cannot stand comparison with the others, but the neo-Baroque interior dripping with heavy cloth and exuberant stucco is unmatched. The art nouveau Café Central, founded in 1887 on Károlyi Mihály utca near Ferenciek tere, was indisputably the most important meeting place for Budapest's literary scene until the Communists took power. After a long period of renovation to renew its former glory the café hopes for the return of the authors. They, however, are not tempted by a stylish ambience alone, but definitely by the laptop connections under the tables; customers still have to bring their own laptops, though.

Arrival of the Modern Age

The arrival of the modern age does not necessarily diminish the appeal of the past. Quite the opposite: should it prove possible to re-establish coffee houses, many of which now resemble museum pieces and are heavily frequented by tourists, as places for artistic creativity, this would signify a return to the origins of the Budapest coffee-house tradition.

Municipal Forest Map

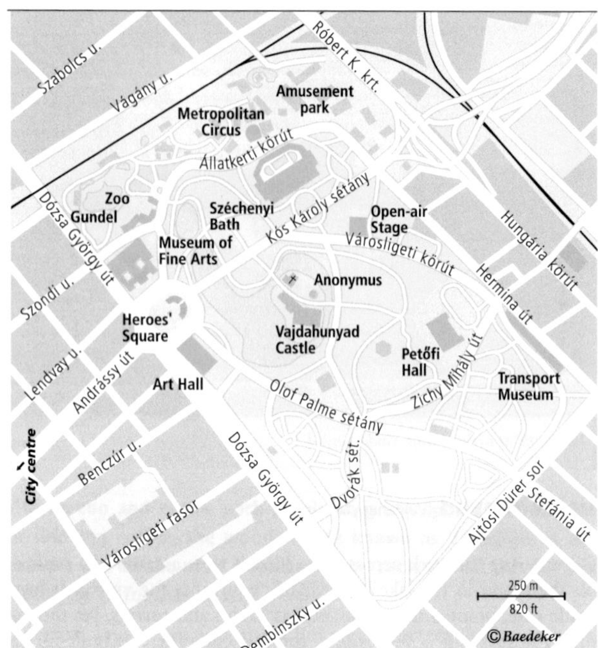

on the theme of animal husbandry, especially the breeding of horses, cows, sheep and pigs; other sections are devoted to wine-growing and viticulture, forest conservation and management, as well as hunting and fishing. Periodic special exhibitions augment the programme. (Opening times: mid-Feb to mid-Nov Tue–Fri and Sun 10am–5pm, Sat to 6pm; otherwise Tue–Fri 10am–4pm, Sat–Sun till 5pm).

Anonymous Opposite the entrance to the Agricultural Museum stands a memorial created by Miklós Ligeti in 1903 in honour of the anonymous 12th–13th-century scribe who wrote Hungary's first chronicle (Gesta Hungarorum), presumably on the orders of Béla IV.

★ Széchenyi Bath (Szechenyi fürdö)

Location: Állatkerti körút 11

Where Hungarians bathe The Széchenyi Bath is not one of Budapest's oldest – it was opened in 1881 – but it is among the most popular. Located in the northern

Chess players in the newly renovated Széchenyi Bath →

Not a mosque, but the Elephant House in the Zoological Garden

section of the Városliget park, its extensive grounds include three open-air pools and one indoor pool in the neo-Baroque style with steam baths and hot tubs. A stylistically matching entrance hall was added to the buildings on the northern side in 1927. The whole complex has been restored to its former glory, and a glance into the entrance hall is recommended to non-swimmers as well! The pool is fed by a thermal spring at a temperature of over 70 degrees Celsius (160°F).

Zoological and Botanical Garden

(Fövárosi Állat-és Növénykert)

Location: Állatkerti körút 6 – 12

Opening hours: May–Aug daily 9am–7pm, April and Sept daily 9am–6pm, March and Oct daily 9am–5pm, Nov–Feb daily 9am–4pm

The Budapest Zoological and Botanical Garden lies on the northwestern side of the Városliget park. It was created by private initiative in 1866, and ownership passed to the city at the end of the nineteenth century. Enclosures and animal houses were built in 1911–12. Of the buildings that have survived from that time, the elephant house, which is reminiscent of a mosque, is particularly worth seeing, as well as the bird house built designed by Károly Kós. The zoo's other attractions include an aviary for birds of prey, a rock garden, a pool for polar bears and sea lions, a baby animal enclosure, the monkey house, lion and bear caves, and the Africa House. The species-rich flora of moderate latitudes can be studied along outdoor footpaths, while tropical plants can be viewed in the architecturally interesting palm house, as well as in the terrarium and aquarium for animals from warm climates.

Metropolitan Circus

The building for the Metropolitan Circus (Fővárosi Nagycirkusz) at the eastern edge of the zoo and opposite the Széchenyi Bath was completed in 1971. It is one of the most visited institutions of its kind in Europe. The world's most renowned circus companies have performed here, and continue to do so. Programme information and performance times can be found at the Budapest Tourist Office (►Practical Information).

Vidám Amusement Park

Vidám Amusement Park, which draws thousands of visitors annually, is located at the northern corner of the Városliget and has a giant wheel, a roller coaster, an enchanted castle, carousels and other attractions. (Opening times: April–Sep daily 10am–8pm, March and Oct 10am–7pm).

Transport Museum

The exhibits of the Hungarian Transport Museum (Közlekedési Múzeum) are housed in a purpose-built property on the eastern edge of the Városliget, which originated in a show for the 1896 millennium jubilee. It is an attractive presentation of the development of transport from ancient times to the present is given: models of old ships from the Danube and Lake Balaton are represented as well as various locomotives and flying machines. (Opening times: May–Sept Tue–Fri 10am–5pm; Sat and Sun 10am–6pm, Oct–April Tues–Fri 10am–4pm, Sat and Sun until 5pm).

Velence Lake

Excursion

Location: 45km/28mi south-west of Budapest

Europe's warmest lake lies at the south-eastern foot of the Vértes highlands, south-west of Budapest. With water temperatures of up to 26 degrees Celsius (79°F), swimmers certainly don't get cold.

Swimming; nature reserve

The lake is 10km/6mi long and, on average, only 2.5km/1.5mi wide. The water is between 1.2m/4ft and 1.6m/5ft deep and quickly warms up to between 22 and 26 degrees Celsius (72–79°F) during the summer. A bird sanctuary has been created on the north-west side of the lake. Bathing, sailing and boating are possible at the southern end, where the resorts of Velence, Gárdony and Agárd are located, but here the landscape is flatter and less appealing. There is a water sports school at Velence and also an area 2300m/2500yd long reserved for kayak, canoe and sailing regattas.

Gárdony, Agárd Gárdony is first mentioned in the 13th century. Today the resort has around 8000 inhabitants, who mostly live from tourism. Agárd is the largest resort on the lake with the largest yacht harbour, as well as being the landing stage for a regular boat service. Visitors will also find a modern thermal bath here.

✶ Vigadó (Pest Redoute)

C 6

Location: V district, Vigadó tér **Underground:** M 1 (Vörösmarty tér)

Pest's Vigadó ballroom and concert hall are among the most impressive creations of the Romantic era in Hungary.

A venue for festive occasions The designs for Pest's Vigadó ballroom and concert hall between ► Vörösmarty tér and the banks of the Danube were supplied by the architect Frigyes Feszl (1821–1884), a commission he received in 1859, ten years after the old concert hall had been destroyed during the 1848–49 revolution. The new ballroom and concert hall was inaugurated with pomp and circumstance in 1864. The richly embellished main façade facing the Danube, with its high rounded arches opening from the large concert hall on the first floor, is decorated by female figures symbolizing music and dance. A frieze above the window arches contains the Hungarian coat of arms as well as representing Hungarian rulers and politicians. The building, which is used for all kinds of festive occasions and musical presentations – Liszt and Bartók, among others, conducted here – was badly damaged at the end of the Second World War; but was re-opened in 1980 after lengthy renovation works, when it celebrated its glittering comeback as a concert and exhibition venue.

✶ Víziváros (Watertown)

A/B 5–6

Location: I district **Suburban train HÉV:** Batthyány tér
Underground: M 2 (Batthyány tér) **Tram:** 19
Bus: 86

Víziváros, »Watertown«, extends along the narrow terrace between Castle Hill and the Danube.

Once liable to flooding Right up to the era of Turkish rule, this quarter was fortified. The Ottomans installed baths in the area predominantly populated by fishermen, artisans and merchants, and turned the existing churches into mosques. The name Watertown is explained by the repeated floods to which Víziváros was once exposed. There was a lot of building here during the Baroque era, when craftsmen and merchants settled on Castle Hill as a result of the construction of the Royal Palace. This is when, among other buildings, St Anne's Church (►Batthyány tér) was erected. The character of the quarter has been permanently changed by the building of multi-storey apartment blocks from the end of the 19th century onwards.

Fö utca 20

The house at Fö utca 20, whose origins reach back to the 15th century, was rebuilt in the 18th century and given its attractive Rococo façade in 1811. The corner bay crowned by a turret is particularly pretty, as are the reliefs under the windows. The Biedermeier interior dates from the mid-19th century.

St Elizabeth's Church

At Fö utca 41–43, a Baroque church was built in 1757 on the foundations of a Turkish structure which originally belonged to the Franciscans. It was transferred to the Elizabethan nuns in 1785, who set up a hospital, which today serves as an old people's home. Details worth seeing are the sculptures on the church façade and the pulpit made by the Franciscan monks.

✶ Kiraly Bath

Still in use today, Király fürdö on Fö utca 82–86 is one of the most interesting facilities of its kind in Budapest. The oldest part of this bathhouse, excellently restored after heavy damage in the Second World War, is the hamam built in 1570 under Mustafa Pasa – a Turkish bath whose octagonal main room is covered by a dome. Smaller domes cover the three side rooms. The bath house was considerably extended in the Baroque era, when it received its beautiful arched passage. After 1827, a classical wing and a pillared courtyard were added.

St Florian's Chapel

The little St Florian's Chapel (Flórián-kápolna) at Fö utca 90 dates from 1759–60 and is the work of the architect Matthäus Nepauer. Today it is used as a parish church by members of the Greek Orthodox community. Beautiful statues of the saints Nicolas, Florian and Blasius adorn the façade of the chapel. The paintings and sculptures that used to be inside the chapel can now be seen in the Historical Museum on Castle Hill (►Royal Palace).

Corvin tér

South of ►Batthyány tér, about halfway to Clark Adam tér, lies Corvin tér. It is lined by several noteworthy buildings from the 18th century (nos. 2, 3, 4, and 5). The former Capuchin monastery stands on the southern side of the square and still shows evidence of Turkish construction and ornamentation.

Foundry Museum

The Öntödei Múzeum at Bem József utca 20, an old foundry established by Abraham Ganz in the middle of the 19th century, was the foundation of the Ganz industrial concern. This company, which became famous far beyond Hungary, built locomotives, wagons and cranes etc. The museum illustrates the history of the Hungarian iron industry (Opening times: Dec–March Tue–Sun 9am–4pm, April-–Nov Tues–Sun 9am–5pm).

★ Vörösmarty tér (Vörösmarty Square)

C 6

Location: V district **Underground:** M 1 (Vörösmarty tér)

Named after the poet Mihály Vörösmarty, this traffic-free square is the lively heart of Pest city centre, where it is a great pleasure to watch the world go by from one of the street cafés.

Lively city centre

Immaculately renovated former office buildings around the square now house all manner of shops. The ugly office block from the 1960s that was built on the west side of the square is today the seat of various cultural institutions, including the central ticket agency for Budapest's concert events. On the other side of the square, on the corner by Deák Ferenc utca, the building of the former Luxus department store is discreet, but nevertheless architecturally interesting for its skeleton construction. Today smaller boutiques and shops are housed here.

Popular with tourists, but also with locals: Café Gerbeaud

Vörösmarty Memorial

At the centre of the square, surrounded by trees, the memorial to Mihály Vörösmarty (1800–1855) shows the author enthroned in an armchair. The figures at his feet – children, adults, old and young – represent the Hungarian people that Vörösmarty's prophetic poem *Szózar* eulogizes. The first line of this work is etched into the marble base of the monument: »Hazádnak rendületlenül légy híve, óh magyar» (Hungarians, always retain love and loyalty to your homeland). To the right, underneath the first stanza's line, a black mark is noticeable, supposedly a »lucky forint« donated by a beggar when the memorial was built. The construction of Carrara marble is the work of the artists Kallós and Telcs from the year 1908.

Christmas market

During the run-up to Christmas Vörösmarty tér is an atmospheric place: the whole square is filled by numerous stalls offering craftwork and food, including warming or refreshing drinks.

Café Gerbeaud

The famous Café Gerbeaud, which was founded by Henrik Kugler in 1858 and later became the property of the Swiss patissier Emil Gerbeaud, is at the northern side of the square. Gerbeaud's original interior survives to this day. The café was temporarily called Café Vörösmarty and was an extremely popular society rendezvous in the early 20th century. In the summer months it is pleasant to spend time here, watching the colourful life on the square from the terrace while savouring a cup of excellent coffee. Nevertheless, even in good weather a look at the beautiful 19th-century interior should not be missed.

INDEX

1

a

c

l

m

n

LIST OF MAPS AND ILLUSTRATIONS

PHOTO CREDITS

AKG p. 22, 31, 36, 45, 50, 51, 53, 54, 57, 105 (above), 106, 155 (left above, below centre), 155 (left below), 159 (above), 159 (below), 195, 216 (above), 221, 223, 226 (above), 226 (below)
Baedeker-Archiv p. 4 (left), 9 (below), 93, 259
Bilderberg p. 2, 10, 13 (above), 13 (centre), 13 (below), 14 (below), 15, 40, 75, 77, 87, 130/131, 139, 235 (left above), 243
Boszó p. 38
Dackweiler p. 151
dpa p. 56, 196
Haafke p. 7, 14, 101, 166, 178, 208, 228, 230, 254
Huber p. 7, 81, 136, 205, 235 (below)
Huber/Gräfenhain p. 236
Hug p. 39, 60, 62, 64, 143, 155 (right above) 163, 169, 172, 177, 190, 261, 263
HB Verlag/János Kalmár p. U2, 4 (right), 5 (below), 48, 59, 69, 72, 73, 83, 105 (below), 122, 140, 145, 162, 164, 170, 176, 185, 189, 196, 201, 206, 219, 229, 231, 234, 239, 285
IBUSZ p. 160
ifa p. 156
Interfoto p. 191(2x), 192, 193
Laif/Kirchgessner p. 12
Laif/Kirchner p. 182
Laif/Kristensen p. 142/143, 240
Laif/Langrock p. 234
Laif/Modrow p. 116
Laif/Neumann p. 3, 9, 129, 154, 155 (left below), 199
Laif/Specht p. 81
Mauritius p. 11, 235 (right)
picture alliance p. 8, 20, 26, 118, 217 (right above), 217 (right below)
Radkai p. 3, 41, 210
Randebrock p. 5 (above) 6 (above) 245, 249, 250, 260, 264, houtside back cover
Renyi p. 8, 247
Silvestris/Stadler p. 84, 184
Skupy p. 75
Transit/Schulze p. 6, 16, 24, 25, 131
Wrba p. 1, 14, 42, 58/59, 167, 179, 216 (below), 255

Cover photo: Blume / www.blumebild.com

PUBLISHER'S INFORMATION

Illustrations etc: 189 illustrations, 27 maps and diagrams, one large city plan
Text: Stefanie Bisping, György Dalós, Odin Hug, Helmut Linde, Silwen Randebrock, Peter Renyi, Monika Wucher, Andrea Wurth
Editing: Baedeker editorial team (John Sykes)
Translation: Natascha Scott Stokes
Cartography: Franz Kaiser, Sindelfingen; MAIRDUMONT/Falk Verlag, Ostfildern (city plan)
3D illustrations: jangled nerves, Stuttgart
Design: independent Medien-Design, Munich; Kathrin Schemel

Editor-in-chief: Rainer Eisenschmid, Baedeker Ostfildern

1st edition 2008

Printed in China

DEAR READER,

We would like to thank you for choosing this Baedeker travel guide. It will be a reliable companion on your travels and will not disappoint you.
This book describes the major sights, of course, but it also recommends the best pubs, as well as hotels in the luxury and budget categories, and includes tips about where to eat or go shopping and much more, helping to make your trip an enjoyable experience. Our authors ensure the quality of this information by making regular journeys to Budapest and putting all their know-how into this book.

Nevertheless, experience shows us that it is impossible to rule out errors and changes made after the book goes to press, for which Baedeker accepts no liability. Please send us your criticisms, corrections and suggestions for improvement: we appreciate your contribution. Contact us by post or e-mail, or phone us:

► **Verlag Karl Baedeker GmbH**
Editorial department
Postfach 3162
73751 Ostfildern
Germany
Tel. 49-711-4502-262, fax -343
www.baedeker.com
E-Mail: baedeker@mairdumont.com

Baedeker Travel Guides in English at a glance:

- Andalusia
- Barcelona
- Berlin
- Budapest
- Dubai · Emirates
- Egypt
- Ireland
- Italy
- London
- Mexico
- New York
- Paris
- Portugal
- Prague
- Rome
- Thailand
- Tuscany
- Venice
- Vienna